The Daily Telegraph

Book of

Military

Obituaries

The Daily Telegraph

BOOK OF MILITARY OBITUARIES

Edited by

DAVID TWISTON DAVIES

GRUB STREET · LONDON

Published by
Grub Street
The Basement
10 Chivalry Road
London SW11 1HT

Jacket illustration supplied by courtesy of
Great Northern Publishing, with thanks to Mark Marsay.

British Library Cataloguing in Publication Data
Davies, David Twiston
   The Daily Telegraph book of military obituaries
   1. Soldiers – Obituaries
   I. Daily Telegrph
   355′.00922

ISBN 1 904010 34 2

Typeset by Pearl Graphics, Hemel Hempstead

Printed and bound in Great Britain by
Biddles Ltd, Guildford and King's Lynn

**To the regimental associations whose
unstinting help is greatly acknowledged**

DRAMATIS PERSONNAE
(in order of appearance)

Brigadier Ian MacAlister Stewart

Major-General F J Loftus Tottenham

Brigadier Tim Massy-Beresford

Brigadier George Chatterton

Major-General "Jack" Bond

Major-General Eric Harrison

Lieutenant-Colonel John Prentice

General Sir John Anderson

Lieutenant-Colonel Phil Strickland

General Paul Freeman

Major Huia Woods

Brigadier Peter Young

Major Gordon Lett

Major-General Roy Urquhart

Brigadier "Arch" Clough

Lieutenant-Colonel Lord Byron

General Sir Horatius Murray

Brigadier James Drew

Brigadier "Loppy" Lerwill

Brigadier "Slasher" Somerset

Brigadier Stair Stewart

Major "Raj" Fowler

Lieutenant-Colonel Stuart Chant-Sempill

Major-General Sir Reginald Scoones

Brigadier Sir Mark Henniker

General Sir Nigel Poett

Book of Military Obituaries

Colonel Basil Groves

Lieutenant-General Sir John Cowley

Major Bill Temple

Major Bill Anderson

Captain "Peter" Clegg

Brigadier Murray McIntyre

Lieutenant-Colonel Dudley Coventry

Colonel Peter Earle

Lieutenant-Colonel Oswald Cary-Elwes

Brigadier Eustace Arderne

Colonel the Reverend Neville Metcalfe

Colonel Kenneth Merrylees

Lieutenant-Colonel Cyril Cochran

Captain Charles Upham

General Stanislaw Maczek

Brigadier Anthony Wingfield

Lieutenant-Colonel Brian Gait

Brigadier Lord Lovat

Lieutenant-Colonel Mahmood Khan Durrani

Lieutenant-Colonel Victor Wildish

Brigadier Bill Bradford

Lieutenant-Colonel "Mad Jack" Churchill

Major-General Brian Daunt

Brigadier "Roscoe" Harvey

Brigadier the Reverend "John" Harris

Major David Floyer

Lieutenant-Colonel Colin Mitchell

Colonel Murray de Klee

Captain Desmond Lynch

Drum Major Philip Buss

Captain Bernard Harfield

Major-General Jack Irvine

General Sir John Hackett

Colonel Mark Dillon

Corporal Ted Matthews

Major Geoffrey Brain

Major Kenneth Balfour

Major Alan Bush

Brigadier "Birdie" Smith

Major Peter Lewis

General Sir Kenneth Darling

Chef Caporal James Worden

Major Bill Davidson

Major-General Sir Charles Dunphie

Major Herbert Warburton

Lieutenant-Colonel "Tishy" Benson

Major John Howard

Sergeant "Tex" Banwell

Major Edward Thomas

Major Jack Pringle

Colonel Brian Coombe

Colonel Ray Nightingale

Captain Bill Hall

Major Dennis Ciclitira

Lieutenant Vivian Bullwinkel

Company Sergeant-Major John Kenneally

Lieutenant-Colonel Thomas Firbank

Colonel Maurice Willoughby

Book of Military Obituaries

Major Richard Coke

Major D F Stone

General Sir Walter Walker

Field Marshal Lord Carver

Captain Sir Roden Cutler

Field Marshal Sir Nigel Bagnall

Lieutenant-Colonel Henry van Straubenzee

Major-General Sverre Bratland

Major Arthur Fearnley

Sergeant-Major Leonard Griffiths

Lieutenant-Colonel "Ronnie" Degg

Major Bob Maguire

Brigadier "Pudding" Pye

Colonel Jimmy Johnson

Major Douglas Witherington

Sergeant William Parkes

INTRODUCTION

During the long, complacent peace which we have enjoyed at home since the end of the Second World War, our Armed Forces have been periodically praised, neglected, downplayed, and occasionally denounced. Yet, when the politicians fail, they still go off without complaint to do their duty, as they did in Iraq earlier this year. In doing so they are part of the great tradition celebrated in this collection of a hundred soldiers' obituaries, which were first published in *The Daily Telegraph* between 1987 and 2002.

The primary task of a soldier is to fight and to inspire others to fight. This book contains some of the finest examples. Here are the New Zealander Captain Charles Upham, winner of a Victoria Cross in Crete and a Bar in North Africa; Lieutenant-Colonel "Mad Jack" Churchill, a Commando leader who liked to take his bagpipes and bow-and-arrow on operations; and Drum Major Philip Buss, the bugler who rallied the Glosters at the Imjin river in Korea.

Exactly what motivates soldiers to risk their lives is a mystery that only deepens if probed. The lure of adventure, the thrill of danger, the thirst for success play a part. There is also the camaraderie of military life and that feeling of loyalty which still draws the Queen's men from the farthest ends of the earth. Whatever the combination, these can be seen in the restless spirit of Lieutenant-Colonel Colin Mitchell, the "Mad Mitch" who upset the Labour government of the 1960s by taking the Crater in Aden with panache and served in Italy, Palestine, Korea, Kenya, Zanzibar and Northern Ireland. They drove Lieutenant-Colonel Dudley Coventry to end a colourful and controversial career as head of the Zimbabwe SAS and inspired Colonel Murray de Klee, who joined the Scots Guards in 1946 and served in eight conflicts.

That motivation lingered on in retirement for Brigadier Lord Lovat's devotion to his clan and love of big game hunting, and could be seen in Brigadier Peter Young who raced his Sandhurst students up the cliffs he had first climbed on the Dieppe Raid and founded The Sealed Knot, to re-enact the battles of the Civil War. On the other hand, Corporal Ted Matthews, who lost two mates on either side of him at Anzac Cove on the first day of the Gallipoli landings, was left convinced of the futility of war when he died at the age of 101.

But the Army provides opportunities for soldiers to do their duty in many ways. Major Gordon Lett led an Italian guerrilla force, made up of fellow escapers and partisans, after being freed from his prison camp. Colonel the Reverend Neville Metcalfe earned a DSO as a chaplain in Burma. One of the least likely heroes is Captain Bernard Harfield, a dentist who treated General Montgomery in Cairo, and 18 months later found his patient pinning an MC to his chest for the gallant way he led a stretcher party in Germany. The staff officer Colonel Peter Earle complained to General Sir Alan Brooke, Chief of the Imperial General Staff, that it would be seen as a black mark later in his career if he had not been in battle. "Silly fellows, soldiers, to think that", said Brooke, but he persuaded Montgomery to take Earle on his staff in Normandy.

Although no soldier's career can be completely free of danger, some make their mark in essentially pacific roles. Brigadier Stair Stewart, a godfather of the Bailey bridge, spent almost his entire career with the Experimental Bridging Establishment, while Colonel Kenneth Merrylees was valued as a dowser in the Army's search for water. Brigadier James Drew contributed to the morale of front-line troops by delivering post to the Normandy beaches. Brigadier "Arch" Clough produced the maps for D-Day, and later wrote a long account of the task on a typewriter he had "liberated" from the Germans in the Cameroons in 1914.

Inevitably, the battles of 1939-45 feature most in these pages, but the number of men here who also took part in the First World War confirms the realisation that both wars were two halves of the same conflict. The first obituary is that of Brigadier Ian MacAlister Stewart of Achnachone, the first British officer to set foot on French soil in 1914, who later commanded the Argylls before the fall of Singapore. Yet the last, written some fifteen years later in 2002, is that of Sergeant William Parkes, who served with the Welsh Bantam Brigade on the Western Front and emigrated to America in 1920. The life of the Indian Army, in which young officers like Brigadier Sir "Honker" Henniker found themselves being saluted by elephants' trunks, now seems remote; yet the efforts of men like Lieutenant-Colonel Victor Wildish to keep peace in Waziristan served as a reminder that essentially little had changed when the Afghanistan conflict began in 2001.

Not the least fascination in these stories are the snippets of military history. When Brigadier the Reverend "John" Harris landed in France in 1915 with the 2nd Lancers, they still carried the sabres and lances which had been part of their equipment since they were raised in India during the early 19th century. Brigadier "Slasher" Somerset found himself involved in a battle on two fronts, just as his regiment, the Glosters, had done during the Napoleonic wars when they earned the right to wear badges on both the front and the back of their caps. Part of the success of British arms, opined General Sir John Hackett, is that men join a regiment, not simply the Army. But this can lead to surprises. Lieutenant-Colonel Henry van Straubenzee was nonplussed, on taking over command of the Oxford and Bucks, to be informed by a corporal that the regiment had mutinied under one of his ancestors in the nineteenth century.

Although some glittering senior figures are treated here, such as the brilliant Field Marshal Lord Carver and the comically outspoken General Sir Walter Walker, all the major British and Commonwealth commanders of the Second World War were dead by 1987. However, two allies are represented here: the redoubtable General Stanislaw Maczek, commander of the 2nd Polish Corps in Normandy, who ended up working as a barman in Edinburgh, and General Paul Freeman, who was highly critical of his fellow Americans during the Korean War. Nevertheless some of the famous can be spotted flitting through the background: Alexander, Mountbatten, Churchill, the actor David Niven and the American General "Vinegar Joe" Stilwell. The legendary Fakir of Ipi, who claimed his warriors were protected against bullets, is to be found making trouble on the North-West Frontier, while Goering demonstrates a German sense of humour by promoting Colonel Maurice Willoughby's hunter to the rank of Reichsmarschall.

Choosing these obituaries has not been an easy task, since they represent only about one-tenth of those published during the past fifteen years, during which they had to compete for space with almost equal numbers of sailors and airmen. One way of reducing the numbers was the decision not to include any which have appeared in earlier collections of obituaries. A consequence of this is that there is only one woman here though no one could doubt that Lieutenant Vivian Bulwinkel, who was machine-gunned in the sea by the Japanese, was as resolute as any of the 99 men.

The mastermind of the obituaries operation is Hugh Massingberd. In 1986 he persuaded Sir Max Hastings, the new Editor of *The Daily Telegraph,* that the paper needed an obituary section with its own set place on the Court and Social page; and I was drafted in unwillingly as his deputy. My irritation about the move lasted about a week, by which time I knew that I desired to do nothing else for the rest of my career; and, perhaps as divine punishment, I soon found myself posted off to other duties, though I continued to contribute obits and to be involved in the department.

It was clear that the column must concentrate on the two great stories of the 20th century, the world wars and the Empire; but Massingberd and I quickly discovered that there was a surprising dearth of information about members of the Armed Forces in the yellowing cuttings files held in the office library. All the same, anything we had relating to events before the Second World War was often unknown to the subjects' families. The reason for this dearth of information was that, as one obituarist remarked dismissively to me of an architect's war service, "They all did that".

By the late 1980s, however, it was clear that "they", the Second World War generation, were beginning to pass from the scene. Massingberd's predecessor the estimable Augustus Tilley, who had struggled to provide a good service within the constrictions of the tightly packed news columns, had allowed Brigadier John Woodroffe to write occasional pieces about Indian Army figures. Hastings's first instruction was that we should turn to reporters in the News Room. But it became clear that they were not interested, usually did not know enough and, anyway, did not have the time to find out. So we looked around for specialist authors who could write in a style appropriate for newspapers.

We found an air obituarist in Edward Bishop and a naval writer in the late John Winton easily enough, but a suitable military specialist proved elusive. When Massingberd encountered the late Philip Warner, a prolific author and long-term Sandhurst lecturer, at a *Daily Telegraph* Books Page party Warner was adamant that, no, he did not think he would like to write an obituary or two. However, after several more approaches he agreed to produce one. He duly arrived at the cramped obituaries department on the first floor in the paper's Fleet Street office at about 4.30 one Friday afternoon after what had clearly been an excellent lunch.

He sat down at a vacant desk, shyly made some desultory conversation with John Winton, who also happened to be paying us his first visit, and produced from his pocket the piece on Ian MacAlister Stewart. He was still not greatly enthused after it appeared; but as a freelance writer he was attracted by the prospect of regular, if hardly generous, payment. Gradually, as his contributions continued, he began to perceive two particular values in what he was doing. One was the opportunity to bypass those whom he characterised as "straight up and down major-generals", in favour of men, whose moment of notable gallantry was all too often forgotten.

One example is Major Edward Thomas who won an MC when he took command of a hundred leaderless members in a sharp action one afternoon in the "Hellfire Gap" of North Africa. The second opportunity relished by Warner was that of illustrating the much derided standards celebrated in that favourite reading of his youth, the *Boy's Own Paper*, as in the obit of the all-round athlete Major-General Eric Harrison. Although Warner's opinions of the Japanese remained sulphurous to the end of his days, he would never talk about his war. However, in a book about the magazine, he paid tribute to the way it inspired him while working on the infamous Bangkok–Moulmein railway of death:

"Food was inadequate and appalling; the work was heavy and exhausting; the Japanese and Korean guards seemed scarcely sane; malaria, dysentery, cholera, beri-beri and a host of other diseases were rife. Sometimes it rained incessantly and there was no protection at night except for a few leaking tents or huts. Men died with steady regularity. Around was the jungle, hot, oppressive, menacing. There was really no hope of survival. Even if the Allies won the war it would take so long that we should all have been long since dead. I remember one day looking round at the scene and saying to myself 'What an extraordinary situation! It's like some strange adventure in the *Boy's Own Paper*'. Suddenly it was less real, more bearable: after all, B.O.P. characters lived to tell the tale. Fantasy perhaps, but in certain conditions illusion may be more genuine than reality."

Warner became one of the hardest working contributors to the obituaries section. He only admitted once that he had a problem, when confronted with a dashing Canadian brigadier. So we co-opted Jeffery Williams, whose work is only represented here by one offering because more is planned in a sequel to the earlier *Canada from Afar: The Daily Telegraph Book of Canadian Obituaries*. It might be thought by now that the great days for obituaries has passed, but when Warner himself died in 2000 the work was still growing apace.

We now have a team of four military specialists in which Williams has been joined by Charles Owen, Julian Spilsbury and Bill Barlow. Several other writers' work is represented here, including George Ireland, our Australian obituarist David Bowman and, in a unique contribution by a regimental officer, Major Jeremy York of the King's Shropshire Light Infantry who supplied us with Major-General Sverre Bratland. This Norwegian officer had so impressed British troops during the Narvik campaign that he was invited to join the KSLI four years later in Normandy, where the sound of his thick accent coming over the field telephone often made listeners think a British unit had been captured by the Germans. Special mention must also be made of Warner's old Sandhurst colleague Sir John Keegan, whose personal recollections appended to several of the obituaries are always valued.

Since Hugh Massingberd had to retire on health grounds in 1994, the obituaries department has grown in numbers, prestige and the space allotted to it. This still leaves him unique in the annals of Fleet Street for having introduced one innovation that did not involve dragging its newspaper down-market; certainly no other journalist has ever been described as having created a new art-form, at least without a heavy dose of sarcasm.

He was succeeded as Obituaries Editor first by David Lewis Jones, then by Kate Summerscale and Christopher Howse before Andrew McKie brought a new panache to the chair just before my return to the heart of the department after twelve years on the nearby Letters Desk. A large number of editor-writers have served with them. They include Robert Gray, Claudia FitzHerbert, Aurea Carpenter, Will Cohu, James Owen, Katherine Ramsay, Georgia Powell, Martha Read, Philip Eade and Jay Iliff, now the painstaking Deputy Obituaries Editor. Teresa Moore, who took over the administration of the department from Diana Heffer, continues to keep us running smoothly, and a special mention should also be made of my secretary on the Letters Desk, which for years was an integral part of the obits department, the incomparable Dorothy Brown. Finally, I must also thank Morven Knowles and her predecessor as publications manager Susannah Charlton for getting the project off the ground, and, not least, Charles Moore, Editor of *The Daily Telegraph,* for unfailing support.

David Twiston Davies
Chief Obituary Writer

The Daily Telegraph

Canary Wharf, London E14

BRIGADIER
IAN MacALISTER STEWART

Brigadier Ian MacAlister Stewart, the 13th Laird of Achnacone, Argyllshire (who died on March 14 1987, aged 91), was the first British officer to land on French soil and the first to be mentioned in despatches in the First World War.

As an 18-year-old platoon commander with the 2nd Battalion, Argyll and Sutherland Highlanders, he led a charge and fell, claymore in hand like his Jacobite ancestors. The next moment his sergeant leaned over him, saying "Poor kid", only to receive Stewart's caustic retort that he had only tripped over his sword.

During the retreat from Mons, he was cut off from the battalion but managed to commandeer a train, ordering the driver to head back down the line. He and his men then fell asleep and woke up to find they had passed the British troops and were almost in Paris. Stewart was awarded the Military Cross in 1915, a Bar in 1917 and was mentioned in despatches for a second time. After being wounded he served the remainder of the war as a junior staff officer to Major-General J F C "Boney" Fuller in the Tank Corps and fought at the Battle of Cambrai.

Stewart then settled down to regimental life, serving in the West Indies, Peking, Hong Kong and India. Characteristically, he passed the Staff College exams but refused to take up his place, saying he never knew an officer who did not come away more stupid than when he went. From 1934 to 1937 he was commanding officer at Stirling Castle, the Argylls' regimental depot, where he introduced several comforts, including a hot water system and a cup of tea for the troops after lunch.

Arriving in Malaya as commanding officer of the 2nd Battalion after the outbreak of the Second World War, he immediately started training his men in jungle warfare, developing those tactics of encircling and driving an enemy up against a roadblock which the Japanese were to employ so successfully in the campaign. The Argylls fought with great distinction on the Malayan peninsula, and were the last troops to cross to Singapore Island. As they passed over the causeway two pipers played 'A Hundred Pipers' and the battalion's march past 'Highland Laddie'.

On the island, Stewart ordered the enrolment of some Royal Marines who had survived the sinking of the battleships *Prince of Wales* and *Repulse* to form what were inevitably known as the "Plymouth Argylls". He escaped capture when Singapore fell on February 15 1942 because he had been ordered away to report to General Wavell, the newly appointed Supreme Commander, South West Pacific, on the best methods of fighting in the jungle. When he arrived in Colombo, he met outside a hotel his wife Ursula, who had been evacuated from the island in a naval intelligence ship three days before the fall.

Awarded a DSO in 1942, Stewart's fighting days were now over. He was appointed colonel and chief instructor at the School of Infantry, and then transferred to South East Asia Command. He was appointed Brigadier, General Staff, responsible for

11th Army Group training, and commanded 144th Infantry Brigade in 1945. In his last two years before retirement he commanded Stirling District and did much for Polish troops stationed locally.

Ian MacAlister Stewart was born in India on October 17 1895, the son of an expert polo-playing medical officer of the Poona Horse. He went to Cheltenham and Sandhurst, from which he passed out in December 1913, to become the youngest officer in the British Army.

On retiring from the army, he started to farm from dawn to dusk the 2,500-acre estate at Achnacone, which had been granted to an ancestor after the Battle of Flodden in 1513. While not a grand house, his home contained an immaculately ordered collection of relics, including those belonging to two ancestors killed at Culloden, one who had been Nelson's flag officer at the Battle of Copenhagen and yet another who was killed in the Peninsular campaign. There was also his mess tin which in 1914 had stopped a bullet, which continued to rattle around inside it.

Ever innovative, he experimented with bringing sheep indoors for lambing and took a keen part in resisting the Forestry Commission's attempts to cover the country with conifers. He led the fight locally against plans to amalgamate the Argylls with another regiment as well as continuing to befriend the local Polish community. A tall modest man, with a fund of stories, Stewart continued to put his organisational skills to good use, running mountain rescue operations. He owned a horse called Mistake the

Second, on which he won many races.

Ian MacAlister Stewart married, in 1931, Ursula Morley-Fletcher, the niece and secretary to the Duchess of Atholl. She died in 1969. He was survived by a daughter.

MAJOR-GENERAL
F J LOFTUS TOTTENHAM

Major-General F J Loftus Tottenham (who died on April 11 1987, aged 88) was a talented jungle commander whose combination of tenacity and tactical sense helped to hold and turn back the Japanese thrust towards India in the Arakan strip of Burma during 1943.

Commanding 33 Indian Infantry Brigade of the 7th Indian Division, he pushed forward on the east of the Mayu Ridge in a series of strongly contested actions. The enemy reacted with a major advance on India, hoping to force a withdrawal by isolating units. But for the first time the British forces dug in, stood fast and fought the enemy to a standstill. In the meantime, the Japanese attack on Assam had cut off the road to Imphal at Kohima. So 7th Indian Brigade was switched by air, rail and road to the northern front where Loftus Tottenham was involved in some of the toughest fighting, including hand-to-hand combat, until the Japanese were routed.

Promoted to major-general, Loftus Tottenham commanded 81 West African Division on the long and difficult march through the Kaladan valley which culminated in the capture of the Japanese base at Myohaung, for which he was awarded a DSO.

Frederick Loftus Tottenham was born on May 4 1898 at Naas, Co Kildare, and had a varied education in France and at Bedford School. At 17, following a course at the Royal Military College, Dehra Dun, he was commissioned into the 2nd (King Edward's Own) Gurkha Rifles. Loftus Tottenham took part in the Mesopotamian Campaign, and was wounded in 1918. From 1919 to 1920 he was back in action in the Waziristan campaign. For two years he served with his regiment on the North-West Frontier then, appreciating the importance of signals in modern warfare, with the Indian Signal Corps.

In 1927, he was attached to the French army in the Pyrenees, and afterwards was Envoy Extraordinary to the King of Nepal in Katmandu. From 1929 to 1934 he served with his regiment on the North-West Frontier then, for the next four years, commanded the Mewar State Forces, which he successfully modernised.

Loftus Tottenham commanded the 1st (King Edward's Own) Gurkhas on the North-West Frontier at the beginning of the 1939-45 War before taking a course in parachuting, then raising and commanding the 1st Gurkha Parachute Battalion. In 1942 he was sent on a special reconnaissance mission to Eastern Persia.

From 1946 to 1947 he was GOC, Iraq, and then GOC 7th Division, in Pakistan after the partition of India, when he had responsibility for internal security. While in no way a brilliant man, the dogged Freddie Loftus Tottenham was a great deflator of the bogus and the pompous. When one officer tried to justify his action, Loftus Tottenham demanded: "Surprise the enemy? Or merely amaze him?"

A thrusting, aggressive horseman, both on the polo ground and out pig sticking, he reached the quarter-finals of the last Kadir Cup before the war. On retirement he commanded the Home Guard in Northern Ireland.

Loftus Tottenham married in 1922 Margorie Dare, who died in 1978; then, in 1980, Isabel Baker, who survived him with a son of the first marriage. His two other sons were killed, one at Monte Cassino and the other in Burma.

BRIGADIER
TIM MASSY-BERESFORD

Brigadier Tim Massy-Beresford (who died on July 21 1987, aged 91) had an adventurous military career which culminated in the organisation of "Massy-force", a highly motivated unit created in 1942 to harass the Japanese before the fall of Singapore, and to wage guerrilla war afterwards.

On arrival in Singapore, he had been astonished by the lack of preparations among senior military and civilian officers, and set about creating a force from about 2,000 men of the 1st Cambridgeshires, 4th Suffolks and 5th/11th Sikhs. But his initial plan was countermanded by Lieutenant-General A E Percival, the Army commander in Singapore, as was his second proposal of a counter-attack by Lieutenant-General Sir Lewis Heath.

When the garrison was surrendered Massy-Beresford believed that a resolute commander would have evacuated most of the million civilians, collected rainwater when water supplies were cut off, and made proper use of the troops who were ready and willing to fight. Whether the idea was feasible can never be known. But the Japanese were close to breaking point, it was learned after the war, and Massy-Beresford was awarded the DSO for his efforts.

As a prisoner of war Massy-Beresford was sent from Changi to Taiwan and then to Moukden. In 1945 he was released by the Russians and returned home, first via Okinawa and then round the Pacific – taking longer, as he said, than had Sir Francis Drake.

Tristram Hugh Massy-Beresford was born on April 10 1896, and educated at Eton and Sandhurst before being commissioned into the Rifle Brigade. He was badly wounded in France in 1915 but succeeded in persuading a medical board to allow him to rejoin his regiment in 1918. He was awarded an MC, but wounded again in October when a bullet passed through his chest and killed the man behind him.

After the 1914–18 War he was in the Dardanelles during the Chanak incident, and then served on the North-West Frontier. At the funeral of King George

V in 1935 Massy-Beresford was the leading figure in the procession, marching 200 yards ahead of the column; "the loneliest man in the world," as he put it. In 1931 he was posted to the Royal Military College at Kingston, Ontario, but returned in 1940 to take up a staff appointment with the 59th TA Battalion.

Tim Massy-Beresford was a lively raconteur, interested in people and very sociable. He played most games, notably cricket and tennis.

In 1927 he married Helen Lindsay Lawford of Montreal, who died in 1979. He was survived by a daughter and two sons.

BRIGADIER
GEORGE CHATTERTON

Brigadier George Chatterton (who died on November 12 1987, aged 75) played a vital part in the establishment of the Glider Pilot Regiment, and won a DSO in the invasion of Sicily in 1943.

When the Sicily landings were in prospect Chatterton, who was in command of the 1st Glider Pilot Regiment, was told by Major-General Hopkinson that his gliders would take part in the action. Chatterton protested that his pilots had an average of only two hours flying experience, had never flown at night and had never co-operated with ground troops. Hopkinson stated firmly that they would take part or Chatterton would be cashiered.

On the night of the invasion Chatterton found his own glider sinking into the sea short of the objective at Cap Murro di Porco; but, although fired on, he managed to swim to the shore where he and his squadron joined up with a boatload of SAS and captured 150 Italian prisoners. Once established, the party was nearly annihilated by a British destroyer firing at the wrong target. Subsequently he insisted that glider pilots must be capable of handling all types of arms and of fighting on the ground as efficiently as the troops they transported.

The same degree of organisation went into the preparations for D-Day – he even made his pilots wear dark glasses so that they would be able to land with limited vision. He himself piloted General "Boy" Browning in the Arnhem operation, landing him close to Nijmegen – which involved fitting the immaculate general into a bucket seat constructed out of a beer barrel. The regiment's heavy losses in the operation were made up by Chatterton borrowing 1,500 RAF pilots, not without high-level opposition.

By this time Chatterton had decided that tactical landings were less costly in casualties than mass landings, and introduced the concept of landing on top of enemy troops rather than before or behind them.

George James Stewart Chatterton was born on December 2 1912 and educated at the Nautical College, Pangbourne, Berkshire. But instead of continuing with a career in the Merchant Navy he joined the RAF, training with types of aircraft which had given distinguished service in the 1914-18 War and which, he recorded, went on to give useful service during the 1939-45 War. He had various mishaps and, after a flying accident, decided to avoid being posted to an unadventurous ground post by joining the Army.

Flying Officer Chatterton was metamorphosed into Lieutenant Chatterton of the Queens (Royal West Surrey) Regiment. In 1939 he was sent to Europe with his company, which was attached to the 3rd Battalion, Grenadier Guards.

Already a supporter of the axiom that a good regiment is a smart regiment, he was so impressed with the Grenadiers in action that he later borrowed some of their NCOs to instil the same qualities into embryonic glider pilots.

After the Dunkirk evacuation he volunteered for the Glider Pilot Regiment, which was being formed under Lieutenant-Colonel John Rock of the Royal Engineers, and was chosen to command the 2nd Battalion. When Rock was killed in a glider crash in 1942 he took over command of the 1st. Rock had been a popular and greatly respected commander, and Chatterton's insistence on spit and polish was resented at first; though his drive, energy and progressive thinking soon won favour.

Chatterton retired in 1946 and for a time became a stockjobber. He also ran the Blue Wings Association, and devoted his drive and energy to the Lady Hoare Trust, raising more than £1 million for thalidomide victims. He was appointed OBE.

In 1962 he published *The Wings of Pegasus*, which

tells his own story and that of the Glider Pilot Regiment.

Now integrated into the Army Air Corps, the regiment owes more to Chatterton than to any other single figure; his leadership and stubborn refusal to be beaten by difficulties enabled it to play a vital operational part in the war.

He was survived by his daughter Julia Hall, who ran the Pinfold Stud at Market Drayton.

———

MAJOR-GENERAL "JACK" BOND

Major-General "Jack" Bond (who died on December 11 1987, aged 85) was known as "the Petrol King" because of his ability to ensure adequate supplies of that essential fuel were always available on the various fronts where he served.

Bond's career in the Royal Army Service Corps took him from Norway to North Africa and North-West Europe to Burma, and involved him in numerous narrow escapes. During the Spanish Civil War he was based at Gibraltar when it was accidentally shelled; and he organised rescue operations for the crew of a German ship, which led him to be embarrassed on receiving a letter of thanks signed by Adolf Hitler.

During the 1939-45 War, Bond revelled in the RASC's dangerous task of conveying by land, sea and air large quantities of petrol and ammunition. The job often required them to be defended, en route and in supply depots, with anti–aircraft and other guns. In 1940, he went to Norway and was one of the last to leave at the conclusion of the campaign. While waiting on the dockside he took one last look round to make sure no-one was left behind; when he returned a few minutes later there was a large hole in the ground where he had left his kit.

Soon afterwards he was sent to North Africa. He served on the staff of General Montgomery, who became a lifelong friend, and was at D-Day planning conferences in Reigate and at St Paul's School.

Bond qualified as a parachutist, but being 6ft 4in tall and accustomed to holding himself erect he gave himself concussion when leaving aircraft, so became a glider pilot instead. In the latter role he took part in the Arnhem operation with 1st Airborne, and when the battle was over was once again fortunate to escape.

His next posting was to Burma, where he was organising supply by aircraft to various units in the jungle. By the end of the war he had been appointed OBE and mentioned in despatches.

George Alexander Bond, the son of a Chief Constable of Dover, was born on December 31 1901 and was educated at Dover Grammar School. He initially qualified as a teacher, becoming head of the Army School at Aldershot, and then won a cadetship to Sandhurst.

After the war he was Director of Supplies and Transport in the British Army of the Rhine from 1950 to 1953, then held a similar post in Southern

Command. He next had the unusual distinction of being concurrently both Director of Supplies and Transport, War Office, and Inspector of the Royal Army Service Corps.

On an inspection tour of Malaya, Bond was met by his eldest son who had been appointed his ADC for the visit. After a somewhat formal greeting the two embarked on an aircraft; the General then took several notes from his wallet and told his ADC to buy himself a new pair of shoes.

Bond retired from the Army in 1957, and became transport manager of Thornycrofts. He was then invited to join the Southern Gas Board to organise its transport on efficient lines. This task took him a week, and soon afterwards he resigned because he had left himself nothing further to do.

A striking, forthright, and highly intelligent character, Bond was a good swimmer, an enthusiastic yachtsman who took part in the Fastnet race, and a keen skier. But perhaps his greatest interest was painting, mainly in oils, which were displayed in many exhibitions.

In 1929 he married Dora Margaret Gray, who had been a fellow teacher; she died 12 days before him. He was survived by their two sons.

———

MAJOR-GENERAL
ERIC HARRISON

Major-General Eric Harrison (who died on December 20 1987, aged 94) enjoyed a life which could have graced the pages of the *Boy's Own Paper*. Besides giving distinguished service in both world wars, he was a remarkable all-round sportsman – a representative rugby player, an Olympic athlete, a legendary rider to hounds, pig-sticker and big game hunter – as well as an artist, author and gardener.

Eric George William Warde Harrison, the son of a major in the Indian Army, was born on March 23 1893 and educated at Cheltenham and Woolwich, where he played rugby for the Army and Kent and was chosen for a tour with the Barbarians. Commissioned into the Royal Artillery he was posted to Shoeburyness and was invited to play soccer for Southend United, then in the Second Division. Taking up hurdling, he was soon selected to run for England against Scotland and Ireland in the 120 yards hurdles.

After the outbreak of the 1914-18 War, he was posted to the anti-aircraft defences of Harwich, and nearly shot down Britain's only airship when it came unmarked over that area. Soon he was sent to France where he was involved in the murderous battles around Hooge, the Menin Road and Polygon Wood; in 1915 he was awarded the Military Cross at Givenchy. By the end of the Battle of Loos, Harrison claimed, "I had shot my guns from every observation post of importance along the whole Corps front."

In 1918 he was made a brevet major, the youngest in the British Army at the time, and was surprised to be put in charge of a Corps Infantry School until a genial Irish colleague assured him: "My dear old boy, remember the worst you can do is make a complete balls of the whole show." Harrison spent the final stages of the war with 58th London Division, and by the Armistice had been mentioned in despatches four times.

On returning to England he was selected to train for the "Mother Country" XV, the forerunner of the British Lions, and scored seven tries, playing wing-threequarter for the Army against Oxford University. After injury ended his football career Harrison concentrated on fishing, riding and hurdling. He was selected for the 1920 Olympics, but at the preliminary medical inspection the doctor said he had "moved his heart" and forbade him to compete.

Harrison received the decision with some scepticism, for two days earlier he had won six events for his unit in an Army championship. A week later he won the 120 yards hurdles for England against Scotland and Ireland. He was then offered the Mastership of the Royal Artillery Harriers. Although a normal day consisted of hunting in the early morning, partridge shooting in the afternoon and fishing in the evening, Harrison still managed to scrape into the Staff College. Despite asthma when training for the 1924 Paris Olympics, which were immor-talised in the film *Chariots of Fire*, he managed to reach a semi-final.

His next posting was to India, where he took up

big game shooting and became Master of the Lahore Hounds, which hunted jackal. Although he only took up racquets after arriving in the country, he won the doubles title in the All India Championship, and also proved himself a fearless pig-sticker. In 1932 Harrison was posted back to England to command a battery at Aldershot, but managed to transfer to Catterick where the hunting was better. At this time he took up painting after reading Winston Churchill on oils, and eventually had two pictures accepted though not hung by the Royal Academy, and three hung by the Paris Salon.

In 1934, to his astonishment, Harrison was appointed to command the OTC at Oxford University where he lectured on military history, and also became Master of the South Oxfordshire Foxhounds. On the outbreak of the 1939–45 War he was given command of the Royal Artillery's 12th Territorial Division at Sevenoaks, where Home Guard units were full of retired generals acting as platoon commanders.

He was relieved to be posted to Northern Ireland which provided some salmon and trout fishing, as well as snipe shooting, and in 1942 was sent to North Africa with 9th Armoured Corps which became involved almost immediately in the forcing of the Fondouk Gap. After working closely with Lieutenant-General Brian Horrocks in the tail end of the North African campaign, he was appointed Commander, Royal Artillery, at General Eisenhower's Allied Forces HQ.

Harrison continued in the post during the Sicily

and Italian campaigns, during which he was mentioned in despatches, but he returned home in 1943 to become GOC, Sussex and Surrey District. He retired from the Army in 1946 to resume his Mastership of the North Cornwall Hounds, and become a noted rhododendron grower. He served as a Deputy Lieutenant, JP and High Sheriff and was a reforming chairman of St Lawrence's mental hospital, Bodmin.

Breeding labradors, trout fishing and travel helped to fill the rest of Harrison's time, but he also wrote three books, including a delightful autobiography *Gunners, Games and Gardens* (1979). He was appointed CBE in 1943 and CB in 1945, and was ADC to King George VI from 1945 to 1946.

Harrison's first marriage, to Audrey Coller, was dissolved; and in 1961 he married Mrs Roza Stevenson, who died in 1967. He used to say "Everyone should be put down at 70", but he belied the words himself. In his nineties he was still fishing, shooting, gardening and painting, and his memory remained unimpaired.

LIEUTENANT-COLONEL JOHN PRENTICE

Lieutenant-Colonel John Prentice (who died on March 9 1988, aged 75) was a gallant Indian Cavalry officer with a reputation for always going flat out in whatever he did. Before the outbreak of hostilities in

1939, Prentice was referred to by his commanding officer as "that lionhearted subaltern", and when war came he took every opportunity to live up to that soubriquet. His first chance came in the Western Desert, on May 28 1942.

That morning Brigadier Filose, commanding the 3rd Indian Motor Brigade, reported that the whole of the Afrika Korps was drawn up in front of him as if for a ceremonial parade. Rommel had taken the Eighth Army by surprise. The brigade, comprising three Indian cavalry regiments, lightly armed with Bren guns and two-pounders and supported by a regiment of artillery (25 pounders), put up a tremendous fight and destroyed about 50 German Mk 4 and Mk 3 tanks. But after three and a half hours of unequal combat, with every anti-tank gun knocked out, it had almost ceased to exist.

Prentice, who was commanding an anti-tank gun squadron, was taken prisoner when he finally ran out of ammunition. But, after being rounded up and disarmed, he felled his German guard with the edge of his steel helmet and escaped – with his Madrassi cook and two other soldiers – to walk across the minefields held by the French Foreign Legion under General Koenig. For this gallant conduct he was awarded the Military Cross.

Finding life too quiet on the staff of the 4th Indian Division, he applied to join the 18th Cavalry in Tobruk, which was then under siege. He got there by "walking aboard a destroyer", taking a special party of five officers (one of them Winston Churchill's son Randolph) and a load of ammunition into the fortress by night; he stayed for four months.

After a course at the staff college in Haifa, Prentice was posted as brigade major to the 43rd Gurkha Lorried Infantry Brigade, which greatly distinguished itself in the Italian campaign of 1944-45. On his arrival Prentice walked into the mess tent and said: "I believe this brigade is commanded by a terrible old boy, Joe something or other." At that point Brigadier "Tochi" Joe Barker appeared. The Gurkha brigadier was known for his uncertain temper and dislike of cavalry officers; but he had met his match in Prentice, and came to think highly of him.

John Wykham Prentice was born on February 26 1913, one of four brothers who all served in the Indian Cavalry. He was educated at All Hallows School, and commissioned in the Poona Horse in 1933. On his return to the regiment in India after the war Prentice was temporarily commanding the Poona Horse when independence was declared in 1947. He transferred to the British Army for a short spell as a gunner, and then retired to farm in Rhodesia.

He began with virgin land and built up over many years a successful cattle and tobacco farm at Marandellas, until selling up and returning to Salisbury, where he became the chief accountant in a manufacturing business. In an independent Zimbabwe he was a cheerful and popular personality. It was typical of his courage and determination that, despite cancer, he continued to work until two months before his death.

Prentice was survived by his wife, daughter and two sons.

GENERAL
SIR JOHN ANDERSON

General Sir John Anderson (who died on April 16 1988, aged 79) was one of that remarkable breed of Ulstermen so disproportionately represented in the upper reaches of the British Army.

In 1940 he was awarded a DSO for conspicuous gallantry during the fighting to the south-west of Abbeville, shortly before the fall of France. Then Brigade Major of 2nd Armoured Brigade, Anderson was required to make contact with the 10th Hussars, who were cut off, and having set off in a scout car had to cross open ground on foot under heavy fire before returning with a vital situation report.

Later the same day he made a second journey to the same regiment, this time in a Cruiser tank. After it had been hit four times, Anderson managed to manoeuvre the flaming vehicle into cover, which allowed the crew to escape. He himself pulled out the wireless operator, who was wounded and unable to walk, and saved his life by dragging him to the shelter of a farmhouse. Although wounded himself Anderson was able to maintain contact between the regiments in the front line and Brigade HQ.

Anderson, who enjoyed a brilliant academic career

without ever appearing to make any special effort, had a host of friends of all ranks and would insist on speaking personally to every soldier on parade even if it upset the schedule. He was also a diplomatist, who, in the words of General Sir John Hackett, "went around with a cruse of oil for pouring on troubled waters". Another officer added, "He could deliver a rocket in the nicest possible way; with a smile he could give you absolute hell."

His career culminated in the 1960s with stints as Deputy Chief of the Imperial General Staff, Military Secretary to the Minister of Defence and Commandant of the Imperial Defence College.

John D'Arcy Anderson, the son of a major in the Royal Garrison Artillery, was born on September 23 1908 at the family seat of Ballyhossett, Co Down, and won a scholarship to Winchester and an exhibition to New College, Oxford, where he read Greats. In 1929 he was commissioned into the 5th Royal Inniskilling Dragoon Guards and 10 years later went to France with the British Expeditionary Force.

After various staff appointments he went to the Middle East with the 8th Armoured Division, with whom he was mentioned in despatches, and returned to England at the beginning of 1944 to take command of the Sherwood Rangers. He landed in France with his regiment on D-Day; and was again wounded. Anderson's wife Elizabeth had often holidayed in the Arromanches area and had kept a photograph of a half-sunken wreck on the beach which was allotted to his regiment for their aiming in the landings.

In November 1944 Anderson joined the Central Mediterranean forces and took part in the Italian campaign, earning another mention in despatches. After the war he was General Officer Commanding 11th Armoured Division and Chief of Staff Northern Army Group and the British Army of the Rhine, before being appointed Director of the Royal Armoured Corps in 1958. He was Colonel of the 5th Royal Inniskilling Dragoon Guards, Colonel Commandant of the Royal Army Educational Corps, and Colonel Commandant of the Ulster Defence Regiment from the time the present troubles started in 1969 until 1979. Anderson was also Honorary Colonel of the Oxford University OTC and Queen's University, Belfast OTC.

From 1966 to 1968 Anderson was ADC General to the Queen. He was a Deputy Lieutenant and High Sheriff of Co Down and an active member of the Commonwealth War Graves Commission and the Army Museum Ogilby Trust. In 1967 he set up the Irish Cavalry Regimental Museum in Carrickfergus.

An accomplished painter, who had a watercolour of sponge fishers at Benghazi Harbour exhibited at the Royal Academy, Anderson was a first-class horseman and cut a dash over fences in point-to-points.

Appointed CBE in 1945, CB in 1957, KCB in 1961, and GBE in 1967 he was particularly proud of his honorary LLD from Queens. He was survived by his wife Elizabeth Walker, whom he had married in 1937.

LIEUTENANT-COLONEL
PHIL STRICKLAND

Lieutenant-Colonel Phil Strickland (who died on April 16 1988, aged 75) earned a reputation for cool courage and tactical ingenuity by his command of the Canadian Highland Light Infantry in some of the heaviest fighting of the 1939-45 War in Holland and Germany.

In October 1944 he was a brigade major during the Canadian assault on "Breskens Pocket" on the south bank of the Scheldt. During the landings, Brigadier John Rockingham, his commander, ordered him to take command of the HLI, who were cut off, saying "They're somewhere over there but the Germans are in between." Borrowing a Bren carrier from another battalion Strickland raced through the enemy to find his unit, which he then led until almost the end of the war.

Fighting in appalling weather through the flooded polder country, the HLI paid a heavy price in casualties for their part in opening Antwerp to Allied shipping. The Scheldt campaign ended for Strickland when he overcame the remnants of the German 64th Division at Knocke. Three months later the HLI were again fighting in water, through the drowned flood plain of the Rhine and earning, with the rest of Canadian 3rd Division, the nickname of "water rats". Operating in "Schwim Panzers", as the Germans called his amphibious Buffaloes, Strickland captured a succession of Rhineland villages and secured the line of the Spoy canal between Cleve and the Rhine. From there he led them in the bloody battles near the Hochwald Forest which smashed the enemy's last hold on the west bank of the Rhine.

Early on March 24 1945, Strickland and the HLI crossed the river to become engaged in a ferocious fight to rescue detachments of the British Black Watch who were cut off in the town of Speldrop. Clearing its houses at the point of the bayonet and blocking the near-suicidal attacks of German paratroops, he drove the enemy out into nearby fields where he completed their destruction. After the break-out from the Rhine bridgehead, Strickland was approaching Zutphen in Holland when he was appointed GSO1 of Canadian 3rd Division, a position he held until the German surrender.

A month later he returned to Canada to take command of the 2nd Battalion, Princess Patricia's Canadian Light Infantry, which was training for the assault on Japan. But the war ended before their departure, and Strickland, the typical militia soldier, lost no time in returning to civilian life.

Phillip Wheaton Strickland was born on April 9 1913 at Saskatoon, Saskatchewan, a descendant of Samuel Strickland who, in 1824, left the comforts of Reydon Hall, Suffolk, for what is now Lakefield, Ontario, where he became a successful farmer and established a college to introduce young men from English public schools to the frontier life. Young Phil graduated as a lawyer from Saskatchewan University and spent a year at Columbia University, New York, before joining an Ontario flour mill. Commissioned into the Artillery before the war, he came to England with the HLI in 1941. Two years later he was appointed to the staff planning Operation Overlord but returned to his regiment as a major in time to land with them on D-Day.

After the war Strickland, who was awarded the DSO and appointed OBE, returned to the flour industry in Ontario and ran his own mill for a time, maintaining an active role in the local reserve. He left a widow, two sons and two daughters.

GENERAL
PAUL FREEMAN

General Paul Freeman, the former Commander-in-Chief of the United States Army in Europe (who died on April 17 1988, aged 79) was a forthright critic of the American army's performance in the opening months of the Korean War when he commanded the 23rd Infantry Regiment.

He described the 24th Division as "a completely defeated ragtag that had lost all will". Of the Republic of Korea's army he said: "It was pitiful. But it wasn't their fault. They lacked the training, the motivation, and the equipment to do the job. Whenever their units were on our flanks, we found they were liable to vanish without notice."

In his book *The Korean War* (1987) Max Hastings wrote: "Freeman was one of the few senior soldiers in Korea who never lost their grip. Freeman watched with pride his own 1st Battalion holding the Chinese on the Chongchon for 30 hours; his regiment undertaking 13 successive deployments without losing a man. In the 2nd Division Freeman's regiment remained the only combat effective unit by the end of the year."

Freeman felt that the United States army had been downgraded by the fact that the best of American youth had been kept out of the infantry, either by the Selective Service Act, or the belief that wars could be won by technical and management functions rather than dour frontline fighting. His frequent advice to officers who had careers on the staff rather too firmly in their sights, was: "Your job is to fight, and don't you forget it."

In February 1951, when the United Nations' forces and the Chinese were battling for the town of Chipyong-ni, Freeman's regiment was surrounded and attacked by five Chinese divisions, but it held on with the help of air supply until eventually the Chinese fell back. He himself was wounded. His indomitable leadership had enabled his men to prove that the Chinese could be beaten by resolute fighting, and in doing so revived the morale not only of the whole of the 2nd Division of which he formed part, but also of the entire American army in Korea.

Freeman subsequently criticised the fact that the Korean War had ended in an armistice and not a victory, and felt that the Chinese should have been decisively defeated, using whatever weapons were thought to be necessary: "I thought there had been a lot of unnecessary blood-letting for a stalemate. To have this thing drag on and on, fighting for every bloody little hill over there, was all wrong. We should have knocked the Chinese out of there, whatever it took. The absurdity of trying to destroy those Yalu bridges without bombing the other side, that isn't the way to fight a war."

The son of an army doctor, Paul Lamar Freeman was born at Manila in the Philippines on June 7 1909, and spent his childhood at the army posts where his father was stationed. He continued to "follow the drum", graduating from West Point in science, and being commissioned into the infantry in 1929.

Freeman spent most of the 1930s in China until the attack on Pearl Harbor, and then became assistant chief of staff to the redoubtable General "Vinegar Joe" Stilwell, the commander of Chinese troops in Burma and assistant to General Chiang Kai-Shek (whom Stilwell liked to refer to as "the peanut"). Being a staff officer to Stilwell required considerable diplomacy for he disliked and despised most of his fellow commanders, and referred to his British allies as "goddam limeys". In 1943 Freeman returned to America to help plan the final assault on Japan, and was himself engaged with the Sixth Army in the conquest of the Philippines.

After the war he was concerned with planning, and visited Brazil for joint discussions. He succeeded to the command of the 2nd US Infantry Division in Europe and was then the senior army member of the Weapons Development Division. Freeman's subsequent appointments included Commandant of the US Infantry School at Fort Benning, Deputy Commander of Reserve Forces in Virginia and Commander of the Joint Task Force at Fort Monroe. He became Commander in Chief of the US Army in Europe, and Central Army Group, NATO, in 1965, and was Commander of the US Continental Army and C-in-C US Army Strike Force before retiring in 1967.

After leaving the army Freeman was a vice-president and then a consultant on operational planning to Litton Industries; his recreation was golf.

Freeman's decorations included the American DFC, DSM, Legion of Merit, Silver Star with oak leaf cluster, Bronze Star with three oak leaf clusters, and the Air Medal and a Purple Heart.

In 1932 he married Mary Anne Fishburn, who survives him with one daughter.

MAJOR
HUIA WOODS

Major Huia Woods (whose death was recorded in *The Daily Telegraph* obituaries column on September 9 1988, aged 56) was a brilliant New Zealand tracker responsible for teaching his skills to the SAS when it was engaged in combating terrorists in the jungles of Malaya and Borneo.

A stocky, dark man of Maori extraction, he was clearly better at tracking than Australian or Malayan aborigines as well as Ibans from Borneo. Until he arrived in Malaya with the newly-formed New Zealand SAS in 1956, terrorists had been able to disappear into the deep jungle after murderous forays with a good chance of never being followed to their remote hide-outs. Woods quickly changed the situation. The notorious Ah Ming gang, which had previously been immune in the Perak Kelantan area, was quickly eliminated; and a similar fate soon followed for the LiHak-Chi gang in Negri Sembilan.

Huia Woods was born at Paroa, New Zealand, in 1932 and attended Auckland Teacher Training School.

He was invariably cheerful, even at the end of a long stint in the arduous conditions of the jungle. He was highly intelligent, and rated a first-class soldier by his comrades. But it was his ability to teach tracking on jungle warfare courses in Malaya and England that made him invaluable for counter-terror operations. Under his tutelage, British soldiers learned to note the tiniest signs that others had passed that way earlier and to apply this aptitude in the Borneo confrontation of 1963-66, when Indonesian infiltrators tried to take advantage of the 700-mile-long border.

Later, during the Vietnam War, in which the New Zealand but not the British SAS took part, Woods also taught Australians and Americans to track the Vietcong in the jungle.

Although his tracking skills were often attributed to his Maori heritage, Woods denied that either his race or background had anything to do with it, saying that the reason was attention to detail and practice.

BRIGADIER
PETER YOUNG

Brigadier Peter Young (who died on September 13 1988, aged 73) was one of the most colourful, creative and influential soldiers of his generation.

He served in the Commandos with distinction in Europe and Burma during the 1939–45 War, was a regimental commander in the Arab Legion and an innovative head of the Military History Department at Sandhurst. He was also creator of The Sealed Knot, the Civil War commemoration society, and the successful editor of part works and author of many incisive books. In addition, he always had time for old and new friends and the life of a bon vivant.

Young's rise from second lieutenant in 1939 to brigadier in 1945 was meteoric; had he been even a little more senior at the outbreak of the war, it seems certain that his acute intelligence and extraordinary gifts of command in battle would have ensured his promotion to general rank and that he would then have reached the highest reaches of the Army.

Peter Young was born on July 28 1915 and educated at Monmouth School and Trinity College, Oxford, where he read Modern History, with Military History as a special subject. He used to recall that, when at Monmouth, he had made up his mind to follow a military career after looking at the statue of Henry V, who had been born in the town. In 1937 Young was commissioned into the Bedford-shire and Hertfordshire Regiment, with which he went to

France, and was wounded in the evacuation from Dunkirk.

On recovery he joined 3 Commando and took part in the raids on Guernsey, Lofoten and then Vaago, where he earned an MC. After a period on the staff at Combined Operations HQ, he became second-in-command of 3 Commando and took part in the Dieppe Raid. Here he managed to take his raiding force up the cliffs on a network of barbed wire, which, as he put it, an over-conscientious German officer had inadvertently provided for them to walk on. Young was the only Commando officer to reach his objective and bring back all his men. At one point, when they were approaching enemy machine-guns through a cornfield, he encouraged his soldiers by telling them not to worry about bullets as standing corn made an effective protection. He was awarded a DSO for his part in the raid.

In 1943 at Agnone in Sicily he was awarded a Bar to his MC and then, when leading 3 Commando in raids in Italy, received a second Bar. In 1944, he was back in Normandy, serving with distinction in the D-Day landings before being posted to the Arakan in Burma. A fellow officer recalled seeing Young's Commandos under attack from an apparently endless number of Japanese at Kangaw and sending a message asking Young if he would like reinforcements. "No thanks," came back the message. "We can see this lot off all right." And he did. In 1945, Young was acknowledged to have been an outstanding commander of 1st Commando Brigade in Burma.

After the war he attended the Staff College, and in

1947 joined 2 War Office Methods of Instruction team. He was then posted as a company commander in his former regiment, which was then serving in Salonika; but, finding normal peace-time soldiering rather humdrum for his tastes, he was seconded to the Arab Legion, where he took command of the 9th Regiment, a Bedouin unit with which he was immediately successful and popular. While commanding the Arab Legion garrison in Jerusalem there was a serious clash between the Arabs and the Israelis, but Young's prompt efficiency defused the situation and earned him high commendation.

He returned to England in 1950 and joined the staff of the Joint Services Amphibious Warfare Centre. His last serving appointment was on the staff of the Regular Commissions Board. In 1959, Young retired from the regular army and became head of the Department of Military History at Sandhurst with the title of Reader, which gave him some pleasure and amusement. His effect on the teaching of military history was dramatic. He recruited outstanding fresh staff – such as the distinguished historians John Keegan, David Chandler and Christopher Duffy – and inspired them and his students to try their hand at writing, often helping to find publishers for their works.

Young believed that a thriving military history department would reflect credit on the academic standards of Sandhurst as a whole. He had always been particularly interested in the English Civil War and he now founded The Sealed Knot to re-enact its battles. At first his friends were somewhat unwillingly pressed into service to dress up and charge with heavy pikes over ploughed fields from Edgehill to Lansdowne; but soon recruits were pouring in and branches were being formed from Scotland to Cornwall. There was no discrimination of sex or age.

The Sealed Knot, with its spectacular cavalry, stiffened by film stunt-men, was in great demand for pageants and shows, and frequently appeared on television. Young, in the genuine Civil War rank of "Captain Generall", presided as a dignified though portly figure. Forcibly directing events from his horse he managed to convince both performers and watchers that, as cannons roared and the stage blood flowed, this was a genuine battle.

Although many of Young's writings were on the Civil War and its battles – on which he spoke with scholarly authority – he also produced excellent works with such titles as *Bedouin Command*, *Storm from the Sea*, *The British Army 1642-1970*, *Commando*, *History of the Second World War* as well as books on "wargaming". He was editor-in-chief of Orbis's *World War II* and a consultant for several television productions, including 'Churchill and the Generals'.

Young's somewhat bluff, hearty, larger-than-life manner concealed a remarkable sensitivity to the problems of others. Virtual strangers would call on him for advice and often be entertained, as well as informed and lent books. His sense of humour invariably matched any occasion. He was perhaps too kind and generous for his own good, but he lived by his own standards, which meant minimising his own achievements and doing his best to assist those of others.

On one of his more tumultuous battlefields he spotted a small boy who was scared by the noise and general frenzy, and gave him a pat on the head and a word of encouragement. When he was at Sandhurst Young liked to take parties of cadets to the 1939-45 War battlefields. At Dieppe he showed them the cliffs he had once climbed. They looked at him disbelievingly. "See if you can do it yourselves," he said, and beat them to the top.

Although Young enjoyed battle, he never forgot that tragedies could be involved. Despite the fact that he was wounded himself, the injury which gave him the most trouble in later life was a blow from a hockey ball on his shin at the age of 14.

He was survived by his wife, the former Joan Duckworth.

MAJOR
GORDON LETT

Major Gordon Lett (who died on October 4 1988, aged 78) won a DSO for putting together and leading a private partisan force of some 300 men in the Apennines during the 1939-45 War. Others may have similarly disrupted and maddened German forces after Italy's capitulation in 1943, but Lett's special achievement was to raise and lead his army without help from outside. It was only after news of his presence in the Rossano valley and on the heights above La Spezia percolated through to MI9, the escape organisation, and to Special Operations Executive, that he received support in arms and supplies.

Lett had been a prisoner of war near Veano when the camp gates were thrown open, and he was invited by the camp commandant to make himself scarce. Heading for the sea in the hope of making contact with Allied landings, he was encouraged by the friendliness of the Rossanesi to raise a partisan force. He was visited by a representative of the Liberation Committee in Genoa, and agreed to lead an "international battalion". This seemed a somewhat grandiose title when applied to the three Poles, two Yugoslavs, a Peruvian, a Somali, three British and two Australian soldiers and an ordinary seaman, RN, who with some Italians formed the nucleus of the battalion.

The group adopted a green scarf as a distinguishing feature and a badge depicting the Union flag and the Italian flag. Soon Lett established a firm authority in the region, not only among his men but also as the "Signor Maggiore" and unofficial governor, making laws, registering births and deaths, mediating in disputes and safeguarding public health. His fine, serious face was framed by a reddish beard, which seemed to be both expressive of a man who thought deeply and to reinforce his natural authority.

Ernest Gordon Appleford Lett was born in British

New Guinea on November 17 1910 to an English writer and his Australian wife. He was educated at Claylesmore. Commissioned into the East Surrey Regiment, he served in India in the 1930s; mountaineering expeditions in the Himalayas were an unconscious preparation for the rigours of his campaign in the Apennines.

In June 1942, Lett was taken prisoner near Tobruk and shipped to Italy. After he had made contact with SOE's 1 Special Force under Commander Gerard Holdsworth, his international battalion took part in a series of successful ambushes. These had the effect of calling down retaliatory fury on his force, but it reduced pressure on other partisan groups.

Lett's personal gallantry became a byword, but he was much remembered in the region for one less spectacular act. Asked by the Bishop of Pontremoli if he could stop Allied bombing of that city, he offered to exchange his good offices for information on German dispositions so that targets could be pin-pointed. The bishop demurred at providing the information personally, but shortly afterwards an Italian partisan handed him the target list. Later Lett received the Freedom of Pontremoli.

His natural humanity also led him to grieve at the barbarous German reprisals for his group's attacks on garrisons, roads, power supplies and telephone lines; so he attempted to simulate an attack by British paratroops to deter reprisals against civilians. In one such ambush he put fair-haired Italians in battledress and shouted: "Fire! Give them all you've got!" Not long afterwards he was selected to receive an SAS parachute squadron to boost his operations.

Lett's partisan professionalism greatly impressed those visitors and messengers to whom he gave short shrift until he was assured of their credibility. One Italian courier was distrusted until he unwrapped a bottle of Scotch sent as a passport by Major Charles Macintosh, Holdsworth's operations officer. Towards the close of the final offensive in Italy, Lett entered La Spezia and found himself in command of the naval base with a handful of his men.

Before leaving Italy he returned to his beloved Rossanesi, who in the rough times had sustained him on chestnut bread, and underwent the "bitter experience of winding up partisan bands." He prepared Pontremoli to face the new problems of peace, then left to begin a fresh career in the Foreign Office: he was vice-consul (Information) in Italy from 1949 to 1950 and first secretary (Information).

Lett wrote a lively account of his subversive activities in *Rossano: an Adventure of the Italian Resistance* (1955), with a foreword by Freya Stark. He was survived by his wife, Sheila, and a son and a daughter.

MAJOR-GENERAL
ROY URQUHART

Major-General Roy Urquhart (who died on December 13 1988, aged 87) commanded 1st Airborne Division in the attempt to capture and secure the vital bridge over the Rhine at Arnhem in The Netherlands on September 17 1944. The operation, codenamed "Market Garden", was for First Allied Airborne Army to capture key bridges and open a way for the British Second Army to outflank the Siegfried Line.

In fact Market Garden was not the complete disaster it is often considered to have been, for the two American divisions, the 82nd and 101st, secured the nearer bridges over the Maas and Waal. 1st British Airborne was landed six miles from the famous "Bridge Too Far", but the main reason for its catastrophic defeat was that it was heavily outgunned by 9th and 10th Panzer and other powerful German forces which had been thought not to be in the area.

Urquhart and his men fought with desperate and heroic courage during the nine days of the battle; but when ammunition was virtually at an end, casualties had risen to an unacceptable level and there was clearly no hope of the Second Army reaching them in time, he ordered the break-out. There was no surrender, and 2,163 men succeeded in crossing the Rhine; some 1,350 were killed in the battle and 6,450 were taken prisoner. Urquhart, always to the forefront of the action, had many close escapes. His first brush with death was when a German shell destroyed the Jeep he had been about to use. Soon after, when he had had to take shelter in a house, a German soldier appeared at the window. Before he could fire Urquhart shot him at point-blank range.

Later, when making a personal reconnaissance, he was cut off from his own headquarters, to which he had to make his way back through fire so intense that he was given up for dead. One part of the division had reached the bridge, where it was holding out against German attempts to eject it. Urquhart, with the main force, set up Divisional HQ in the grounds of a large hotel, the Hartenstein. Here, in spite of having the lighter armament of an airborne unit, they clung on desperately in the face of heavy German attacks, hoping that the Second Army – then making the best possible speed through the constricted roads and strong German opposition – would arrive in time to cross the bridge. As the days passed, the airborne forces found themselves short of ammunition, food and water, surrounded by the dead and dying and under constant heavy bombardment.

Urquhart's personal example of resolution and courage was a great inspiration, but he finally decided that there was no hope of relief for the remnants of the division and sent a signal informing GHQ that, although the operation had failed, he was not going to surrender and would attempt to break out and cross the Rhine. On receipt of orders approving this course of action, he hastily planned an evacuation towards the river that night. The route to the boats was marked with parachute tapes, and the survivors of the Airborne Division made their difficult journey through heavy rain over marshy ground in pitch darkness.

To deceive the Germans about the break-out, Urquhart ordered diversionary shots to be fired. The survivors, who had blackened their faces so as to be invisible in the darkness, finally reached the river only to find that the worst part of their journey was yet to come. A violent wind and a swift current made the crossing extremely hazardous in the small, heavily over-laden boats. But, guided by tracer bullets, 2,000 made the crossing although some boats were lost, and others, broken down in midstream, had to be propelled by using rifle butts as oars. Although Urquhart's leadership and example had made the best of an impossible situation, there was subsequently some criticism of his tactics during the battle.

Urquhart was a brave, modest and good-looking Scot, 6ft tall and 14 stone. He was extremely popular at all levels both inside and outside the Army. He addressed his men by their first names or, more casually, as if (one recalled) "he was a general who didn't mind doing the job of a sergeant." One of the few virtues of *A Bridge Too Far*, Richard Attenborough's film of the Arnhem operation, was Sean Connery's portrayal of Urquhart, which caught a good deal of the character, as well as the appearance, of the man.

A doctor's son, Robert Elliott Urquhart was born on November 28 1901 and educated at St Paul's and Sandhurst. He was commissioned into the Highland Light Infantry in 1920. He served in India between the wars, passed the Staff College course at Camberley in 1937, and held staff appointments in India until 1940.

Urquhart's outstanding leadership qualities were demonstrated when he commanded the 2nd Battalion, the Duke of Cornwall's Light Infantry, from 1941 to 1942; was GSO1 of 51st Highland Division in North Africa from 1942 to 1943, and commanded 231 Brigade in Sicily and the Italian landings in 1943 – for which he was awarded a DSO and Bar. In 1944 – to the surprise of many, including himself – Urquhart was appointed GOC, 1st Airborne Division. Although popular and known to have an excellent fighting record, he had no experience of airborne warfare, had never parachuted and was considered to be too heavy to begin.

He also suffered badly from air sickness, a particular liability in the gliders which would normally be used for airborne operations. There was a strong feeling that the experienced parachutist Brigadier Lathbury should have been preferred to Urquhart; but it was reasoned that, though Lathbury was more familiar with the airborne role, once the division had landed Urquhart's experience as an infantry soldier would be more valuable.

With memories of a disastrous scattered airborne landing in Sicily, Urquhart was anxious that, for Market Garden, 1st Airborne should be landed as close as possible to the target area. But he was overruled on the grounds that German anti-aircraft fire would make this too hazardous. Many later thought that if the landing had been closer to the bridge then 1st Airborne could have held out until help arrived, but the point remains highly controversial, as the bridge was known to be well protected by anti-aircraft guns.

After the war Urquhart was Director of the Territorial Army and Army Cadet Force until 1946;

Commander, 16th Airborne TA, from 1947 to 1948; Commander, Lowland District, from 1948 to 1950 and Commander, Malaya District and 17th Gurkha Division, in 1950. He was then appointed GOC, Malaya, for the worst period of the Emergency, from 1950 to 1952. His last appointment was GOC, British Troops, Austria, from 1952 to 1955. He was Colonel of the Highland Light Infantry from 1954 to 1958, resigning when the regiment was threatened with merger with the Royal Scots Fusiliers.

He then began a successful second career in heavy engineering, and became a director of Davy & United Engineering from 1957 to 1970.

Urquhart's personal account of Arnhem was published in 1958, but shortly before his death he gave a revealing interview to Tom Pocock in *The Daily Telegraph*. He summed up the matter tersely: "We did all we were asked to do. And when we were not relieved, as we expected to be, those of us who survived fought our way out." Asked if Operation Market Garden could have succeeded, Urquhart replied: "Perhaps, but the port of Antwerp should have been opened first so that all the supplies did not have to be brought up from the Channel ports. We should have arrived in a single lift and we should have dropped a strong coup de main party at the bridge.

"Air support should have been given high priority. Wireless communications should have been far better, and the relieving force should have been able to fight its way through. We learned that you could not successfully launch an airborne division against an enemy who could put up that sort of fight."

Urquhart was appointed CB in 1944 and received the Netherlands Bronze Lion and Norwegian Order of St Olaf.

In retirement he was an enthusiastic golfer. His wife, the former Pamela Condon, survived him with a son and three daughters.

BRIGADIER "ARCH" CLOUGH

Brigadier "Arch" Clough (who died on January 5 1989, aged 100) was a remarkable sapper surveyor with the rare distinction for an Army officer of having been awarded the Sea Gallantry Medal at the beginning of the 1914-18 War.

A member of the Anglo-French force engaged in the arduous task of capturing the German Cameroons, he was attached to a party of marines making early morning raids on the coastal villages where enemy troops were suspected of being in residence. Returning from one of these they saw an open boat, carrying the Senior Naval Officer and others from the Government yacht *Ivy*, capsize while trying to come in through heavy surf. Clough's own ship was grounded on a sand bank but a boat was launched from it and managed, "with a clever coxswain", to get through the surf and rescue the SNO and four others.

The *Ivy* incident was only one of many perilous

moments Clough encountered during a campaign in which most of the fighting took place along the railway line, where the Germans had prepared a variety of ambush positions. Clough and another subaltern had the task of working their way through the bush by night and getting behind the German positions. Clough's GOC said that he was "a most energetic and capable young officer ever ready to undertake difficult duties. On more than one occasion he displayed conspicuous gallantry thereby rendering most valuable service."

Although Clough had originally been sent to West Africa as a surveyor there were no local facilities, and the only way of reproducing the maps they made was by a sun-printing frame. As the Germans retreated they removed vital parts of their locomotives and buried them; but their former African employees soon showed the British where they had been hidden, and Clough and his colleagues rapidly had the locos running again.

In 1916, he went home on leave but was not allowed to return to the tropics on health grounds. Instead, he was posted to France, where it was presumably thought to be healthier. He arrived in the closing stages of the Battle of the Somme and was in the trenches for the next two years, mainly to the north of Arras. Here he was awarded a MC in 1917 when commanding 210 Field Company, Royal Engineers.

At the end of the war Clough became RE Instructor at the Senior Officers School at Aldershot. In 1925, he was appointed British Commissioner on the International Commission for the Boundary Delimitation between Albania, Yugoslavia and Greece. After returning home Clough received "a magnificent Albanian decoration, the Order of Skenderke, with an illuminated address signed by King Zog". But on reporting this to the War Office, he recalled, "I was instructed to return it, which seemed a bit of an insult, but was apparently normal Govern-ment policy."

Next he was sent to Africa as senior British Commissioner for the boundary between the Belgian Congo (now Zaire) and Northern Rhodesia (Zambia). The boundary ran along the watershed and was, he said, "trees, trees, trees, literally for hundreds of miles"; but the recent discovery of a rich copper belt below made the exact definition of ownership in all areas vital. During the 1930s, Clough was seconded to the Ordnance Survey in Southampton, to be in charge of the publications division, and was deputy director for five years.

On the outbreak of the Second World War, he was appointed Director of Survey for the British Expeditionary Force, an organisation which he had to reform as it had been disbanded in 1918. Despite the difficult weather conditions of 1939-40 it managed to produce up-to-date maps, not only of France, but also, with the help of high altitude aerial surveys, of Belgium and parts of Germany.

After evacuating from Dunkirk, Clough returned temporarily to Ordnance Survey to supervise the printing of all necessary maps for the home forces in case the Germans invaded. When this threat subsided he began planning 21st Army Group's maps for the invasion of Northern France. These, made with the help of earlier aerial surveys from an RAF Spitfire squadron, were produced in millions, and once the North-West Europe campaign was well under way they were dropped to advanced units by air. They were printed on silk for parachutists and special forces, and later became sought after for women's headscarves.

The son of a colonel in the Royal Munster Fusiliers, Arthur Butler Clough was born at Hamilton, Lanarkshire, on August 8 1888, and educated at Clifton and Woolwich. He was commissioned into the Royal Engineers and spent his subaltern years in Ireland during what he described as "those, peaceful, golden pre-First War years".

After the Second World War Clough worked for 15 years with the Pyrites Line in Portugal. He was required to raise a battalion of the Home Guard when the Cold War looked like becoming hot; he also became chairman of the Romsey Conservative Association, president of the local SSAFA and a voluntary visitor to disabled and war pensioners.

In 1952, his monograph, *Maps and Survey: the Second World War*, was published by the War Office. In some 330,000 words it covers not merely the areas of Europe for which Clough personally had been responsible, but all other theatres too. Writing it took him nearly three years; he typed it all himself on an Adler typewriter which he had "liberated" from the Germans in the Cameroons in 1914. It became a standard work on the subject.

Clough was mentioned in despatches in both world wars, appointed OBE in 1930 and CBE in 1945, and awarded the French Croix de Guerre with palm, and the American Legion of Merit. "Arch" Clough was in full command of his faculties even after passing his 100th birthday when he was sent a telegram by Queen Elizabeth the Queen Mother, at whose wedding he had been an usher in 1923. He had a splendid sense of humour, enjoyed life to the full, and was a lively though never boring raconteur.

In 1918 he married Doris Canning, who died in 1976, and was survived by two daughters.

———

LIEUTENANT-COLONEL
LORD BYRON

Lieutenant-Colonel the 12th Lord Byron (who died on June 15 1989, aged 89) commanded the 4th/7th Royal Dragoon Guards when they landed on Gold Beach in the first wave of the Normandy invasion on D-Day, June 6 1944.

The regiment, which was equipped with amphibious Sherman tanks, had the complicated task of coming ashore in the centre of the landing area, where the sea was very rough and the tide high enough to conceal the lethal underwater obstacles which the Germans had thoughtfully provided. Byron, who had spent the previous two years training for this moment, displayed courage and imperturbability which approached the legendary:

he was awarded an immediate DSO. He continued to command the regiment in the advance through northern France, displaying the same indifference to personal danger and unwavering attention to the efficiency and well-being of his men.

The son of a colonel in the King's Royal Rifle Corps who won a DSO in the South African War, Richard Geoffrey Gordon Byron was born on November 3, 1899, and educated at Eton and Sandhurst. He joined the 4th Royal Irish Dragoon Guards a fortnight after the end of the 1914–18 War, and found himself the only person among all the officers and soldiers not entitled to wear a medal ribbon; he was probably more conscious of that fact than they were.

Subsequently he served with the Army of Occupation in Cologne. In 1922, the 4th was amalgamated with the 7th (Princess Royals) Dragoon Guards to form the 4th/7th Royal Dragoon Guards. After service in Ireland the regiment was posted to India and stationed in Secunderabad. During the same year Byron was appointed ADC to the Governor of Bombay, Sir George Lloyd. On his return to Britain in the 1930s he became adjutant of the Duke of Lancaster's Own Yeomanry in Manchester.

In 1937, Byron was appointed military secretary to Viscount Galway, the Governor-General of New Zealand, and developed a deep affection and affinity for the Dominion's countryside. At the outbreak of war he rejoined the regiment in France, where he commanded a squadron. On May 10 1940, when the Germans launched their invasion he was billeted with the parish priest of Verd, a small French village. When the regiment moved up to confront the Germans, Byron left his wireless and bicycle in the priest's care. Four years later, he found himself in the vicinity of Verd and called on the priest. His wireless was returned to him, but the bicycle had been commandeered by the Germans.

In 1942, he took command of the 4th/7th and displayed exceptional skill in training for a type of warfare which was new and untested. It was said that few could have achieved so much. When commanding in action later it was noted that Byron never lost his equanimity under the most intense pressure and in the most hazardous situations. In September 1944, he returned to England where he was once more engaged in training.

Soon after retiring from the Army in 1948 he inherited the Langford estate in Essex from Anna Lady Byron, widow of the 10th Baron. Twenty-five years later he succeeded his kinsman, the 11th Lord Byron, a grazier in Western Australia, in the peerage. This was created in 1643 for a faithful adherent of King Charles who was Field Marshal of the Royalist forces in Worcester, Salop, Chester and North Wales; the 9th baron was the scapegrace great poet of the 19th-century.

A tall, lean, aristocratic figure, extremely modest and shy, Geoffrey Byron was so reserved that he could give the impression of distancing himself; but he had great charm and had the welfare of others at heart, particularly when commanding troops.

His first marriage, to Margaret Steuart, was

dissolved in 1945; his second wife, the former Dorigen Esdaile, died in 1985. There were two sons of the second marriage, of whom the elder, Richard, was killed aged 37 in an air crash and is buried at Timbuctoo. The younger son, Robert James Byron, born 1950, succeeded in the peerage.

———

GENERAL
SIR HORATIUS MURRAY

General Sir Horatius Murray (who died on July 2 1989, aged 86) became Commander-in-Chief, Allied Forces, Northern Europe, at the end of a military career in which he had been brilliant at all levels and in all aspects of command.

Although an infantryman, "Raish" Murray had been given command of 6th Armoured Division in Italy in 1944 in somewhat bizarre circumstances. While commanding 153 Infantry Brigade in the Normandy battles, he objected vigorously when ordered to use it in an attack which seemed both pointless and suicidal. While this conflict of views was taking place, General Montgomery appeared, heard both sides of the story and supported Murray, who was subsequently given his command when a sudden vacancy occurred. The future Field Marshal Sir Gerald Templer had been injured by a looted grand piano, which had fallen from a passing truck on to his car. (Templer's comments were unsuitable for setting to music.)

It was not unknown for an infantryman to command an armoured division (Brian Horrocks had already done so), but Murray's performance in the gruelling Northern Apennines winter and later in the Po Valley was exceptional by any standards. Not only did he show a grasp of the intricacies of armoured warfare, he paid so much attention to the morale and welfare of the division that it was able to outfight and outlast the resourceful and skilful German troops who confronted it.

Horatius Murray was born on April 18 1903 and educated at Peter Symonds School, Winchester, and Sandhurst. In later life when asked where he had been at school he would answer "Winchester" then add, as the questioner nodded approvingly, "but not the one you're thinking of". He had a strong sense of humour and delighted at taking a dig at snobbishness or pomposity.

In 1923, he was commissioned into the Cameronians (Scottish Rifles), with whom he served until 1936 after which, owing to accelerated promotion, he was transferred to the Cameron Highlanders with whom he served in Shanghai, India and Egypt. His Army nickname "Nap" (short for Napoleon), was conferred early in his career because of his dedication to soldiering, which led him to install a "sand table" (a deep metal tray used for demonstrating tactics) in his bedroom. A fellow subaltern thought this was being unduly professional, and once buried a dead cat under one of the sand hills for Murray to discover at leisure.

After qualifying as an interpreter Murray served

with a German regiment on an officer-exchange, an experience which proved of great value in understanding German military psychology later. When asked, condescendingly, by his Wehrmacht contemporaries whether his regiment had been in existence for long, Murray would reply: "Only since 1689."

He attended the Staff College at Camberley, Surrey in 1936, and then served at the War Office and in 3rd Division before being appointed to command the 1st Gordons in the Western Desert. He was wounded at Alamein and, after spending six months in hospital, discharged himself in time to take part in the final battles of North Africa and the Sicily campaign. He returned to Britain with his brigade for the Normandy invasion and subsequent battles. At the end of the Italian campaign he accepted the German surrender on the borders of Austria. But in spite of his distinguished record with an armoured division he always felt his heart and place was with the infantry.

From 1946 to 1947, Murray was Director of Personnel Services at the War Office but found the post boring and contrived to lose it by mislaying so many files and Army Council Instructions that he was soon transferred to the more active post of GOC, 1st Infantry Division, which was then in Palestine. His next appointment was GOC, Northumbrian District, before becoming Commander of the Commonwealth Division in Korea. This post required all his qualities of tact, attention to welfare, practical common sense and ability to maintain morale and efficiency. From 1955 to 1958 he was GOC-in-C, Scottish Command, and Governor of Edinburgh Castle, and finally retired after three years as C-in-C, Allied Forces, Northern Europe.

Murray was awarded the DSO in 1943 and appointed CB in 1945, KBE in 1956 and GCB in 1962. He was the last Colonel of the Cameronians.

Dignified in appearance, Murray appeared somewhat aloof on first acquaintance but he had a warm personality and a special ability at getting on with the younger generation; his tolerance of long hair and other foibles of junior officers surprised many, but it typified his understanding of what was important and what was not.

In retirement he maintained strong links with the Royal Hospital for Incurables. He enjoyed golf, cricket and classical music. In his youth he had been a good soccer player, having represented both Sandhurst and the Army Crusaders as a very bulky goalkeeper.

In 1953, Murray married Beatrice Cuthbert, an artist who specialised in pastels and murals; some of them, which she signed "Lotus", appeared on walls in stations and prisons. She died in 1983.

BRIGADIER
JAMES DREW

Brigadier James Drew (who died on January 2 1990, aged 77) overcame formidable problems of logistics during the Second World War as director of the

Army Postal Services which, in 1944, dispatched some 340 million letters, 95 million packets and 13 million parcels overseas.

Letters from home were considered so important to morale that Montgomery ordered mail deliveries to begin on D-Day. As a result of his directive, some of the first Army postmen to arrive in France were transported by parachute and glider before many troops had landed on the beaches. Instant post offices were set up in slit trenches and barns, even in areas still full of snipers; and some soldiers were soon using the return service to send home packets of butter wrapped in cabbage leaves in emergency ration tins.

A surgeon tending a badly wounded man on the beach at D-Day heard his name spoken, and looked up to be handed a buff envelope by a triumphant lance-corporal who had located him with great diffi-culty. He opened it to find an income tax demand.

The growth and efficiency of the Army Postal Service during the war was little short of miraculous. When Drew joined in 1939 it had set up a centre at Mount Pleasant in London, from which postmen were dispatched to France according to the size of their feet. There was a shortage in the stores of boots above size 9 and below size 8, so anyone with bigger or smaller feet could not be posted overseas although a few gallant volunteers with smaller feet managed to clump off in 8s.

After many temporary homes the service was moved to Nottingham, where it coped with distribu-tion to remote and often top-secret locations. Security problems were enormous before invasions such as "Torch" in North Africa and D-Day in France. But tank crews in the desert, riflemen in the Burmese jungle and men and women in every part of the Services could be sure that their mail would reach them.

A tall, powerfully-built man with an awe-inspiring handlebar moustache, Drew's ability to achieve apparently impossible objectives made him a legendary figure. James Norris Drew – known usually as John but sometimes as Norris – was born on June 8 1912 and educated at Queen Mary's School, Walsall; he entered the Post Office as an assistant traffic superintendent (telephones) in 1933. Five years later he became assistant surveyor, and as a Royal Engineer officer in the Army Supplementary Reserve he became closely involved with the Army Postal Services. When Montgomery issued his instruction to 21st Army Group in 1944 Drew rose to the challenge.

After the war Drew stayed on in the Army with a regular commission, and was Director of Army Postal Services when it combined with the Royal Navy and RAF to become the British Forces Post Office; at the same time he took over responsibility for the Forces Courier Service. He was mentioned in despatches and appointed OBE in 1945; the CBE followed in 1964.

In his youth Drew was a keen rugby footballer and represented both Walsall and Staffordshire; a useful bat, he went on to captain Army cricket XIs. He was also a knowledgeable student of the Turf, and acquired a valuable collection of paintings.

He was survived by his wife, Pamela, two sons and a daughter.

———————

BRIGADIER
"LOPPY" LERWILL

Brigadier "Loppy" Lerwill (who died on January 19 1990, aged 79) won an immediate MC for his stalwart defence of Datta Khel on the North-West Frontier in the summer of 1938. The fort, 10 miles from the Afghan frontier, was a regular target for attacks by Wazir tribesmen well equipped with rifles and artillery.

Lerwill's command consisted of 150 trained Tochi scouts and a small garrison of Khattacks, Mohmands and Yusufzais. But the sieging force of several thousand had blown up bridges and mined the only road along which relief could come and, as the whole frontier was ablaze thanks to the incitement of the Fakir of Ipi, the chance of early reinforcements were negligible.

Every night the besiegers shouted exhortations to the inhabitants of the fort to kill their *faranghi* (English) officer and join the Ipi; they were encouraged to come closer and then greeted with grenades. Under the cover of darkness and in the early morning, members of the garrison would sally forth, patrol and set up ambushes. On one occasion Lerwill led a patrol which climbed to a summit of a crag and surprised 50 Afridis who were completing their ablutions as they suddenly came under fire.

All depended on Lerwill's leadership, for those inside the fort came from the same tribes as the besiegers. But their loyalty to him never faltered, and six weeks later a relief column broke through. Lerwill's achievement was subsequently reported in the Press, and brought him a large amount of fan mail; one letter from a complete stranger contained a proposal of marriage.

Godfrey Lerwill came from a military family, and was born on September 14 1910. He was educated at Eastbourne College and Sandhurst before being gazetted into the Sikh Regiment in 1931. He attended the staff college at Quetta.

His leadership came to the fore again when he was appointed to command the machine-gun battalion of the Sikh Regiment in Burma in April 1945. The battalion, which was in 19 "Dagger" Division, contained two companies of Sikhs and two of Punjabis who would normally have been quite happy fighting each other; but under Lerwill they were welded into a co-operative team, proving more than a match for the Japanese in the fighting around the Singi bridgehead which had just been established on the far side of the Irrawaddy.

A large man with a strong sense of humour, "Loppy" Lerwill kept in touch with the men in the foxholes while showing complete indifference to personal danger. As the battle occurred during the monsoon and most of the Japanese attacks were at night, maintenance of morale was particularly important. The battalion was first into Mandalay and subsequently distinguished itself in the bitter fighting along the Mauchi Road and in the Toungu area. After the partition of India, Lerwill transferred to the Middlesex Regiment and was later seconded to command the 2nd Battalion of the (Royal) Nigerian Regiment. His last command was 168 Infantry Brigade.

In retirement he was employed by Cornwall County Council as emergency planning officer, and found himself with a major disaster on his hands when the Kuwaiti oil tanker *Torrey Canyon* ran aground, polluting 70 miles of coastline. He was appointed OBE and was a Deputy Lieutenant for Cornwall. "Loppy" Lerwill was survived by his wife, Dorothy ("Dee"), and two sons.

BRIGADIER "SLASHER" SOMERSET

Brigadier "Slasher" Somerset (who died on February 7 1990, aged 96) served with distinction in both world wars, winning the DSO and the MC and being mentioned in despatches four times.

In August 1914 he went out to France as a platoon commander in the 1st Gloucestershire Regiment, and had his first encounter with the enemy at Haulchin, just south-east of Mons. In 1940, when commanding the 2nd Glosters, he was sent up to Alsenburg, also just south-east of Mons, once again to face the Germans in the same area. During the subsequent fighting withdrawal, he was surrounded at Cassel, and spent the next five years as senior British officer in various prisoner-of-war camps; as such he was at the centre of all complaints by the Germans about the British and of protests by all the PoWs about the behaviour of their captors.

Nigel FitzRoy Somerset was born at Cefntilla Court, Usk, on July 27 1893, the youngest son of the 3rd Lord Raglan, whose grandfather, the 1st Baron, gave the imprecise order which led to the fatal Charge of the Light Brigade in the Crimean War. The 1st Lord Raglan, himself the youngest son of the 5th Duke of Beaufort, had lost an arm at Waterloo; after it was amputated without an anaesthetic, he observed an attendant carrying the limb from the room, and called out: "Hi! Bring that back. It's got a ring on the finger that I want."

The 3rd Lord Raglan was Governor of the Isle of Man, and young Nigel was educated at King William's College on the island before going to Sandhurst. He was commissioned into the Gloucestershire Regiment in 1913.

During the 200-mile Great Retreat of 1914, the regiment fought in the rearguard action at Landrecies before finally halting at Roziers. In the subsequent fightback he received a bullet through his pack while he was crossing the Aisne River, and then was wounded in the head by shellfire on the next day at Chivy Wood (where the trenches were only 15 yards apart). After being discharged from hospital, Somerset rejoined his regiment in trenches knee-deep in water in January 1915 for a month of continuous snow and rain.

He was involved in the action when the regiment was attacked from both front and rear – a repetition of its experience in the Battle of Alexandria (1801) when, as the 28th, it was surrounded and fought back to back; the regiment was therefore granted the privilege of wearing two cap badges, one front and one back. Somerset was in almost continuous action in the murderous trench battles of Festubert, Neuve Chapelle, Richebourg, Givenchy and Cuinchy, being wounded again in the last by shrapnel.

On coming out of hospital he served for six months in a machine-gun motorcycle unit, and was then sent to Mesopotamia to command 14th Light-Armoured Motor Battery (of which there were only two), in spite of protesting that he knew nothing about armoured cars. The unit's vehicles were Rolls-Royces dating from 1908 to 1913, with such names as "Yellow Demon" and "Golden Eagle"; they were "marvellous", Somerset recalled.

He was awarded an MC in the unsuccessful attempt to capture Ramali (on the Euphrates) in July 1917 and an immediate DSO in October 1918 at Quiyarah, where his coolness and initiative led to the capture of 500 Turks, 10 machine-guns and one field gun. Attached to his battery was Kermit Roosevelt (son of the former American President "Teddy" Roosevelt), "a great classical scholar, apart from being a gallant and good all-round soldier" who also won an MC before leaving to join the American Army.

During the campaign the "Lambs" were almost

continuously in action against the Arabs who, though theoretically on the side of the Allies, would attack British or Turks impartially in the quest for loot; when a Lamb captured German prisoners, they told them to go to the British base to receive some ammunition to protect themselves from marauding Arabs.

At one point the Lambs linked up with Russians who, despite having just turned Bolshevik, were very "friendly and agreeable". Somerset took in all the major actions, including the capture of Baghdad. After the Armistice he escorted the surrendered Turkish commander from Mosul to Nisidin; here he encountered some British survivors of the siege of Kut, who had been prisoners since 1916.

In 1919, Somerset was with the Armoured Motor Brigade in the third Afghan War and the Waziristan campaign. The following year he became ADC to the Governor of Western Australia, Sir Archibald Weigall, and on returning from Australia, served in the Army of Occupation in Germany. He was assistant military secretary at HQ Southern Command, Poona, in 1926. Subsequently he commanded the depot of the Gloucestershire Regiment and went to Egypt with the regiment during Mussolini's invasion of Abyssinia in 1935, when it was not known how far the situation would develop.

Somerset's fourth mention in despatches came in 1945 on his return from being a PoW, but related to his action in the 1940 campaign; he was also appointed CBE at the end of the Second World War. Finally he became Brigadier with special duties in BAOR before retiring in 1949.

"Slasher" Somerset was a tall, dark, slim, very good-looking and extremely popular man. He was thoughtful, compassionate and deeply conscientious, with a cheerful temperament and a strong sense of social responsibility. After retirement he took an active part in the local affairs of Hailsham district in Sussex.

In 1922, he married Phyllis ("Fif") Irwin, an Australian doctor's daughter who died in 1979. They had a son (David Somerset, who became Chief Cashier of the Bank of England) and a daughter.

BRIGADIER
STAIR STEWART

Brigadier Stair Stewart (who died on May 1 1990, aged 86) was a member of the brilliant team of designers at the Experimental Bridging Establishment at Christchurch, Hampshire. One of its best-known products was the Bailey Bridge, without which Field Marshal Montgomery said, "We should not have won the war."

Soon after the outbreak of hostilities in 1939, it became apparent that existing military bridges were inadequate for carrying the weight of the latest kind of new tanks. The new bridge bore the name of Donald Bailey, a civil servant, but it was produced by a team working on his design for a "panel" bridge, and Bailey was the first to acknowledge the part played by others in the project.

The bridge was assembled from welded steel panels linked by pinned joints. No special mechanical aids were required, and each unit was light enough to be carried by six men. It could span a gap 240ft wide and, with pontoons, cover a much wider area. The Bailey first came to public attention in the Italian campaign where its ability to go over fast-flowing, wide rivers proved invaluable. Later, in north-west Europe, as fast as existing bridges were blown up by the retreating Germans, they were replaced by Baileys, thus enabling the Allies to keep up the pressure.

After the war the Bailey bridges, which could be adapted for many other purposes apart from crossing rivers, had a vital part in the reconstruction of devastated Europe: 2,000 had been built by the end of 1947. There were many other successful projects at the Experimental Bridging Establishment, and Stewart was involved in all of them.

A brigadier-general's son, Stair Agnew Stewart was born on April 23 1904 and educated at Winchester, where he was an exhibitioner, and at Woolwich, where he won many prizes. He was commissioned into the Royal Engineers in 1924, and two years later was selected to join the Experimental Bridging Establishment.

Stewart subsequently had three more tours of duty in the establishment and finally became super-intendent. He recalled that at the interview to recruit Donald Bailey into the establishment in 1940, Bailey had produced a sketch of the bridge on the back of an envelope. He and his colleagues then worked out with him the calculations and detailed design.

After the war Stewart became deputy director of fortification and works at the War Office from 1950 to 1953; deputy director of works in Middle East Land Forces from 1953 to 1956, and at the Ministry of Supply from 1956 to 1959.

He subsequently became director of the British Road Tar Association for 12 years, a post which involved him in close liaison with the Road Research Laboratory and the British Road Federation in the motorway era. He also served on numerous committees to do with road-making, chaired the Flexible Road Group and was a member of British delegations to overseas conferences on road transport.

But Stewart's forte was personal invention and practical work. Among his many creations was the lawn-edge trimmer, which was patented and manufactured successfully by Webbs; the flickering lights which are now used to guard hazards on roads; and a variety of toy models. Early in life he built a portable workshop and transported it around on the back seat of a Raleigh 9 tourer – a motorcar of which it was said the owner needed to be a rich man or a mechanic. He built an explosive model battleship which disintegrated when it reached a certain point or was torpedoed; managing directors would lie on the floors of their offices to play with this vessel when Stewart arrived to demonstrate it. He is also credited with inventing windscreen washers.

A brilliant mathematician, Stewart was extremely quiet, modest, and anxious to give credit to others;

and he had a pleasant sense of humour. He was immaculate in appearance, with never a hair out of place, even though he was an engineer. After retiring from the Army he took up repairing clocks, mainly long-case, and when vital parts were unobtainable, made them himself. Stewart repaired some 250 clocks in eight years, keeping meticulous notes, but never charged for his work. His motto was: "Engineering is fun".

Stair Stewart was appointed OBE in 1949 and CBE in 1956, and was ADC to the Queen from 1957 to 1959. He was also awarded the American Legion of Merit. An enthusiastic cricketer and tennis player, he took great pride in the fact that his wife was selected to play tennis for Hampshire. She predeceased him; he was survived by a daughter.

MAJOR "RAJ" FOWLER

Major "Raj" Fowler (who died on March 5 1991, aged 69), inspired his Sikh company in the 4th/15th Punjabis on the night before the attack on Kohima Ridge by reciting appropriate passages of Shakespeare in Urdu. Morale in his company was already high, but his Urdu version of "Come these three corners of the world in arms/And we shall shock them/Nought shall make us rue" was particularly electrifying.

To the music of their *dhols* and *surnais* (Pathan

drums and fifes) the soldiers launched into the assault at dawn with tremendous dash and courage. Several days of continuous fierce fighting followed, during which Fowler was a tower of strength, showing tireless initiative and enthusiasm with no regard for his own safety. As the advance through Burma continued, the regiment was in action for the next 12 months. His company was among the leading assault troops to cross the Irrawaddy (the longest opposed river-crossing in the Second World War) and, on the far bank, Fowler accepted surrender of the 15,000-strong "Indian National Army", the force organised by the Japanese from captured Indian soldiers.

In March 1945, two of Fowler's men won VCs in separate actions – Sepoy Nand Singh of the Sikh Regiment and (posthumously) Abdul Hafiz of the 9th Jats – and in April he himself won his second MC. On this occasion, he had been ordered with his company to establish a roadblock behind Japanese lines.

Reaching the appointed destination, they found themselves in what appeared to be an enemy administrative area, and were immediately attacked by 100 Japanese. During the bitter and confused fighting which followed, Fowler was given the option by his seniors of retiring. Instead, he led his Sikhs with such skill and determination that they secured the position and resisted all Japanese attempts to dislodge them.

Richard Anthony James Fowler was born in Birmingham on September 20 1921 and educated at

St Philip's Grammar School and Birmingham University. He joined Esso Petroleum and, on the outbreak of war, volunteered for military service.

Fowler attended the Officer Cadet Training Unit at Bangalore, and was then posted to the 4th Battalion of the 15th Punjabis. Joining this elite regiment was, he always maintained, the most important and exciting event of his life. In addition to HQ, it contained four companies – one Sikh, one Jat, one Punjabi Mussulman and one Pathan – and Fowler won the respect and affection of them all. He saw minor action on the North-West Frontier before setting out east with 7th Indian Division for jungle training and the Arakan battles of March 1944.

By now Adjutant, Fowler won his first MC when two platoons had been repulsed with heavy casualties from a large and strongly-held enemy position. He volunteered to reorganise the remainder, and then led them up a precipitous slope under continuous fire to capture and consolidate the position.

At the end of the war, Fowler was selected to be interpreter at the presentation of Indian holders of the VC to King George VI. On leaving the Army, he returned to Esso, where eventually he became director of the company's international and industrial business, which included responsibility for world-wide aviation and marine sales. During the 1960s, he made a significant contribution to the extensive use of naptha in the manufacture of gas and of heavy fuel oil in electricity generation. In 1975, Fowler joined Esso Europe and became responsible for their bulk oil trading division. After leaving the company, he remained for several years actively involved in cargo oil trading, with assignments in the Far East and Australia.

Tall, dark, energetic and cheerful, "Raj" Fowler was overjoyed to be invited to Pakistan in 1990 as a guest of honour of his old regiment, and was greatly impressed by the way his high standards were being maintained.

He was a Liveryman of the Worshipful Company of Coachmakers and Coach Harness Makers.

Fowler married, in 1947, Valerie Littleales; they had three sons and a daughter.

LIEUTENANT-COLONEL STUART CHANT-SEMPILL

Lieutenant-Colonel Stuart Chant-Sempill (who died on July 27 1991, aged 74) led the demolition team in the St Nazaire raid of March 27/28 1942, one of the most important and daring actions of the Second World War.

Chant-Sempill and his Commandos destroyed what was then the largest dock in the world – the only haven on the Atlantic coast for the German Navy's capital ships – by ramming the gates with the destroyer *Campbeltown* then blowing up the ship with five tons of ammonal, thereby putting the dock out of action for the rest of the war. Chant-Sempill was wounded three times in the raid, first in the arm and twice in the legs. The last bullet completely immobilised him – and in the event saved his life.

His party's objective was to destroy the pumping station and complete the general devastation of submarine pens, inner lock gates and winching apparatus. The *Campbeltown* crashed into the lock gates at 20 knots after slicing through anti-submarine nets and other obstacles. The Commandos then ran over the decks, now sloping at 20 degrees, clambered over debris and corpses and dropped 18ft onto the quayside carrying their equipment. All this was accomplished under intense German fire.

They then blew open the locked gates of the main pump house, which was 75 ft high and 150 ft long, laid charges with a 90-second fuse and ran for it. Outside they paused for breath for a few seconds and moved on – just before the explosion hurled huge blocks of concrete on to the ground where they had been standing. Some of the destruction was achieved by delayed charges, so that much of the damage occurred after the Germans, assuming the raid was only a partial success, had reoccupied the area in strength. In the general panic which ensued after the later explosions, the Germans shot many of their own workmen, having mistaken their uniforms for those of British soldiers.

A hundred and sixty-nine British officers and men were killed in the raid, and 200 were wounded and captured. The surviving raiders had hoped to make their getaway in motor launches, but discovered that these had all been destroyed by German counterfire. With half of them already wounded, they decided to make their way inland, link up with the Resistance and escape overland. But as Chant-Sempill was now completely immobilised he was left behind on the dockside.

At that point he realised he was only a few yards from the *Campbeltown*, which he recalled contained the five tons of ammonal, fused to explode within a short time and destroy everything around it. But before that happened, he was taken prisoner by the Waffen SS, who shot a soldier next to him on the dockside for unwisely rising to his feet on the order to put up his hands. Even though he could not move, one of the Germans wanted to kill Chant-Sempill with a sword, but was prevented from doing so by the others.

When the *Campbeltown* blew up it killed 400 Germans who had gathered round to assess the damage caused by the ramming, which they assumed to be the sole purpose of the raid. Although the casualties were high, the operation ensured that the mighty battleship *Tirpitz* would not now dare to leave the shelter of the Norwegian fjords, lest it suffer the fate of the *Bismarck*, and that other powerful ships would not be able to use St Nazaire as a base in the critical Battle of the Atlantic.

He was born Stuart Whitemore Chant on March 11 1917 and educated at Mill Hill before becoming a "blue button" on the London Stock Exchange. Young Stuart joined the Artists Rifles (now 21 SAS) as a private soldier, and was commissioned into the Gordon Highlanders in October 1939. He served in France as a member of the British Expeditionary Force and escaped from Bray Dunes, a seaside village near Dunkirk, in a rowing boat.

In October 1940 he volunteered for the Commandos, and trained intensively in Scotland and at various docks in Wales and England before embarking on the *Campbeltown*, a former American destroyer which at a distance resembled the Mowe Class destroyers of the German Navy. All of those taking part in the raid were informed that they were expendable but that their task was of vital importance. Having been taken prisoner and suffering various horrendous operations, Chant tried to escape: first by a tunnel, which was disclosed by an informer; secondly, in a swill cart under potato peelings, in which he was detected by a guard's sniffer dog. In 1943, though, he was repatriated as a *grand blessé*.

Chant was the first officer to return to Britain after the St Nazaire raid, which until then, for various inexplicable security reasons, had been given little publicity. This enabled German propaganda to describe the raid as a failure, so Chant was promptly sent to America to give lectures about it, travelling some 9,000 miles by train before returning to the War Office. In 1945 he was discharged from the Army as unfit for active service. Chant was then taken on by the Rank Organisation and worked for five years with David Lean, Noel Coward and other luminaries of the film world. But as he spoke fluent French he was suddenly recalled to the Army, and appointed liaison officer at SHAPE in Paris, where he worked with General Eisenhower and Field Marshal Montgomery.

On retiring again in 1955, Chant formed a public

relations agency with Prince Galitzine and others. Later he became director of public relations with C T Bowring, and was instrumental in that firm's sponsorship of the Oxford and Cambridge match at Twickenham, for which the "Bowring Bowl" is the annual trophy.

Although paralysed on his right side by a stroke in 1977 he taught himself to write with his left hand and completed a book on the raid entitled *St Nazaire Commando* (1985). In appearance Chant-Sempill, as he became in later life, was fair, stocky and of medium height. As a younger man he had been a passionately keen rugby footballer and had played in all the Wasps' 10 teams, from 1st XV to Extra C; later he became vice-president of the club. He was also, from 1966, honorary secretary of the Pilgrims, the Anglo-American society, as well as an enthusiastic and talented painter in oils.

He was awarded the Military Cross in 1945 for his services in the St Nazaire raid and the OBE (Military) in 1952 for his services with SHAPE.

In 1948 Stuart Chant married Ann (née Forbes-Sempill); they had two sons and a daughter. In 1965 his wife succeeded to the Barony of Sempill, and by decree of the Lyon Court at Edinburgh he assumed the name of Sempill – which he said was "in order to keep up with the Joneses, as it were".

MAJOR-GENERAL
SIR REGINALD SCOONES

Major-General Sir Reginald Scoones (who died on October 6 1991, aged 90) won the DSO in 1945 for his brilliant leadership against the Japanese in Burma. When General Bill Slim and the 14th Army were charged with the task of driving the enemy back from the borders of India and out of Burma in 1943, many doubted that tanks could be employed effectively in the offensive.

But "Cully" Scoones – who had commanded a machine-gun battery alongside the Camel Corps in Sudan between the wars and had later fought in the Western Desert – believed there might possibly be ways of making good use of tanks. He talked it over with his brother, Lieutenant-General (later Sir) Geoffrey Scoones, then commanding 4 Corps in Burma, and set off for Assam to examine the prospects. As a jockey walks a racecourse before the race, Scoones reconnoitred the jungle in the teak forests of the Kabaw Valley on foot and climbed the hills on the Tiddim Road, terrain which was to figure prominently in Slim's advance.

Scoones then returned to GHQ in India, where he reported that there was good reason to believe that tanks might be able to operate in limited numbers. After defying the sceptics and winning approval for the scheme, he received command of 254 Tank Brigade, comprising the 3rd Carabiniers (Prince of Wales's) Dragoon Guards and the 7th Indian Light Cavalry. Towards the end of 1943 Scoones moved the brigade and its Lee Grant heavy and Stuart light tanks up to Imphal.

He was renowned in the Army for his thorough preparation and the issuing of clear and concise orders. An impressively lean and hard figure, he also exercised a quiet humour to relax tense situations. This was needed as the tanks experimented with ways of negotiating swamps, scaling jungle hills and, accompanied by infantry, attacking enemy bunkers.

They were put to the test the next spring at Nungschigum – a commanding eminence more than 1,000 ft above the Imphal plain – when tasked with tackling the steep slopes in support of infantry. The tanks, in turn, were supported by artillery and Hurricane fighters operating as bombers. Slipping and skidding, their tortured engines took them up the hill at little more than 1 mph. The angle of climb denied the drivers a view of the ascent so that their commanders stuck their heads out of the turrets to call directions.

As the armour inched its way upwards with heavy fighting alongside, Scoones's wireless crackled with reports of the exposed commanders being killed or mortally wounded until five out of six were dead. Yet the surviving members of their crews pressed on and, together with Indian infantry, took the hill and its defending bunkers.

In a later action, Scoones – forward, as ever, to watch his tanks in action – wriggled alongside a Gurkha in the front line. The rifleman saw a dove in a tree, and let fly with a catapult. He missed. When he looked over his shoulder, there were the red tabs of the brigadier. Scoones suggested he reload – the rifle, not the catapult – and get on with the war.

Reginald Laurence Scoones was born on December 18 1900 and educated at Wellington and Sandhurst before following his father, Major Fitzmaurice Scoones, into the Royal Fusiliers. In 1923 young Scoones transferred to the Royal Tank Corps. Five years later he was attached to the Sudan Defence Force, where he remained for eight years, in command of its mobile machine-gun battery. Then in 1935 he returned home to become Adjutant of the 1st Royal Tank Regiment. By 1938 he had moved up to the staff of the Mobile Division.

Scoones began the Second World War as a brigade major in Cairo and, in 1940, he was GSO2 of the Western Desert Corps. The next year he consolidated his reputation as CO of 42nd Royal Tank Regiment with the 7th Armoured Division. Then, following a spell on the staff at the War Office and as deputy director of Military Training, Scoones headed east.

After the war he resumed his post in Military Training before returning to his beloved Sudan as assistant Kayid (Head) of the Sudan Defence Force. In 1950 he was promoted major-general commanding British troops in Sudan and Commandant of the Sudan Defence Force. He also served on the executive council of Sudan. But in the summer of 1954 the new Sudanese government suddenly decided to implement the "Sudanisation" of the Defence Force. So Scoones, the last British C-in-C to command its 5,000-strong men, duly handed over command to his deputy, Lieutenant-General Ahmed Mohamed. Scoones's last act before boarding the aircraft at Khartoum back to Britain was to inspect a guard of honour formed by the Camel Corps.

Three years later, after retiring from the Army, the general was to be found under the pseudonym of "Mr R. Smith", sitting a London County Council examination on the running of a public house, complete with questions on how to pull pints of ale. Sir Reginald passed the test with honours, but he had no intention of keeping a pub. With the thoroughness that had distinguished his military career, he had decided to do the course anonymously in order to brief himself for his new post as director of the National Trade Defence Association – a joint organisation of brewers and licensed victuallers which later changed its name to the Brewers Society. He remained in the job for 12 years.

Scoones was appointed OBE in 1941, CB in 1951 and KBE in 1955. He married, in 1933, Isabella Nisbet; they had a daughter.

———

BRIGADIER
SIR MARK HENNIKER, BT

Brigadier Sir Mark Henniker, 8th Bt (who died on October 18 1991, aged 85) was a sapper awarded an MC on the Indian Frontier in 1933 and an immediate DSO in the North-West Europe campaign during the Second World War. A highly intelligent professional soldier with a notable sense of humour and a ready compassion for all victims of war, he was a keen admirer of Montgomery and Horrocks, with whom he shared imperturbability and resourcefulness in moments of great personal danger.

Henniker wrote several books, including *Memoirs of a Junior Officer* (1951), which described his early life in India. "One of the tests by which the Commandant at Roorkee chose his officers," he recalled, "was their willingness to play polo." Most of the polo ponies were paid for by the Indian government because they appeared on the books as "chargers", which officers were required to possess for wartime duties. Two elephants were also kept for heavy work. Each would salute by raising his trunk if he met an officer. If in uniform the officer would acknowledge by saluting, and if in plain clothes by raising his hat.

"The youngest second-lieutenant from England," wrote Henniker, "felt quite a nabob – though ignorant people were sometimes seen to smile."

A scion of the family of the Lords Henniker, Mark Chandos Auberon Henniker was born on January 23 1906. His father had served in the Indian Civil Service, and his great-great-grandfather, Lieutenant-General Brydges Henniker, had been created a baronet in 1813. Young Mark was educated at Marlborough, Woolwich and King's College, Cambridge. In 1926 he was commissioned into the Royal Engineers, where he found himself landed with the sobriquet of "Honker". Two years later he began his service in India with the Bengal Sappers and Miners.

In 1933, when the Mohmands disturbed the uneasy peace of the Frontier by various hostile acts against their neighbours, Henniker's unit was one of those chosen to restore the situation. His responsibility was to supervise the building of a road up the Karappa Pass from the Vale of Peshawar, a distance of some 20 miles. This gave him the experience of being shot at without having the least idea from where the bullets were coming.

At the outbreak of the Second World War Henniker was sent to France to build pill-boxes, which in the event were never used. He was at home on leave when the Germans invaded Belgium and France and rushed back to the front with some difficulty, only to find himself taking part in the general retreat. Seeing little prospect of getting away from Dunkirk, he took his unit further along the coast where they found a large rowing-boat, in which they made their way back to England.

His next post was as Chief Royal Engineer, 1st Airborne Division, working closely with General "Boy" Browning. In 1942 Henniker took part in the raid on Bruneval near Le Havre, the site of an important German radar station. The raiders were required to land by parachute, capture the station and bring away pieces of advanced technical equipment – a task they accomplished with minimal casualties. Later that year Henniker was involved in the disastrous raid on the Norwegian heavy water plant at Rjuken. He was one of the few survivors, only because the Halifax aircraft carrying him developed engine trouble and had to turn back.

During the Sicily landings in 1943 Henniker was unhurt when his glider crash-landed, but soon afterwards he was wounded in seven places, as well as sustaining a broken arm; he continued to fight, though swathed in bandages. Later, without having spent any time in hospital, he took part in the invasion of Italy.

Some of his letters home to his parents now read strangely: "On October 9 1943 I had a captured German army 'people's car', with an air-cooled engine under the back seat, but now order has been given for all captured German vehicles to be returned to HQ. So I now have an American thing called a Jeep. It has no doors and if you fall asleep you may fall overboard going round a corner." He lived in a captured German tent – "a tame hen lays an egg in it just before dawn every day, but an Italian policeman, who guards our enclosure, creeps under the flies of the tent and steals the egg as soon as he hears the hen lay." The policeman was not the only unauthorised visitor. On October 21 Henniker recorded: 'Today I killed a snake in my tent. A *carabiniere* pronounced it to be a *vipri*."

On his return to England Henniker was posted to 43 (Wessex) Division, and took part in the race to reach Arnhem before the rest of his former comrades in 1st Airborne were overwhelmed by the Germans. At Nijmegen he had another narrow escape, driving over the bridge five minutes before it was blown up by German frogmen. Subsequently he was involved in the battles of the Rhineland and the Ardennes and the final drive into the heart of

Germany. The last few battles were as dangerous as any before them, for the German engineers from Bremen had mined all the culverts along the roads.

Henniker was in India during the last days of the Raj, then was posted to Malaya during the worst period of the Emergency. He was involved in the Suez operation and mentioned in despatches before retiring from the Army in 1958.

Honorary colonel of the Parachute Engineer Regiment (TA) from 1959 to 1968, and of REME (TA) from 1964 to 1968, he was appointed OBE in 1944, CBE in 1953 and a Deputy Lieutenant for Monmouthshire (later Gwent) in 1963. In 1958 he succeeded his cousin, Lieutenant-Colonel Sir Robert Henniker, 7th Bt, in the family baronetcy. "Honker" described his recreations in *Who's Who* as "appropriate to age and rank". A talented writer, he contributed to *Blackwood's Magazine*. His other books were *Red Shadow Over Malaya* (1955), *Life in the Army Today* (1957) and *An Image of War* (1987).

He married, in 1945, Kathleen Anderson; they had a son and daughter. The son, Adrian Chandos Henniker, born 1946, succeeded to the title.

GENERAL
SIR NIGEL POETT

General Sir Nigel Poett (who died on October 29 1991, aged 84) commanded 5th Parachute Brigade when it landed in Normandy on the night of June 5/6 1944.

The 6th Airborne Division, to which the brigade belonged, had been allotted the task of capturing the Orne and Caen bridges at Benouville and Ranville in order to prevent them being destroyed by the Germans to hinder the Allies' advance inland. The assault, spearheaded by gliders, involved dropping 2,000 men in darkness into hostile territory during appalling weather.

Poett recalled crossing the Channel in an Albemarle, in which his "stick" of parachutists were so closely packed that movement was almost impossible. He personally opened the double doors in the floor and jumped out first. On the ground he made contact with the other units of his brigade just as the Germans were launching a counter-attack, which was beaten off.

Although all the division's tasks had been accomplished by midday on June 6, more than two months of heavy fighting followed as the Allies tried to move inland and the Germans battled desperately to prevent them. In August Poett's brigade took a vital part in the break-out. They captured the strongly-held position of Putot-en-Auge in another night attack, secured Pont L'Eveque, established a bridgehead over the River Touques and finally secured the west bank of the River Risle and Pont Audemer.

A physically strong man, Poett contrived to spend much of his time in forward and exposed positions without losing his grasp of the overall pattern of the battles. After it had suffered many casualties, the brigade was sent back to England to be re-formed and reinforced, pending the next airborne assignment. But when the Germans unexpectedly broke through the Ardennes sector in December it was hastily dispatched to plug the gap in what became known as the "Battle of the Bulge". Although an airborne unit, they arrived by sea and road and then plunged into a bloody battle in which the Germans failed to hold on to their gains.

The brigade was then withdrawn, reinforced again and prepared for the Rhine Crossing on March 24 1945. The "drop", which was timed to cover the waterborne crossing and extend the bridgehead, took place in broad daylight and was fiercely resisted by high-quality German troops, many of them also parachutists. Although 5th Para had studied the terrain meticulously on sand models, the landmarks were almost entirely invisible when they fell among the firing and the smoke. Nevertheless the brigade's battle experience served it well, and casualties were limited to about 20 per cent of those who jumped or landed by glider. "Morale was high", Poett recalled, "and long distances were subsequently covered, knowing that this way casualties could be kept to a minimum. Fifty miles were covered on foot during the first three days. This included two night attacks and almost continuous fighting or marching. It was a tremendous achievement and the troops had every reason to be proud of themselves."

They drove on, reaching Coesfeld, Greven and Osnabruck, seizing important bridges at Wunstorf and Neustadt while pressing on to Wismar on the

Baltic. Here they met the Russians, with whom their relations were cordial.

Poett's subsequent leave was interrupted while he was fishing on the Tweed, by a message telling him to return and prepare the brigade for the forthcoming assault on Malaya. He discussed dropping zones with General "Boy" Browning, whose job was to seize the causeway between Singapore and the mainland. Browning wanted him to land in a pineapple plantation, but Poett thought a rubber estate might be less prickly. When they eventually landed the war was over, and they disembarked by boat on beaches which turned out to be knee-deep in sticky mud.

The son of Major-General J H Poett, Joseph Howard Nigel Poett was born on August 20 1907 and educated at Downside and Sandhurst. He was commissioned into the Durham Light Infantry in 1927 and sent to Egypt before being posted to Razmak on the frontier of Waziristan, where he learned soldiering the hard way. Later Poett served with the regiment in the Sudan, before spending the early years of the Second World War at the War Office. Having applied to return to regimental duty, he was given command of the 11th Battalion of the DLI in 1942. Then, to his surprise, he was appointed to form and command 5th Parachute Brigade in the 6th Airborne Division. As he had never parachuted before he first had to qualify himself.

After the war Poett's brigade was first charged with the task of reorganising the Malayan Police. Next they were sent to Batavia (Jakarta), where there was an extremist anti-Dutch rebellion. Then they went to

Semarang, where they incorporated into their command a battalion of 500 Japanese who had just fought a successful battle to protect the Dutch against rebels who wished to massacre them.

In 1946 Poett returned to Britain as Director of Plans at the War Office, where he attended meetings of the Chiefs of Staff. As he recalled, it was "a most unhappy organisation. Monty and Tedder disliked each other intensely. Sir John Cunningham was clever but did not hit it off with Monty." After this Poett was sent to the Imperial Defence College where, in contrast to the long hours of his previous post, "they took the broad view from 10 to 4." He subsequently sat on the Harwood Committee to decide on the future shape of the Armed Forces; in 1949 Poett was appointed deputy commander to the military mission in Greece.

The following year he became Chief of Staff, Far East Land Forces, for two years. This was the period when the Malayan Emergency was at its worst and the situation in Vietnam was deteriorating fast. Next he was given the command of 3rd Division in the Suez Canal Zone which, among other responsibilities, was involved in protecting the Tel-el-Kebir base from wily thieves. To add to the difficulties some of Poett's units were based as far away as Cyprus, Tripoli and Kenya.

He was Director of Military Operations at the War Office when the Suez crisis erupted: "a political disaster which many of us would like to forget", he commented afterwards. By contrast Poett found his posting as Commandant of the Staff College at

Camberley relaxed and happy, though it was a busy time. In 1958 he was appointed GOC-in-C, Southern Command, for three years before his final appointment as C-in-C, Far East Land Forces.

After retiring in 1961 Poett became director of the British Productivity Council, and was Colonel of the Durham Light Infantry from 1956 to 1965.

Nigel Poett was a professional soldier to his finger-tips, a man of indomitable spirit and great compassion. He worked tirelessly for SSAFA, the Services welfare organisation, and latterly gave much time to assisting the Airborne Assault Normandy Trust, which identified battle sites and recorded tapes of the events of them. He took a course to make himself fluent in French and wrote an autobiography, *Pure Poett*, which was published a few weeks after his death.

Poett was awarded the DSO and Bar in 1945, appointed CB in 1952 and KCB in 1959. He also received the American Silver Star. In 1937 he married Julia Herrick; they had two sons and a daughter.

COLONEL
BASIL GROVES

Colonel Basil Groves (who died on March 4 1992, aged 95) won an immediate Military Cross as a tank officer at the Battle of Passchendaele in 1917, followed by an immediate Bar at Cambrai three months later.

The citation for the first recorded that "on August 23 1917, at Clapham Junction [the nickname given to one of the notoriously dangerous places on the battlefield], this officer displayed the greatest gallantry in guiding his tanks on foot over very difficult ground under heavy shell fire. After the action, hearing that one of his officers was lying wounded in front of our line, he twice crawled out at great risk to get him. On both occasions he reached the officer but failed to get him back owing to hostile machine-gun fire. The night of 23/24 he went out again but found the officer dead.

"On August 24 at 4.30am the enemy counter-attacked. Seeing that parties of our infantry were retiring, Captain Groves rallied them and materially assisted in repelling the attack."

The area between Passchendaele and Ypres contained huge areas of liquid mud into which men, horses, guns and tanks could sink without trace. Guiding tanks through the few firm places or log roads in the morass required exceptional skill and courage. Some months later, Cambrai became the first place where tanks were used in mass assault. Since half of them broke down on the first day and they could manage at best a top speed of four miles per hour, most of the remainder became easy targets for enemy gunners.

Groves's second citation ran: "For conspicuous gallantry in action near Marcoing on November 20 1917, when in command of a section of tanks. To ensure that all his tanks kept to the right routes and reached their objectives he directed them on foot in spite of the fact that he was exposed to machine-gun and rifle fire. He showed remarkable coolness and daring and it was largely due to his skill and devotion to duty that the infantry were able to reach their objectives with slight casualties. This officer throughout the action showed a total disregard for his personal safety."

Henry Basil Melvin Groves was born in Buckinghamshire on April 21 1896 and educated at Nottingham High School. He was commissioned into the Scottish Rifles in 1915, and the next year transferred to the Heavy Section, Machine Gun Corps. The latter was a codename for the unit then training to be the crews of the new, top-secret tanks with which Field Marshal Haig hoped to achieve a significant breakthrough on the Western Front. The MGC was re-christened the Tank Corps in July 1917.

Some of the Corps's early training in gunnery took place on naval shipping, since the roll, yaw and pitch of moving tanks was roughly similar to that on small ships. The Navy was accustomed to coping with the problems of other forms of transport, and Groves was interested to see the instructions – signed by Captain Percy Scott, the gunnery expert – addressed to naval officers who rode horses in reviews:

"The animals should be checked when rounding corners and extreme deflection never applied except at slow speeds. In mounting and dismounting, only the port side of the horse should be used and spurs are not to be used to hold on by. The animal is steered in the same way as a boat with a yoke, but whereas in a boat the yoke is at the stern, with a horse it is in the bows. The yoke lines are called reins."

Although these instructions did not seem immediately applicable to riding in a tank, Groves noted that they were accompanied by more relevant instructions in gunnery, which later stood him in good stead.

Having survived Cambrai, where the tanks captured 400 guns and took 10,000 prisoners, Groves went on leave and nearly died of Spanish 'flu. On his recovery he was appointed to the staff at Bovington. After the war his unit began intensive sports training. Groves practised the 440 yards for the next Olympic Games, but as he was an experienced oarsman (he had won the All India Sculls) he was made to row, and competed at Henley. In 1919 he went back to running and won the 440 yards in the Empire Day sports meeting at Stamford Bridge.

In 1924 he was posted to Lahore, and then commanded a section of tanks at Parachinar on the North-West Frontier. Further postings took him to Kirkee and Poona before he returned to England in 1927; he had various staff and instructional duties before becoming chief instructor at the Army School of Physical Training at Aldershot in 1936. Two years later Groves joined the 1st Battalion, Royal Tank Regiment, in Cairo. After commanding the depot he was appointed to command 7th Battalion, RTR, in General Wavell's "Operation Battleaxe" to relieve Tobruk in 1941. Near Capuzzo the battalion was attacked by low-flying Messerschmitts, in spite of having been previously informed that there was complete air superiority.

Rommel's forces had better guns and armour, and in brisk fighting Groves had several narrow escapes before his tank was knocked out and he was obliged to walk back. He was eventually picked up by a lorry bearing the bodies of dead soldiers.

In September 1941, Groves was chosen by General Bernard Freyberg to command the New Zealand Armoured Fighting Vehicles School in the dominion. On arriving at Waiouru he found that the only equipment the school possessed was a pencil and some paper. The camp was close to an active volcano, and the surrounding terrain was covered with pumice dust, which was very damaging to vehicles. Nevertheless, he organised training, work-shops, radios, instructional films and a gunnery range; he also invented some ditch–crossing devices, which were later adopted by the American Marines for use in the Pacific.

During his tenure Groves also formed and trained the New Zealand Armoured Brigade, which subsequently distinguished itself in the Middle East. He received a glowing report from the New Zealand GOC: "Frankly I am very favourably disposed towards this officer, partly because of his pleasing personality but chiefly because of his keenness, ability and devotion to duty as commandant of the AFV school which I have often described as the most impressive, best organised and most efficient training establishment I have ever seen and which has made a notable contribution to the efficiency of New Zealand forces both abroad and at home."

In 1947, Groves was invalided out of the Army and the next year he moved to Cape Town, where he set up a productive market garden and subsequently ran a company which manufactured motorcar number plates.

He was survived by his wife, and a daughter and a son.

―――――――――

LIEUTENANT-GENERAL
SIR JOHN COWLEY, GC

Lieutenant-General Sir John Cowley (who died on July 1 1992, aged 86), was a staff officer of outstanding physical and moral courage.

As a subaltern he won an Albert Medal during the Quetta earthquake of 1935 in which 25,000 people were killed. The local hospital collapsed. When Cowley arrived on the scene with the first relief team they were too few in number to remove the roofs, so while his men lifted them up for short periods, he crawled in and dragged out from under the debris of the walls many survivors, who were pinned to the floor and known to be suffering from all manner of contagious diseases.

Cowley remained a man of strongly-held convictions, which he never hesitated to express even when they made him unpopular and risked his position.

An Army chaplain's son, John Guise Cowley was

born on August 20 1905 at Mussoorie in the foothills of the Himalayas, where his birth coincided with an earthquake. Later, travelling to England by ship, he won a contest for the ugliest baby on board. Young John was brought up in a Dorset village, where Thomas Hardy was a neighbour. He remembered the writer as a sad, wizened old man who spoke seldom. Although an atheist, Hardy occasionally attended church services, at which he always asked Cowley's father to read the passage from the Bible about Elijah's vision of the earthquake.

Cowley was educated at Wellington and Woolwich, neither of which he enjoyed. He was commissioned in 1925 and posted to Aldershot, where he thought very little of the whole organisation and equipment of the British Army: "The cooker was pulled by a horse. On a route march the cook walked behind the cooker trying to prepare a meal for the company. He always arrived absolutely black in the face with the smoke."

During the General Strike of 1926, Cowley was sent with a platoon of sappers to guard the waterworks at Luton. His company commander, a serious man, told him: "If you have to shoot, shoot to kill." Instead, Cowley arranged a football match between his men and the strikers, whom he found "an extremely pleasant and reasonable lot of men".

In 1932, he joined the Madras Sappers and Miners at Bangalore, and later went to Quetta, where he learned Urdu. After four years he was appointed an instructor at Woolwich, which he now found more enlightened, and then became a student at the Staff

College, Camberley. But before he had completed the course he was posted to the War Office, where he organised the dispatch of the Cavalry Division (with 2,000 horses) to Palestine. A year later all the division had been mechanised except for one brigade, which made the last cavalry charge by the British Army – against the Vichy French in Syria.

In 1940, Cowley was posted to the North African desert. He recalled having to wake up General Wavell in the night to tell him that the Australians had captured Sidi Barrani; Wavell then wrote a personal note to Churchill. "The interesting thing about this story," Cowley later wrote, "is that I was sitting four feet from the Commander-in-Chief for half an hour, and he never said anything, not even 'Good night' or 'Thank you very much'. Not a word. A strangely silent man."

When Rommel counter-attacked Cowley was besieged in Tobruk, but after two months he was evacuated by sea and put in charge of the docks at Alexandria. He recalled the arrival of an officer in the Military Police who had come to stop pilfering on the dockside. Cowley warned him that this might be difficult, as it had been going on for thousands of years. Six days later the officer reappeared, saying he could no longer continue as all the equipment and stores had been stolen.

Cowley's next appointment was to the staff of 7th Armoured Division (the Desert Rats), which left him with the belief that Rommel could have been defeated at the Battle of Gazala if the Army's tactics had been more flexible. In 1942 he was posted to the

Staff College at Haifa, but the day after his arrival he was summoned back to join the staff of 30 Corps. After the Alamein battles he was sent to lecture about the war at Fort Leavenworth, Kansas, then posted to Allied Forces HQ in Algeria, which was moved to Caserta, near Naples.

He joined the staff of 21st Army Group in Brussels to help refugees, before moving to Minden, briefed to restore the German economy after the cease of hostilities. The Ruhr was a mass of rubble, with people living in holes in the ground. The Volkswagen factory lay in the British zone, and as it had never functioned in peace time was inspected by various British military experts. They concluded that the car was inefficient, had no future, and that neither the works nor the VW design should be acquired for use by British industry.

Cowley then spent a year at the Imperial Defence College, followed by a stint on the Defence Research Policy staff before going on to become Director of Administrative Planning at the War Office, where he felt that the civil servants were more likely to be right than the soldiers. From 1953 he was Chief of Staff, HQ, Eastern Command, working with General "Frankie" Festing – "a big man with bright red hair and a very quick temper, who was rarely on time for appointments and wore unusual clothes". At one inspection Festing "arrived late, dangling a beautiful Japanese sword from his belt, and wearing field boots which must have belonged to his grand-father in the Crimean war. On his red hair he wore a green beret. He really was a most impressive sight."

In 1956 Cowley returned to the War Office as Vice-Quartermaster General, just in time for the Suez Crisis. Anthony Eden struck him as "exhausted and mentally ill". The Army wanted to land at Alexandria but Eden insisted on Port Said, which proved a disaster.

The next year Cowley was appointed Controller of Munitions at the War Office, where he soon clashed with Duncan Sandys, the Minister of Supply. Sandys thought that Blue Streak, the British nuclear missile, should be used in a crisis. Cowley argued that it should never be used, as nuclear war would mean the end of civilisation. Sandys asked Harold Macmillan to sack Cowley, but the Prime Minister refused. When the row died down, Cowley was made Master General of the Ordnance.

It was during this time, in the early 1960s, that Cowley met Werner von Braun, the German rocket expert, who told him that at the end of the Second World War he had fled from Peenemunde with his documents and staff and surrendered to the Americans. But the American divisional commander had never heard of Peenemunde; he sent the papers to the nearest Russian HQ and von Braun and his staff to America under arrest, where they were not allowed to do secret work for many years. Von Braun was convinced that the Russian lead in space technology came from their use of these papers.

Cowley retired from the Army in 1962, and was appointed a director of British Oxygen and of Bowmaker the day he left. He soon joined other companies, including C T Bowring. He also found time for the presidency of the New Forest Preservation Society and the chairmanship of the governors of Wellington College and several other schools. He was Colonel Commandant of the Royal Pioneer Corps from 1961 to 1967, and of the Royal Engineers from 1961 to 1970.

As a young man Cowley had been an accomplished games player; he was one of the first squash players to be elected to the Jesters, and had a handicap of three at golf. In retirement, he became a competitive bridge and croquet player. Possessed of an inquiring mind, he traced the history of snooker back to Woolwich in 1889, when the Snookers, as junior cadets were called, were allowed to play with extra balls after their seniors had finished at billiards.

Cowley was appointed OBE in 1943, CBE in 1946, CB in 1954 and KBE in 1958. He was also mentioned four times in despatches; his Albert Medal was converted to a George Cross in 1971.

He married, in 1947, Sybil Millen; they had a son and three daughters.

MAJOR
BILL TEMPLE

Major Bill Temple (who died on November 5 1992, aged 71) was awarded the Military Cross in Greece for gallantry while destroying tactical bridges on the route of the advancing German armoured columns in April 1941.

Between demolitions he and his troops took part in the fighting withdrawal. At one stage they were defending the ground at Thermopylae (the gateway to southern Greece, where Leonidas and his 300 Spartans had fought in 480 BC) against a vastly superior invading force. Even at the time, Temple wondered what the Spartans would have made of the Ju-87 divebombers and Sturzkampflugzeug (Stukas), which made constant, screaming, near-vertical bombing runs on their positions.

The RAF's six Hurricanes (including one flown by the author Roald Dahl) had already been knocked out, and the enemy had complete operational freedom of the skies. Temple had several railway wagons loaded with gun cotton under his charge. Any one of these could have been detonated by enemy fire, but he used them for 18-hour and 52-hour delayed-action charges, which he buried in the abutments of bridges. They would thus cause maximum devastation to the advancing Germans as they attempted to repair the original destruction.

On one occasion, Temple's troop was surrounded by a heavily-armed group of Greek patriots, who hoped to save a bridge near Thermopylae. He persuaded them that it was quite safe before nonchalantly leading his men away. Just after they had left the scene the bridge went up, sending debris whirling above their heads.

Landing on Crete, Temple and his troop were soon involved in a bloody fight against the German parachutists and glider forces. He recalled that he owed his life to an officer in the Welch Regiment who stayed behind to cover his withdrawal. Of the 21 officers and 830 other ranks of the Welch who fought in Crete, only seven officers and 161 men escaped back to Egypt.

Temple's next appointment was to reorganise water supplies at base camps in the Canal Zone. He applied to join the fledgling SAS but instead was suddenly rushed up the coast road to join General Auchinleck's November offensive, "Operation Crusader". His troop marked out two advance landing grounds for fighter aircraft near Fort Maddalena, although these were dangerously close to German-held positions, and then worked closely with the attacking armour.

When Rommel turned the tables in a surprise counter-attack early in 1942, Temple retreated with the 4th Indian Division's armoured fighting vehicles, and was making ready to crater the roadway near Benghazi when he was suddenly confronted by Panzer tanks, supported by mechanised Panzer Grenadiers. Severely wounded in the brisk action which followed, he was pinned down by heavy machine-gun fire on the "wrong" side of a sand dune, and captured. But by this time his troop had blown up vital supplies of fuel, ammunition and vehicles, to prevent them falling into Axis hands.

A scion of a Co Monaghan medical and military dynasty, William Vere Temple was born on March 5 1921. His father was Lieutenant-General R C Temple, formerly of the Royal Marines, and his grandfather, Colonel William Temple, won the VC at Rangiriri as a surgeon-lieutenant in 1863. Young Bill was educated at Wellington and Woolwich. Commissioned into the Royal Engineers in 1940, he first instructed newly enlisted sappers in minefield clearance. His next assignment was to fortify RAF radar stations against the threat of German invasion. This was followed by a posting to the staff of 2nd Division, and then to be OC 3 Troop (3rd Cheshire) Field Squadron, a TA unit which, he said, appeared to have been raised from the members of Birkenhead Rugby Club.

After a brief period in Egypt, the troop landed at Piraeus and joined the British 1st Armoured Brigade on the Yugoslav frontier, where they were soon in action along the River Axios. After his serious injuries in the desert, which turned septic, he was given massive blood transfusions and intensive care by the German army medical staff, who refused to hand him over to the PoW organisation until his wounds were healed.

Temple was repatriated in 1943 and after further hospital treatment (including skin grafts) returned to duty. He was posted to Washington to work with Military Intelligence, assessing what military technology the Germans might have given the Japanese, then attended a technical staff course at the Royal Military College of Science, Shrivenham, where he took a degree in engineering. He next joined the Weapons Development Executive, working first at Teddington, Middlesex, and then at Woomera in Australia, where he was engaged in the proving and development of British rocket weapons, including Blue Streak.

Invalided out of the Army in 1956, Temple began a new career in civilian engineering and rose to be director and head of research and development with Mather & Platt. He was active with SSAFA and the British Legion, and was chairman of the Macclesfield Conservative Association and the Manchester Advisory Committee of the Lord Chancellor's Department. Bill Temple was a church sidesman, and a lector. He walked with a limp, wore a monocle, and was an excellent shot and an experienced sailor, often chartering a catamaran to take his family to the Scillies and across the Channel. He was captain of the RE Yacht Club and was a member of the Royal Ocean Racing Club. In 1947 Temple married Barbara Mason; they had one son and three daughters.

MAJOR
BILL ANDERSON

Major Bill Anderson (who died on December 1 1992, aged 73) was a gallant and versatile soldier with prodigious energies, which he demonstrated most notably behind enemy lines in North Korea and then, after his retirement from the Army, by taking part in an Antarctic survey, climbing in the Andes and spending several weeks in the jungle after being shipwrecked off the coast of South America.

In 1950, when Anderson's regiment, the Royal Ulster Rifles, was sent to Korea, he was appointed an instructor at 29th Brigade, Battle Training School.

The idea was mooted to send an SAS unit but General Douglas MacArthur thought better of this, and decided instead to raise a similar organisation from American Marines and Rangers. Nevertheless Anderson was welcomed to the new unit, for which he recruited 20 South Koreans whom he trained in parachuting, sabotage and intelligence gathering.

In March 1951, accompanied by two Americans and four Koreans, he parachuted into North Korea, where they blew up a train inside a tunnel on the Kwongwan railway. They then set off for the coast, where the US Navy was due to pick them up. When this did not happen, the party embarked on a three-night march through enemy lines. Two of the Koreans were lost, but the others were eventually rescued by helicopter.

Anderson set about training a second party, and soon narrowed down a group of 20 Koreans to 14. Later that day he was presented with a petition to reinstate the discarded six: they had all signed in their own blood. For the next operation, codenamed "Vixen", the section was divided into an advance party and a main body. The advance party, led by Anderson, parachuted blind into a mountainous area on which there was no intelligence. Just before take-off he had severely burnt his hand and arm, so he had to jump with one arm in a sling; the interpreter was badly injured in the landing.

Leaving his two American sergeants in a hiding-place, Anderson began to recce the area by daylight – highly dangerous for a European behind the lines in an oriental country. He found a suitable dropping zone for the main party, and also met a North Korean youth who said he was on the run from the army and would like to join them. The new recruit guided him to a valley camp of hundreds of Chinese and Korean soldiers, on to which Anderson, with the help of radio, was able to direct a successful air strike.

When Anderson returned to base he was disturbed to find that his seniors wanted to put in more people without adequate training. So he asked for a transfer, and was sent to Cho-Do, an island off the North Korean coast, to train more guerrillas. He was later posted back to England to devise escape routes for PoWs, but the Korean war ended before these could be put into effect. Anderson won the MC, was appointed MBE, and awarded a number of French and American decorations.

An ecclesiastical architect's son, William Ellery Anderson was born at Cheltenham on July 30 1919 and educated at Beaumont. He joined the Royal Gloucestershire Hussars as a trooper in 1939, and the next year he was commissioned into the Worcestershire Regiment. He volunteered for parachuting, and served with the Parachute Regiment in North Africa, Sicily (where he was wounded) and Italy, where he won his first MC. In June 1944, by now with the SAS, he dropped into occupied France to sabotage installations, communications and railway lines, and so hinder the Germans from bringing up reinforcements after the D-Day landings.

This involved him in a series of narrow escapes. Once he was obliged to hide in a heap of manure while the Germans were engaged in a search-and-destroy operation. He subsequently remarked that French manure heaps stank 10 times worse than English ones, and that the French Resistance had refused to have anything to do with him until he had washed and changed all his clothing. At the end of the war Anderson served with the SAS in Norway, where he was responsible for arresting quislings.

From 1947 he began to serve on the War Crimes Commission in Germany, and the following year he joined the Royal Ulster Rifles with which he subsequently went to Korea.

Anderson retired from the Army in 1954 to spend two years as base leader and meteorological observer of the Falkland Islands Dependencies Survey Expedition, at Hope Bay, Antarctica. He was once attacked and nearly killed by a team of huskies when he fell through a hole in the ice: they had mistaken him for a seal.

In 1956 he assisted refugees at the Austro-Hungarian border during the Hungarian Uprising. The next year he set off with Eric Shipton, the Everest climber, as part of an expedition to cata-logue plant life in the Andes; on his return he was elected a fellow of the Royal Geographical Society.

In 1958 Anderson set sail for Australia from Falmouth with a crew of six in the 40-footer *Solent Swan*. Just off British Guiana a storm blew up and they were shipwrecked. After reaching a remote beach at night, he wandered through the jungle for several weeks before reaching civilisation. Back in England in 1961 Anderson joined the Prison Service and was appointed Governor of Durham, which then housed the Great Train Robbers.

Ten years later he became secretary of the Naval and Military Club in Piccadilly. On the evening of his wife's birthday, Anderson was entertaining a guest at the club when a message was brought to him that his wife had just been mugged on the corner of nearby Half Moon Street, and had had her necklace torn off. Anderson excused himself and made for the scene, where he came upon a group of youths waiting for their next victim; he grabbed one and banged his head on a parked car, before returning to the club and resuming his conversation.

Although completely fearless, Bill Anderson was not an insensitive man. His compassion and insight were particularly evident in his two books, *Banner of Pusan* and *Expedition South*. He married first, in 1948, Baroness Brigetta von Bourgstorf; they had a son. The marriage was dissolved in 1954 and he married secondly, in 1960, Dilys Roberts; they had a daughter.

CAPTAIN
"PETER" CLEGG

Captain "Peter" Clegg (whose death was recorded on June 5 1993, aged 74) won an immediate MC at Alamein in 1942 and a Bar at Arnhem two years later.

In October 1942, as the Eighth Army was poised to attack Rommel's Afrika Korps, the 1st Royal Sussex was holding the main Ruweisat Ridge, with the task of dominating No Man's Land and obtaining information about the opposition, on which the battle plan might be based. When orders were received to raid a strong enemy outpost at Point 62, Clegg was given the job of reconnoitring the position, which he did on four successive nights.

The main enemy position comprised a group of *sangars* (defensive fortlets), one of which was used as an observation post by night. The position was strongly wired and mined, and artillery could make little impression on it. One night Clegg managed to slip through a gap in the wire around the OP and capture two Germans, whom he brought back safely to the battalion lines. The information gained enabled Clegg's company to rehearse the raid and, on the night of October 5 he led an assault force which completely cleared the enemy outpost, killing or severely wounding at least 28 Germans.

Clegg led one section against the main *sangar*, and killed the occupants with grenades and pistol fire. Although wounded in the hand by a bullet which had shattered his pistol, he managed to throw two grenades into the *sangar*, killing most of the occupants. Two who attempted to escape he shot with an Italian pistol he was carrying in his unwounded hand. When his force had cleared the position with grenades and bayonets he led them back to safety. The citation for the MC emphasised that Clegg's "leadership, bravery and devotion to duty were the main reasons for the success of the operation". Winston Churchill, who as Warden of the Cinque Ports was Honorary Colonel of the

5th Battalion of the Royal Sussex, sent Montgomery a congratulatory cable to pass on to Clegg's company.

In September 1944 Clegg was in the 10th Battalion of the Parachute Regiment at the Battle at Arnhem. Outnumbered and outgunned, the Airborne Division fought desperately to capture and hold the vital bridge so that 30 Corps could outflank the Siegfried Line. But the ground forces never reached it, and the odds against the airborne force were too great. "On the afternoon of September 19", declared the citation for his Bar, "Clegg took over command of B Company, in which only one subaltern was left. Almost immediately he had to conduct a very difficult disengaging action across a very exposed piece of ground which was covered by machine-gun and mortar fire; and by personal example and leadership and complete disregard of all personal danger managed to withdraw his company with a minimum of casualties.

"At dusk the same day the enemy launched a very strong attack against the 10th Battalion's new positions before they had time to dig in properly. It was largely due to Captain Clegg's example in moving from section to section, particularly where the fighting was fiercest, and encouraging the men to greater efforts that the enemy was unable to break through.

"Again, in the late morning of September 20, Captain Clegg led his company in a most spirited bayonet attack, in the final stages of which he personally attacked and destroyed a German machine-gun post." In the late afternoon the battalion, by now sorely depleted in strength, was ordered to attack and capture a crossroads held by the enemy on the divisional perimeter at Oosterbeek. To secure the crossroads it was necessary to clear eight houses and a garden.

"Captain Clegg personally led the assault and cleared three of the houses against bitter opposition from the enemy. In the third house he was very seriously wounded in the jaw by machine-gun fire, but insisted on carrying on until all the enemy were exterminated and the three houses cleared and organised in a state of defence. During this time he was losing a great deal of blood and was in great pain. He finally consented to have his wounds dressed and had just handed over his company to the senior sergeant when he collapsed.

"Captain Clegg in this period of very bitter and confused fighting carried out his duties in an exemplary manner. The leadership of this gallant officer was outstanding, and his own personal courage and complete disregard of danger were an inspiration and example to his men".

At the end of the battle Clegg was hidden by the Dutch Resistance who took him to a Dutch hospital, then returned to England where his jaw was repaired by the surgeon Sir Archibald McIndoe, who became a friend; Clegg was invalided out of the Army in 1946.

The son of a pharmacist Benjamin Beattie Clegg, always known as Peter, was born on October 7 1918 and educated at Middlesbrough High School; in 1936, when money was short, he joined the

Coldstream Guards in the ranks. The next year he was posted to Palestine for anti-terrorist operations, and in 1939 to Egypt.

Clegg took part in the desert campaign against the Italians, and was then commissioned into the Royal Sussex, with whom he stayed until the end of the North African campaign in 1943. He was wounded again on the Mareth Line, this time in the back, shoulder and left leg by a mortar bomb when escorting a party of Indian sappers to blow gaps in the anti-tank ditch. After recovering in hospital he rejoined his battalion in Tunisia.

After retiring from the Army Clegg ran T & J Hutton, manufacturers of scythes and sickles, which was founded in 1660 and closed in 1988. Although Peter Clegg was undemonstrative, the notes he made in the desert show that he was also sensitive and imaginative. "I remember the size of the desert, the lightness of the night when the moon was full, the stars and the depths of the night sky, the coldness of the nights and the hardness of the sand to sleep on, endless dawns and false dawns . . . The smell of cordite, the smell of unwashed troops, the wind off the sea at night as the desert cooled, the spotter planes, the moans and helplessness of the wounded, the torn bodies on the battlefield. I remember what it was like to tell the men you would see them at breakfast and wonder if you would, and how many, and whether you would see the dawn yourself."

Clegg married first, in 1944, Rosemary Anne Coles, who died in 1955; they had two sons. He married secondly, in 1957, Jane Wright; they had a daughter.

———————

BRIGADIER
MURRAY McINTYRE

Brigadier Murray McIntyre (who died on August 13 1993, aged 100) earned the nickname "Mad Mac" for his exploits in the Western Desert in 1941, when he proved himself equally indifferent to both personal danger and bureaucratic interference.

Commanding 51st Regiment, RA, McIntyre used the British 3.7 anti-aircraft field gun to devastating effect, regularly destroying the notorious German 88mms. The 3.7 outranged the 88 by some 5,000 feet and was highly esteemed by the Germans, who used captured 3.7s whenever possible and even manufactured special ammunition for them when captured stocks ran out. During the siege of Tobruk McIntyre's regiment destroyed 12 German 88s and 280 Stukas and Junkers. The War Office, however, persistently discouraged the use of the 3.7s as a field or anti-tank gun.

On being severely wounded McIntyre was evacuated by boat, protesting vehemently from his stretcher that he was still fit enough to fight. Once recovered he returned to take part in the battles from Alamein onwards. In Tunisia he created an effective unit of captured German 88s – designated "Mactroop" with its own badge – which created havoc by engaging the Germans at close quarters before they realised it was British-manned. The name McIntyre was well known to the Afrika Korps.

Hugh Murray Johnstone McIntyre was born on September 11 1892 at Bangalore, where his father was serving in the Indian Army. He was sent home to Scotland at the age of five to begin his education at St Andrews. Later he went to the United Services College at Westward Ho, Devon, which was immortalised by Rudyard Kipling's novel *Stalky & Co*. Young Hugh proceeded to Woolwich, from which he was commissioned into the Royal Artillery in 1910.

He served as a mountain gunner on the North-West Frontier before 1914, and then went with his regiment to Mesopotamia (now Iraq), where he fought in the major battles of the First World War. He returned to Iraq in 1920 during the Kurdish rebellion, and later became a gunnery instructor at Shoeburyness. From 1932 to 1935 McIntyre was in Hong Kong; then returned again to Iraq to train artillery officers. He was put in charge of the Gibraltar guns just as the Spanish Civil War was beginning, then was sent back to Egypt to which he returned yet again after fighting in the abortive Norway campaign of 1940.

He subsequently advised on the anti-aircraft defence of Crete, which would have prevented the German airborne landings had his suggestions been implemented. After the Desert campaign – in which he had been awarded a DSO, mentioned twice in despatches, and had a CBE conferred on him in the field by Montgomery – McIntyre was in Sicily.

Although by now a brigadier, he remained a front-line man, and kept in touch with his former regiment until it was finally disbanded at Arezzo, having fired some half a million 3.7 million rounds.

In December 1944 McIntyre returned to Britain, and retired from the Army two years later to settle down to lecturing and gardening. A humble man, approachable and hospitable, with a strong sense of humour, he had a wide range of interests. In earlier days, he had played rugby for Harlequins and had been a useful hockey player, oarsman and cricketer. He was also an excellent horseman, a good polo player and a competent mountaineer, climbing Mount Fujiyama. McIntyre was particularly fond of opera, and attended performances whenever possible during the Italian campaign. Interested in all forms of music, he sang well and engaged in Scottish country dancing until he was 92.

Murray McIntyre married, in 1922, Gladys Keating, who died in 1977; they had a son.

LIEUTENANT-COLONEL
DUDLEY COVENTRY

Lieutenant-Colonel Dudley Coventry (who died in Harare on September 6 1993, aged 78) had a brilliant, though stormy military career; much of it with Special Forces operating behind enemy lines.

The son of a police officer serving in India, Edgar Walter Dudley Coventry was born on March 26

1915 and educated at Bryanston. His father wanted him to be a banker or a doctor. When young Dudley showed no interest in either profession, Coventry senior lost patience and parted company with his son, who then joined the Royal Norfolk Regiment in 1937.

He was commissioned into the East Lancashire Regiment in 1938, and served on the North-West Frontier and in Afghanistan before the outbreak of the Second World War. In 1942 he was with the East Lancs in the Madagascar campaign and then joined 5 Commando and Parachute Troop before being seconded to Special Raiding Forces. His duties included diverting the attention of the Germans while experts landed on the future D-Day beaches in Normandy in order to obtain soil samples which would indicate whether the surface would support tanks and other vehicles.

In 1944, when there was no longer a need for raiding seaborne forces, he joined 45 Royal Marine Commando, with whom he served in North-West Europe. One of the unit's tasks was to harass German troops attempting to retreat with their weapons; Coventry once stumbled upon a German SS soldier, whom he killed with a single punch. At the end of the war he rejoined the East Lancs in India, where they were endeavouring to preserve order in the period up to independence, and subsequently served in Cyprus, Palestine and Suez. He then transferred to the Parachute Regiment, and broke his back on a training exercise, but made a miraculous recovery.

Coventry next commanded the squadron from the Parachute Regiment which joined 22 SAS in Malaya, where his dedication, skill and warmth of character made him very popular. Although a large man (6 ft 4 in and more than 14 stone) he adapted extremely well to rigorous jungle patrolling. In 1960 he went to Rhodesia, where he became one of the founder members of the country's first modern Commando battalions, the Rhodesian Light Infantry. Three years later, when the Rhodesian squadron of the SAS was formed, Coventry became its first CO. During the next seven years he was engaged in frustrating the attempts of the guerrilla forces which were trying to overthrow Ian Smith's regime. He fought several fierce battles against nationalist leaders, some of whom later became members of the Zimbabwe government.

In 1970, Coventry was moved to the Rhodesian Central Intelligence Organisation, working with such units as the Selous Scouts. He also formed the Mozambique resistance movement, RENAMO, to fight against the Marxist-Leninist government which was to come to power when Portugal granted the colony independence in 1975. Although he was now 60, there was no-one better qualified to teach by example, and Coventry therefore spent long periods in the bush training his recruits and worrying the Frelimo forces. During this period he was wounded several times, often seriously. When Rhodesia was granted its independence from Britain and became the Republic of Zimbabwe, Coventry and a number of other officers prudently withdrew to South Africa.

However Robert Mugabe, the President, announced a "reconciliation" policy and Coventry returned to form and command a Zimbabwe SAS. This took him to the rank of lieutenant-colonel – a rank he might have attained many years earlier, had his career been less turbulent. After wounds and failing health forced him at last to give up his beloved military life, Coventry became the director of a transport company although he had only one eye and imperfect hearing.

Coventry was a heavyweight boxing champion and won a trial cap for England at rugby in his younger days. His good looks made him attractive to women; the late Ava Gardner was said to be among his many conquests. He was twice married.

Finally his skull was crushed by an intruder, who broke into his home in Harare one night and hit him with one of his own rifle butts. Coventry died in hospital after being in a coma for a month. The Zimbabwe government ordered him to be given a funeral with full military honours.

COLONEL
PETER EARLE

Colonel Peter Earle (who died on December 10 1993, aged 76) had a remarkably lucky escape from death in an ambush in Germany in April 1945 when he was one of Field Marshal Montgomery's liaison officers. He had been ordered to drive to General

Barker's 8 Corps HQ and obtain his plans for crossing the Elbe, and was on his way back near the
Lüneberg Forest with another officer, who had come
along to share the driving, when they ran into some
Germans.

Earle was wounded in the arm and temple but
drove their Jeep straight at the German machine-
gunner ahead, killing him; he and Peter Poston were
then thrown from the vehicle and quickly
surrounded by German soldiers. As Earle tried to
wipe 8 Corps' disposition from the chinagraph map
he was carrying he was shot in the back. Poston, who
was also wounded, had emptied his Sten gun into the
Germans and was lying on the ground a few yards
away, trying to eat the recent orders; he was
bayoneted to death.

Earle was picked up later by a German farmer and
taken to a German field hospital, from which he was
soon liberated. Monty's team of liaison officers –
young men mostly of the rank of major – were vital
for keeping him in touch with the various parts
of his huge army, with the authority to go anywhere
and ask any questions they wished. Personable,
tenacious and courageous, they travelled between
200 and 400 miles a day on their various missions,
using Jeeps and Auster aircraft.

Earle noted in his diary: "This is mentally easy –
provided one is not confused by detail – but physically it is exceptionally tiring. Long drives in Jeeps
from dawn to dusk through battle areas, pitted and
cratered roads, past dust and noise, belching guns and
tanks. Getting entry to all commanders and getting a

concise picture is also difficult. The long grind back, not in the least knowing the way and no one except the enemy to ask, the sudden limelight of the caravan with Monty as your audience, everything must be crystal clear by then."

Peter Beaumont Earle was born on April 9 1917 and educated at Eton (where he was nicknamed "Puma" because his physique and movements were perceived to be feline), and then Sandhurst. Commissioned into the King's Royal Rifle Corps in 1937, he served with the 2nd Battalion, partly in Palestine, until 1939.

Lord Annan, who worked alongside Earle in Military Intelligence, recalled their association: "At the outbreak of the war Peter Earle was one of only three regular officers who had been trained to interpret air photographs. In 1940, he found himself posted to MI14, the German section of Intelligence in the War Office, and became a crucial figure in analysing the evidence of Hitler's plans to invade Britain. There was no lack of speculation at what point and when the invasion would be launched – even an astrologer and a water diviner were consulted; but there was practically no hard evidence. The cryptographers at Bletchley had not yet broken the German Army 'Enigma' and their army used land-lines.

"Our networks of agents in Europe were scattered and air reconnaissance was almost the sole reliable source. Earle interpreted the photographs of the building of heavy gun emplacements on Cap Gris Nez and from September 1 the growing number of barges and invasion craft in the Channel ports; yet perhaps even more important was his work in 1941. For long the head of the German section and the Director of Military Intelligence took the view that Hitler would order the invasion of Britain before he attacked the Soviet Union. Earle showed, however, that, despite German deception plans, there was no evidence that this was so. No build-up of barges was revealed, and the troops sent to the West were second-class divisions. In the end, his contentions that invasion was not on the cards prevailed and may have affected a decision by the Chiefs of Staff to send divisions to the Middle East.

"When in 1943 Sir Alan Brooke, as CIGS, began to look for a new personal assistant, he took Peter Earle. He now found his duties included listening to every telephone call, especially those from the Prime Minister, and to be prepared to lay the relevant papers and facts and figures before his chief. The hours were long and unpredictable and Earle's war diary (which he later deposited at the Imperial War Museum) gives a lively account of life at the top. As it became clear in 1944 that the end of the war was in sight, he begged the CIGS to release him. If, as a young regular soldier, he had not seen action, his career would have a black mark against it. 'Silly fellows, soldiers, to think that,' said Brooke; but he interceded with Montgomery to accept Earle as one of his liaison officers."

Before working for Monty, Earle had thought him "raucous, loud-acting, narrow-minded", but when he came to know him better found him more complex. Although "a bounder and a complete egoist", he was also a kind man, thoughtful to his subordinates, a lucid tactician and a great commander.

After recovering from his wounds, Earle was posted to the Political Intelligence Department of the Foreign Office, and then to the Joint Intelligence Bureau of the Cabinet Office. From 1947 to 1949 he was in the Defence Research Bureau in Canada. He then spent a few months with the 1st Battalion of the Rifle Brigade before retiring from the Army and beginning a civilian career. Moves were made to interest him in the newly-emerging world of commercial television, and he worked for Sidney Bernstein for a few years.

Then he turned to the City, where he became the director of Henry Kendall & Son, commodity brokers, who, among other interests, imported sugar from Peru. Earle was awarded the Peruvian El Merito for distinguished services and became president of the Anglo-Peruvian Society. His strong visual sense found some fulfilment in his houses in London and the country. But, although he had an amazing eye, he refused to put it to commercial use, even though he was not well off.

He did take on a refurbishment of the St James's Club, however, and took great pride in rebuilding the Davies Street Territorial Centre. In 1949 Earle became Adjutant of Queen Victoria's Rifles (7th KRRC). From 1953 to 1958, when he commanded them, Earle's leadership undoubtedly attracted the "right type" of officers and men to stay on after

National Service. Not untypical was the occasion when he drove his half-track vehicle to a nightclub after a dinner night at Davies Street. Earle was immensely attractive to women, a fact which he did not ignore.

He was awarded an MC in 1945 (as well as the Croix de Guerre) and was Deputy Lieutenant, London, from 1967 to 1992. In 1962 he became a churchwarden of St George's, Hanover Square, and encouraged its use as a regimental church. He skilfully refurbished the fabric, advised on property disposals and put the finances on a sound basis.

"Puma's" diary gave a clue to his character. He showed ability as a planner when he worked at 21st Army Group HQ in 1943. But two years later he wrote: "I can no longer feel anything but intense boredom for demonstrations of this kind [tank and infantry co-operation], however well they are done. All the old jargon and clichés – how I dislike it." He recalled the pain he had suffered when wounded, and that it had taught him he could endure anything if the need arose.

Peter Earle married first, in 1940, Ursula, eldest daughter of Felix Warre, chairman of Sotheby's (and son of Dr Warre, headmaster and Provost of Eton); they had a son and a daughter. He married secondly Judith MaKinnel Childs.

LIEUTENANT-COLONEL
OSWALD CARY-ELWES

Lieutenant-Colonel Oswald Cary-Elwes (who died on January 1 1994, aged 80) served with the SAS in France during the Second World War and made a notable contribution to good relations between the French and British armies throughout his career.

When the SAS was expanded into a brigade in 1944, Cary-Elwes was posted to HQ at Sorncastle in Ayrshire as liaison chief. The brigade comprised the Belgian company (commanded by Capitaine Blondeel), the 3rd and 4th French parachute battalions (the latter commanded by the one-armed Commandant Bourgoin), and 1 and 2 SAS1. Cary-Elwes was the main link with the Free French, in which role his good humour, tact and firmness served him well; he was also the link between the civilian authorities and his French SAS comrades.

Their task was to drop into France ahead of the main force on D-Day and hinder the German counter-attack. On the night of June 5 the 4th French SAS parachuted into Brittany, and Bourgoin set up a base at St Marcel to train a maquis army. Thirteen days later the Germans attacked the base unsuccessfully and sustained heavy losses, but afterwards took savage reprisals on the civilian population. Bourgoin therefore dispersed his men among the maquis, and closed down all radio contact.

On June 23 Cary-Elwes and his batman Corporal

Eric Mills, who had served with him since 1934, made a blind parachute jump into the area east of Vannes to locate Bourgoin and his men. The Germans were by then especially vigilant, and it was difficult to avoid capture by the Gestapo or the Milice (the French police working for the Germans), but Cary-Elwes eventually succeeded in finding the French regiment and reopened contact between Bourgoin and London.

He moved on to contact Capitaine Marienne's group at Tredion and Capitaine Deplante's at Pontivy, from whom he was to collect plans of the German defences at Vannes, Lorient and Morlaix and take them to London, where a second D-Day in Brittany was being considered. A few hours after he left Tredion, Capitaine Marienne was betrayed by a collaborator and tortured to death by the Milice. His men were all executed.

Cary-Elwes and Mills aimed to leave France through the Shelburne line, the most effective escape route of the war, which entailed the descent of precipitous cliffs to "Bonaparte" beach near Plouha. But as they waited in a safe house, its owner opened the front door to a German patrol of two White Russian conscripts led by a German. When the patrol spotted tell-tale equipment they demanded that Cary-Elwes and his group come out. The two Russians opened fire, and in the confusion their German leader was hit. His companions were so concerned that they took him away to safety. Cary-Elwes then hastily led out his group, including their host. At 3am they were shown down to the beach by a young girl, who had placed white handkerchiefs on the sand to mark each mine. After boarding a waiting gunboat, they were in London by noon. That night Cary-Elwes dined at the Dorchester, where he found that Bollinger '28 had never tasted so good.

Two weeks later Cary-Elwes parachuted back into Brittany, and joined forces with Bourgoin once more to spend most of the rest of the war in operations with 4th SAS in northern France and Belgium. He was awarded the Croix de Guerre with palm and the Legion d'Honneur, and was mentioned in despatches.

Oswald Aloysius Joseph Cary-Elwes was born on November 14 1913. His father and maternal grandfather were champagne shippers, and Cary-Elwes became a fluent French speaker and a wine connoisseur. Like his elder brother Evelyn (Dom Columba Cary-Elwes of Ampleforth Abbey whose obituary was printed in *The Daily Telegraph* on the same day as his), young Oswald was educated at Ampleforth. From Sandhurst he was commissioned into the Lincolnshire Regiment in 1933; then served on Malta and in Palestine, where the regiment was engaged in counter-insurgency operations. In 1937 he returned to England.

On the outbreak of hostilities Cary-Elwes was sent to Lagos as brigade major of the Nigerian Brigade, and in 1942 he was posted to the First Army, which landed in North Africa and liberated Algeria. The next year he was invited by Colonel Bill Stirling (brother of David) to join SAS2, and took part in operations in Sicily and Italy.

After the war he attended the course at the Staff College, Camberley, served briefly in Oldenburg and was posted to the British military mission in Paris. Two years later he rejoined his regiment for anti-terrorist operations in Palestine before the end of the Mandate. Then he was assistant military attaché in Cairo, followed by a period as an instructor and liaison officer at the French School of Infantry at St Maixent. In 1955 Cary-Elwes returned to his regiment to serve in Goslar and Berlin, and next year was posted to Fontainebleau as Chief of the C-in-C's secretariat in SHAPE. He was head of the British Military Mission to the C-in-C, French Army, in Germany, then returned to England to become Commandant, Army School of Civil Defence, before being involved, finally, in the standardisation of NATO equipment at the MoD.

In retirement he often visited France with David Stirling and SAS colleagues as guests of the French parachutistes. In 1984 he was awarded a Medaille de la Ville de Paris by Jacques Chirac. In his younger days Cary-Elwes was a useful boxer, and won many cups for golf. He married, in 1938, Pamela Brendon; they had six children, one of whom predeceased him.

BRIGADIER
EUSTACE ARDERNE

Brigadier Eustace Arderne (who died on March 30 1994, aged 94) was awarded the DSO and Bar, twice mentioned in despatches and appointed OBE (Military) during the Second World War. A South African, he had joined the British Army in 1918; fought in Russia in 1919; was seconded to the King's African Rifles in the 1920s; and served in many parts of the world in the 1930s.

His first DSO came when he was commanding 1st Durham Light Infantry on the night of December 7 1941 during an attack on the El Adem escarpment, south of Tobruk. The citation read: "They were met with heavy defensive fire from mortars, artillery and machine-guns, causing a certain amount of con-fusion. Arderne reorganised the position and made personal contact with the tanks following up. When touch had been lost with the left forward company he rode off on the back of a tank, gained touch and brought them to Point 157, where he organised a defensive position." It stressed his "utmost coolness, complete disregard for his personal safety under heavy fire and high standard of leadership enabling the position to be captured with the minimum number of casualties."

The Bar for his DSO came for an action on the night of October 19 1944 at Roversano at the crossing of the River Savio in Italy.

Eustace Aldford Arderne was born in Cape Town on December 14 1899 and educated at the Diocesan

College, Rondebosch, and Sandhurst before being commissioned into the Durham Light Infantry in 1918. He was posted first to France and then to Germany, where he recalled that his men ignored the "no fraternisation" order, and were soon playing games with the village children.

He volunteered to join a force of Royal Fusiliers which was going to Russia, and landed at Archangel. "The Communists, or Bolos as we called them, were well established," wrote Arderne. But in their first encounter the British force surprised the Communist troops while they were dressing – "I don't think that we fired a shot: you can hardly shoot a man running away and holding up his trousers with his hands." The British force, however, was vastly outnumbered by Trotsky's Red Army, and as the latter approached the British were withdrawn to Archangel again, to abandon the fruitless campaign.

Arderne was then posted back to Germany and stationed in Silesia, where 60,000 Poles had begun fighting an equal number of Germans over the division of their district; fortunately the League of Nations ruling was accepted and peace prevailed. His next posting was to Arusha in Tanganyika, where he was seconded to the King's African Rifles. He was allotted a bungalow which had a roof of banana leaves and walls of interwoven saplings plastered with mud. It did not contain a single nail or rope. When on leave, Arderne walked most of the way from Tanganyika to South Africa. He was astonished to find that the native porters could walk for 15 miles over hilly country without rest, carrying on their heads loads so heavy that they needed help in lifting them; they would drop these and run when a rhinoceros appeared. Arderne simultaneously contracted cerebral malaria, dysentery and tick fever, which left him unconscious for four days.

He recovered and returned to his regiment, then in Belfast. Shortly afterwards he moved with it to Egypt, where he played polo for what was soon the best team in the country. He also learned Arabic – which he practised by frequenting a cafe in the low part of the town, dressed in shabby clothes. Arderne's next posting was with the 2nd Battalion to the North-West Frontier. He took the opportunity to visit Tibet, including the town of Phari Jong, which he described as "the highest and dirtiest town in the world". The inhabitants, however, were friendly enough, smiling and sticking out their tongues in respect.

The regiment moved to Bombay, and thence Khartoum. Arderne was posted to the 1st Battalion, which was on its way to Shanghai when he joined it in 1937 at Port Sudan. From Shanghai he went to Tientsin for five months and then to Peking, where, in the International Settlement during the early days of the Second World War, the British were on quite friendly terms with the Germans and the Vichy French.

When the regiment returned to Egypt Arderne took command at Mersah Matruh. But the troops he confronted there surrendered in their thousands – he assumed that this was due to the Churchill tank and the presence of the Gurkhas. "A Gurkha with a kukri in his hand and a smile on his face," he recalled, "was enough to frighten anyone." But when Rommel appeared with better tanks, the troops were pushed back to the Egyptian frontier, leaving Tobruk besieged. After heavy fighting and numerous casualties Arderne's battalion was suddenly ordered to Syria, now under the Vichy government.

They were expecting to fight the French Foreign Legion which then agreed to an unconditional surrender; the Durhams decided that "the Legion were not quite the heroes they were made out to be and certainly not as good as we were". From Syria Arderne took his regiment to besiege Tobruk, where they encountered more determined Italians as well as Germans. They were next withdrawn and sent to Malta, which was under constant aerial attack. The Germans bombed the runways used by the British fighters, and the Durhams rushed out and filled in the craters after each raid.

In the summer of 1942 Arderne was flown out of Malta in darkness to take over 25th Infantry Brigade in the desert before sailing to Cyprus for further training. The brigade's first ship was torpedoed and sunk. Many years later, when sailing off Cape Town, Arderne was approached by a German wanting to be part of his crew. In subsequent conversations he learned that the German had been the commander of the submarine which had sunk the ship; Arderne was magnanimous and accepted him as a member of his racing crew.

After the sinking the brigade was picked up and returned to Cairo. The men then completed their mountain warfare training in Lebanon and were posted to Italy. From Taranto they fought their way up the peninsula. Having reached the River Po the brigade was suddenly posted to Trieste to prevent the Yugoslav partisans occupying the town. Arderne was then sent as Commander, North Iraq Area, to Baghdad, where his Arabic proved useful. Here, to everyone's astonishment, he caught a 40lb perch in the Euphrates.

At the end of the war Arderne decided to soldier no more, and retired to South Africa. He was an excellent games-player and a first class shot. In 1933, he married Margaret Hennessy; they had a son and two daughters.

COLONEL
THE REVEREND NEVILLE METCALFE

Colonel the Reverend Neville Metcalfe (who died on June 21 1994, aged 80) was awarded an immediate DSO in March 1942 as chaplain to the 7th Hussars, who were fighting a rearguard action in the epic 1,000-mile retreat from numerically superior Japanese forces in Burma.

Metcalfe had arrived in Rangoon when it had been bombed and set on fire, and was stinking from the dead bodies in the streets. The 7th Hussars found released lunatics prowling the streets and ferreting in rubbish dumps for food. Criminals were looting. Wild dogs were gnawing the dead. Lepers from the hospital were begging, and vultures hovering overhead. Animals in the zoo had also broken out. Metcalfe was about to sit on a convenient log when he discovered just in time that it was an alligator.

When one of the doctors was killed by a sniper Metcalfe did his best to replace him, working under heavy fire. He collected identity discs from the dead. After their trek along burning roads and slippery, thorny jungle paths the men reached Imphal, where they lay on bare ground, plagued by mosquitoes and leeches in monsoon rain. Metcalfe conducted a communion service attended by Generals Alexander and Wavell. Army biscuits were used as wafers and some local whisky was procured from friendly Naga headhunters, to be used in lieu of wine. Despite being watered down, it took the lining off a silver sports cup which had been pressed into use as a chalice.

The citation for Metcalfe's DSO recorded that after conducting a burial service close to the firing-line, he returned to Pegu to administer first aid throughout the day, and throughout the night of March 6/7 Captain Metcalfe continued to look after the wounded and perform burial services for the dead. On the morning of March 7, when the 7th Hussars had withdrawn, he remained behind to assist in loading the wounded into lorries and sending them across the bridge at Pegu.

Metcalfe remained with the last ambulances, and succeeded in getting them away under heavy fire. South of the bridge they again came under heavy fire and were held up. He then collected some food from a knocked-out tank and went around distributing it among the wounded. Metcalfe was himself slightly wounded by mortar fire. After the ambulances had got clear he walked back with the last infantry to withdraw along the railway and subsequently arrived at Hlegu, a distance of 25 miles. Metcalfe marched the last 12 miles barefoot, having lost his boots in an explosion which also wounded and deafened him. A member of the retreating column said: "In spite of his difficulties he plodded cheerfully along, radiating good spirits and encouraged and undoubtedly inspired all around him."

"The conduct of this chaplain has been magnificent throughout the operations," declared the citation. "His courage, unfailing cheerfulness and complete disregard for his own safety have been an inspiration and encouragement to all ranks."

Neville Sidney Metcalfe was born on March 23 1914 at Westward Ho, Devon, where his father was Vicar. He was educated at St John's, Leatherhead, and St Peter's Hall, Oxford. After attending Wycliffe Hall, Oxford, he was ordained deacon in 1938 and began his clerical career in Nottinghamshire.

In 1939 he joined the Royal Army Chaplain's Department and was appointed chaplain to the 7th Battalion, Green Howards. The next year he served in France, at first near Arras. After the German invasion of Belgium he found himself employed as a dispatch rider. In the retreat he helped to destroy the regimental transport with a sledgehammer, work which first appalled and then exhilarated him, and was evacuated from Dunkirk.

At the end of 1940 Metcalfe was posted to the 7th Hussars in Egypt. He was provided with a motorcycle but after losing his way in the desert several times while visiting his parishioners he took off the silencer so they could hear and guide him. He tended the wounded and buried the dead at the Battle of Sidi Rezegh, where the regiment was outgunned and lost many tanks. Re-equipped, it was dispatched to Burma. On the three-week voyage he was entertainment officer, organising whist drives and a boxing tournament in which he himself collected two black eyes.

The regiment went on to Basra and Baghdad, where he organised carol singing at Christmas. It also played rugby on iron-hard pitches, sometimes with Iraqis joining in. The next stop was Aleppo, from where the regiment moved to Baalbek, where he led climbing in the Lebanon mountains. Returning to Egypt for further training, Metcalfe organised expeditions to Mount Sinai. A visit to the charnel house in the monastery nauseated even the most battle-hardened Hussars but at the summit their escort, a monk, produced a bottle of arrak from beneath his cassock and toasts were drunk.

In May 1944 Metcalfe landed in Italy at Taranto and began the advance up the Adriatric coast. The regiment lost a number of tanks and sustained heavy casualties against well dug-in Germans. In September 1944 they were withdrawn to Lake Bracciano, where they trained with amphibious tanks before being sent to Ostra to fight as infantry on terrain unsuitable for tanks.

The following March they returned to Bracciano for a refresher course and then crossed the Po, where all the bridges had been demolished. Before the assault they were bombarded with propaganda leaflets describing the horrors of what would happen to them if they tried to advance. In the event they had only two casualties, both from drowning, as the enemy had withdrawn. Their campaign ended in Venice.

After the war Metcalfe stayed on in the Army and was posted to the Duke of York's Military School at Dover in 1945. Three years later he became chaplain to the Rifle Brigade at Minden BAOR, and in 1949 Senior Chaplain to the Forces at Hanover. In 1951 he moved to Verden, BAOR, as Senior Chaplain to 7th Armoured Division. After a spell at Deepcut Garrison Church he was successively Deputy Assistant Chaplain General, Highland District, at Perth, and Senior Chaplain in Jamaica.

This was followed by a three-year appointment as DACG in South-East District, based at Aldershot, and another three at Lübeck, BAOR. Before his retirement in 1972 Metcalfe was DACG, South-East District; Assistant Chaplain General, Western Command, Chester; and Assistant Chaplain General, Northern Command, York. He remained at York as a hospital chaplain and a curate. A keen gardener, he also worked in the city's museum gardens and then in the grounds of the Rowntree Trust.

Neville Metcalfe was not merely a man of outstanding courage and endurance, but a person who kindled and reawakened faith in men whose war experience might well have made them cynical. He was totally unpompous, a good all-round sportsman (boxing, rugby, cricket and hockey) and an intrepid mountaineer. In addition to his DSO he was twice mentioned in despatches, in France in 1940 and in Burma in 1942.

He married, in 1940, Hilda Mary Atkinson; they had four sons. Secondly, in 1975, he married Frances Munro.

COLONEL
KENNETH MERRYLEES

Colonel Kenneth Merrylees (who died on July 1 1994, aged 97) worked as a bomb-disposal expert during the Second World War, when he used his skills as a dowser to find bombs with delayed-action fuses which had penetrated deeply into the ground. The many such bombs dropped by the Germans – which often left no trace of their presence on the surface – would have caused great disruption if Merrylees and his team had not detected and defused them; one 500-pounder which he discovered, had burrowed under the swimming pool at Buckingham Palace in September 1940.

During Merrylees's early years as a dowser he used hazel twigs and whalebone, but after women ceased to wear corsets, and whalebone was no longer available, he changed to nylon rods. He did not attribute his astonishing success to any special gift, but to knowledge of practical engineering combined with an ability possessed by many. When in the Middle East and India, his skill at finding water in barren areas gave him the title "God of the water". He could even detect the presence of water from maps of places he had never visited, and proved it at a demonstration with a map of Corfu.

Merrylees's skill was not limited to detecting the presence of unexploded bombs but extended to inventions for defusing them safely. Several of his methods and devices – such as the fuse extractor – are still in use today. Even in his nineties he still regarded himself as on the active list in case he was needed for an unusually difficult bomb.

Kenneth William Merrylees was born on October 7 1896 at Launceston, Tasmania, where his father was a successful banker. Young Kenneth was sent home to be educated at Charterhouse and Woolwich, and was commissioned into the Royal Engineers in 1915. He served in France, seeing action at the Battle of the Somme, and was wounded in July 1917 when leading a night raid to blow up an enemy strongpoint blocking the advance of the British infantry. One piece of shrapnel from an overhead shell penetrated his shoulder and ricocheted around his body. When it was extracted it carried the imprint of the Royal Engineers' badge on his shoulder, which it had struck before entering. Merrylees later had the shrapnel mounted on a silver plinth.

After recovering from his wounds Merrylees was posted to Italy where he was again wounded, this time by artillery fire. After the war he was in charge of workshops at Chatham for a while before going up to Corpus Christi, Cambridge, where he read mechanical sciences. He then returned to Chatham to complete an electrical and mechanical course, became an instructor at the Electrical School, and was posted to India as garrison engineer, constructing roads and bridges. From 1929 to 1930 he was employed in the construction of the Kalyan Power Station, and for the next five years served in the Punjaband Frontier Province, working on roads and water supplies.

For two of those years he was stationed in the Khyber Pass, where he was entrusted with maintaining 200 miles of road. He was field engineer in the Mohmand Campaign in 1935. The next year he returned to Britain and spent three years at the War Office, working on such projects as the underground refrigeration plant and guns at Gibraltar and other installations abroad, from West Africa to Singapore.

In 1939 Merrylees went to France with the British Expeditionary Force, on the Engineer in Chief's staff, and was evacuated in May. He then joined GHQ, Home Forces, as an experimental officer on the staff of the Director of Bomb Disposal. His next posting was to the Middle East to construct lighter wharves at Suez, from where he moved to Syria in 1941 to build camps and roads. He went to Turkey to construct 30 bomber and fighter airfields, and 300 miles of roads through the Thurus Mountains to Ulukisla. As the Turks were officially neutral, and did not wish to antagonise the Germans, political delays compounded the engineering difficulties.

In 1944 Merrylees moved on to India to build more airfields for use in the projected invasion of Malaya, and the next year returned to Britain to become Deputy Chief Engineer in Scottish Command. Subsequently he became DCE in Pakistan, where he was responsible for all the roads, camps, cantonments and airfields in the North-West Frontier Province during Partition. The following year he retired from the Army and joined Sir Alexander Gibb and Partners, building airfields and water supplies in Iraq. In retirement he moved to Lavenham in Suffolk, where his sympathetic and sensitive reconstruction of cottages and conversions earned him the Civic Trust National Award for his "outstanding craftsmanship and infinite care".

Kenneth Merrylees was a talented water-colourist and etcher, skills he inherited from his mother, Mary Eyres, who was an artist. During the Second World War he produced posters for those engaged in bomb disposal. His skill was noted from an early age. When he was serving in Italy in the First World War he was described by a senior general as "one of the most talented and capable young officers I have ever met." He not only possessed initiative, courage and sound common sense, but was unusually kind, considerate and patient.

Merrylees's talents at dowsing were undoubtedly exceptional – he could detect a bomb 50 feet below the surface, and differentiate between different types of water supplies – but he considered that he was always learning. He was adamant that his ability to find water did not extend, as people often assumed, to finding minerals, detecting diseases, or tracing missing people or objects. He was in great demand as a lecturer and appeared on television, but never sought publicity or fame. "I am not exceptional among 'sensitives' in that I am, after a short time, acutely uncomfortable if I stay on the lines of a fair-sized flow, and I know from experience it's impossible for me to sleep over one. I found it impossible to accept a purely physical explanation of the dowser's ability. I am forced therefore to look beyond the limitations of orthodox physics and the five senses."

He dismissed the idea that the dowser's skills were supernatural, though he maintained there was "a connection by the dowser's mind with some sort of knowledge beyond all physical existence limits". But success in dowsing, he said, required "effort, study and practice". He felt that dowsing was sometimes discredited because dowsers made avoidable mistakes. In Rawalpindi a borehole for a hospital ran dry but Merrylees found a source 50 yards away which is still flowing. He believed that there were vast underground supplies in many countries, and that when modern boring methods had failed to locate them dowsers should do so. Merrylees was chairman of the British Society of Dowsers. He was appointed OBE.

He married, in 1938, Nina, daughter of Sir Theophilus Shepstone, who had arranged the annexation of the Transvaal, and whom the Zulus called Sontseu (white father). She died in 1980. He married secondly, in 1988, Diana Stedman.

LIEUTENANT-COLONEL CYRIL COCHRAN

Lieutenant-Colonel Cyril Cochran (who died on September 11 1994, aged 82) won a DSO in the Western Desert for rallying demoralised and wounded South African stragglers and organising them to make a fighting escape in November 1941. When General Sir Claude Auchinleck launched Operation Crusader against the Axis forces in Libya Major Cochran was second-in-command of the South African Irish Regiment, one of the 5th South African Brigade infantry battalions that made up Major-General George Brink's 1st South African Division.

In the opening days the British and South African forces became dispersed, leaving 5th SA Brigade virtually unprotected by armour when Rommel's tanks attacked its flank near Sidi Rezegh on November 23; the commander, Brigadier Armstrong, was captured and his brigade destroyed. Despite the chaos Cochran had under him a group of about 200 men after three days. Although it was caught up in a furious tank battle, only 13 men had been lost to enemy action when it eventually joined up with New Zealand units.

After reporting to General Bernard Freyberg VC, Cochran was placed in command of a battalion-strength group of South Africans and New Zealanders. For 10 days his mixed force held a position under what was described as "heavy shelling and a succession of actions"; his brother Captain

Frank Cochran, a forward observation officer with the SA artillery, played an important anti-tank role. When the time came to evacuate the position Cyril Cochran was one of the last to leave, remaining in range of German guns as he destroyed vehicles. The recommendation for his DSO noted that "throughout the heavy fighting he displayed admirable coolness and leadership and a complete disregard for his own safety under intense machine-gun, anti-tank and artillery fire. He was a great inspiration to his men and kept them in fighting spirit."

Cochran was then promoted to lieutenant-colonel and given command of the Botha regiment. During the Gazala Gallop (as it became known to the troops), when Rommel put the Allied forces to flight eastwards, Cochran was in charge of elements of the rearguard, and it was said that he was one of the last men in the Eighth Army to get back to Egypt. When Auchinleck stopped Rommel at Alamein in the early days of July 1942 the Botha regiment occupied a key position in the Allied defences. Later that month, as Auchinleck switched over to the offensive, Cochran personally led several raids on German positions. He was a great admirer of Auchinleck, and believed that "The Auk" never received the credit he deserved for his conduct of operations in Crusader and at the first Battle of Alamein.

Before the third Alamein in October 1942 Cochran was severely wounded by shrapnel during lunch in a mess tent. His liver was pierced and a lung damaged, and the surgeons expected him to die within a month. But he survived through force of will, and after three months returned to South Africa. By March 1943 he was fit enough to take command of the 2nd Botha regiment. When this was amalgamated with another to form a new South African armoured formation Cochran moved on to staff work. After the war he returned to civilian life, commenting "we had a job to do and we did it".

Cyril Monalty Cochran was born on May 14 1912 and educated at King Edward VII School, Johannesburg, and Witwatersrand University, where he studied dentistry and won half-blues for boxing and hockey. He earned an MC at the Battle of Mega in East Africa before going to the desert.

On demobilisation he worked briefly in Johannesburg; then opened a practice at Greytown, Natal; later he took up a pastoral position at Natal University. An opponent of apartheid, he believed the multi-racial general election of 1994 was a vindication of the fight for which he had volunteered in 1940.

Cochran was an enthusiastic, convivial host until his last days. He refused to make any concessions to old age or to the discomfort resulting from his wounds. Cyril Cochran married Olive Jean Moll, who survived him with their four children.

CAPTAIN
CHARLES UPHAM, VC

Captain Charles Upham (who died on November 22 1994, aged 86) won the Victoria Cross twice.

Only three men have won double VCs. The other two were medical officers, Colonel A Martin-Leake, who received the decoration in the Boer War and First World War; and Capt N G Chavasse, who was killed in France in 1917. The Chavasse family and the Uphams were related.

For all his remarkable exploits on the battlefield, Upham was a shy and modest man who was embarrassed when asked about the actions for which he had been decorated. "The military honours bestowed on me," he would say, "are the property of the men of my unit." In a television interview in 1983 he said he would have been happier not to have been awarded a VC at all, as it made people expect too much of him: "I don't want to be treated differently from any other bastard."

When King George VI was conferring Upham's second VC at Buckingham Palace after the war he asked Major-General Sir Howard Kippenberger, his commanding officer: "Does he deserve it?"

"In my respectful opinion, Sir," replied Kippenberger, "Upham won this VC several times over."

A great-great nephew of the writer William Hazlitt and the son of a British lawyer who practised in New Zealand, Charles Hazlitt Upham was born in Christchurch on September 21 1908. He was educated at Waihi preparatory school, Christ's

College and Canterbury Agricultural College, which he represented at rugby and rowing. He then spent six years as a farm manager, musterer and shepherd, before becoming a government valuer in 1937.

When war broke out in 1939, Upham volunteered for the 2nd New Zealand Expeditionary Force as a private in the 20th Battalion, and became a sergeant in the first echelon advance party. Commissioned in 1940, he went on to serve in Greece, Crete and the Western Desert.

He won his first VC on Crete in May 1941 while commanding a platoon in the battle for Maleme airfield. During the course of an advance of 3,000 yards his platoon was held up three times. Carrying a bag of grenades (his favourite weapon), Upham first attacked a German machine-gun nest, killing eight paratroopers, and then destroyed another which had been set up in a house. Finally he crawled to within 15 yards of a Bofors anti-aircraft gun before knocking it out.

After the advance had been completed he helped to carry a wounded man to safety in full view of the enemy, and then ran half a mile under fire to save a company from being cut off. Two Germans who tried to stop him were killed. The next day Upham was wounded in the shoulder by a mortar burst and hit in the foot by a bullet. Undeterred, he continued fighting and, with his arm in a sling, hobbled about in the open to draw enemy fire and enable their gun positions to be spotted. With his unwounded arm, he propped his rifle in the fork of a tree and killed two approaching Germans; the second was so close that he fell on the muzzle of Upham's rifle.

During the retreat from Crete, Upham succumbed to dysentery and could not eat properly. His commanding officer noted that the effect of this and his wounds made him look like a walking skeleton. Nevertheless he found the strength to climb the side of a 600ft deep ravine and use a Bren gun on a group of advancing Germans. At a range of 500 yards, he killed 22 out of 50. His citation recorded that he had "performed a series of remarkable exploits, showing outstanding leadership, tactical skill and utter indifference to danger".

Even under the hottest fire, Upham never wore a steel helmet, explaining that he could never find one to fit him.

His second VC was earned on July 15 1942 as the New Zealanders were concluding a desperate defence of the Ruweisat Ridge in the 1st Battle of Alamein. Upham ran forward through a position swept by machine-gun fire and lobbed grenades into a truck full of German soldiers.

When it became urgent to take information to advance units which had become separated, Upham took a Jeep on which a captured German machine-gun was mounted and drove it through the enemy position. At one point the vehicle became bogged down in the sand, so Upham coolly ordered some nearby Italian soldiers to push it free. Though they were somewhat surprised to be given an order by one of the enemy, Upham's expression left them in no doubt that he should be obeyed.

By now Upham had been wounded, but not badly enough to prevent him leading an attack on an enemy strongpoint, all the occupants of which were then bayoneted. He was shot in the elbow, and his arm was broken. The New Zealanders were surrounded and outnumbered. But Upham carried on directing fire until he was wounded in the legs and could no longer walk.

Taken prisoner, he proved such a difficult customer that in 1944 he was confined in Colditz Castle, where he remained for the rest of the war. His comments on Germans were always sulphurous.

For his actions at Ruweisat he was awarded a Bar to his VC. His citation noted that "his complete indifference to danger and his personal bravery have become a byword in the whole of the New Zealand Expeditionary Force".

After his release from Colditz in 1945, Upham went to England and inquired about the where-abouts of one Mary ("Molly") McTamney, from Dunedin. Told that she was a Red Cross nurse in Germany, he was prepared, for her sake, to return to that detested country. In the event she came to England, where they were married in June 1945.

Back in New Zealand, Upham resisted invitations to take up politics. In appreciation of his heroism the sum of £10,000 was raised to buy him a farm. He appreciated the tribute, but declined the money, which was used to endow the Charles Upham Scholarship Fund to send sons of ex-servicemen to university.

Fiercely determined to avoid all publicity, Upham

at first refused to return to Britain for a victory parade in 1946, and only acceded at the request of the New Zealand Prime Minister Peter Fraser. Four years later he resisted prime ministerial persuasion that he should go to Greece to attend the opening of a memorial for the Australians and New Zealanders who had died there – although he eventually went at Kippenberger's request.

In 1946, Upham had bought a farm at Rafa Downs, some 100 miles north of Christchurch beneath the Kaikoura Mountains, where he had worked before the war. There he found the anonymity he desired.

But in 1962, he was persuaded to denounce the British government's attempt to enter the Common Market: "Britain will gradually be pulled down and down," Upham admonished, "and the whole English way of life will be in danger." He reiterated the point in 1971: "Your politicians have made money their god, but what they are buying is a disaster." He added: "They'll cheat you yet, those Germans."

Upham and his wife had three daughters, two of them twins.

GENERAL
STANISLAW MACZEK

General Stanislaw Maczek was the last surviving senior army commander of the Second World War when he died in Edinburgh on December 11 1994, aged 102. He led the 1st Polish Armoured Division which, in August 1944, blocked the Falaise Gap in Normandy and prevented the escape of most of the German 7th Army. Subsequently Field Marshal Montgomery told the division that it was "like the cork of a bottle in which the Germans were trapped".

On August 7 1944, two months after the Allied invasion of Normandy, the Germans launched a counter-attack in the direction of Avranches, in the hope of destroying the armies which had broken out of the beach head. This 70,000-strong German force was held at Mortain while the Allied armies made converging sweeps to ensure that it did not emerge from the trap. Suddenly aware of their danger, the German forces tried to disengage and force a way back through the remaining outlets.

On August 15 General Maczek's tanks crossed the river Dives at two points north-east of Falaise and went on to cut one of the three remaining German escape routes. They then raced south to the other two, and blocked the second. The last gap was at Chambois, which the Poles captured on August 19. There followed an inferno of death and destruction as the enemy tried to hammer a way through the sector held by the Poles, and the Allies launched salvo after salvo of bombs and shells on to the 7th Army's men, tanks, guns and vehicles. Though other Allied units were approaching as fast as possible, the Poles were virtually isolated as the German 1st and 12th Divisions, fighting with the desperation of the doomed, launched repeated attacks. As tank fought tank at close range, and men engaged in hand-to-hand struggles the Poles were running short of food and ammunition, and their wounded could not be evacuated. Not until August 21 was the pressure relieved.

Writing that day, *The Daily Telegraph* correspondent, H D Ziman described the battle: "The entire German force, with supporting infantry, bore down on the Poles, who were temporarily out of touch with their allies on either flank. The Poles stood their ground. Compelled to face about – for the enemy force had approached them in their rear as well – and with both their flanks exposed, they fought back all day against the Germans, who emerged in wave after wave from the cover provided by the forest of Gouffen." After six days of dogged fighting the Poles had taken 5,000 prisoners, including a general and 140 officers. In the Falaise "pocket" as a whole the German losses amounted to 50,000 prisoners, 10,000 dead, and the equipment of an entire army.

Although some 20,000 Germans had managed to slip out before the encirclement was completed by the arrival of Canadian and American troops, the drive, initiative and fighting quality of Maczek's men were responsible for one of the greatest disasters which the German army suffered in France. After the battle the much-battered Polish Division was given six days to rest and replace damaged equipment, before again setting off on the drive towards Germany. Having crossed the Seine it pushed northwards, liberating Abbeville, St Omer, Ypres, Passchendaele and Roulers, and then finally relieving the 7th Armoured Division at Ghent. It was next ordered to clear the enemy from the area north of Ghent and west of the Scheldt. Though the terrain was unsuitable for armoured vehicles, after hard fighting the division reached Terneuzen, on the south side of the Scheldt estuary. From here the Poles linked up with 1st British Corps, and captured Baarle Nassau, Alphen and, on October 29, Breda.

Maczek liked to command his troops from the leading tank. He always sought to minimise the damage to the towns which he liberated, and took Breda through a surprise attack from the east, without firing a single shot into the town. He earned the undying gratitude of the inhabitants, who awarded the whole Polish Division honorary citizenship; and it was at Breda that he chose to be buried among his fallen comrades.

Moerdijk, which was heavily fortified and stubbornly defended, fell shortly afterwards, and by November 9 all the division's objectives had been achieved. It was then ordered to hold the 30-mile Maas front through the winter, an assignment which demanded patience and alertness in the face of boredom, as the Germans frequently tried to slip across during the long winter nights. Maczek left his troops in no doubt of the importance of their unglamorous vigil, and assured them they would be to the fore when the Allies entered Germany – a promise fulfilled on April 9. The Poles doubled back for further operations in Holland, but were soon in Germany again. Finally, on May 6, after slogging through countryside cluttered with the detritus of war, the division hoisted the Polish flag over Wilhelmshaven, where Maczek was one of the officers who accepted the surrender of German forces.

During the campaign in north-west Europe the division captured 17,000 prisoners and suffered 5,000 casualties. Yet Maczek's men knew him as *Baca* – or Chief Shepherd – for the care he took with their lives. "He never lost a battle from 1939," remembered one of his soldiers, "and we lost fewer men because of his brains."

Stanislaw Maczek was born on March 31 1892 at Szczerzec, near Lwow in south-eastern Poland, which was then part of the Austro-Hungarian empire. He was educated at Lwow University, where he read history and philosophy.

His first military training was as a member of a clandestine unit. Called up into the Austro-Hungarian army in the First World War, he served in a ski regiment, and saw action on the Italian front. At the end of the First World War Poland gained her independence, only to be immediately invaded by the Bolsheviks. Maczek fought in infantry and cavalry regiments during the two-year conflict, and developed the style of mobile fighting that became his trademark. In August 1920 Poland defeated the Red Army in the decisive Battle for Warsaw on the River Vistula.

Between the wars Maczek graduated from the Staff College, commanded an infantry regiment and was second-in-command of 7th Infantry Division. In 1938 he returned to the cavalry as commander of the 10th Motorised Cavalry Brigade, which he transformed within a year into Poland's first professional mechanised outfit. When the Germans invaded Poland in 1939 Maczek launched his men with considerable effect against better-equipped German forces. The brigade, clad in black leather coats, berets and boots, were nicknamed the "Black Devils" by the Germans. But their efforts could not prevent the country being overwhelmed. When the Russians also invaded Poland, Maczek led his depleted, yet still effective force into neutral Hungary, where it was interned.

By October, though, he had managed to take the brigade to France to join General Sikorski, the Polish GOC. Here Maczek was promoted Major-General and awarded the Gold Cross of the Virtuti Militari, the highest Polish decoration, in recognition of his courage and skill during the German invasion. In France Maczek started to train and equip a Polish armoured division. While still only at half-strength, and only partially equipped, it went into action to cover the retreat of the Allies in May 1940. After the fall of France, Maczek, though blue-eyed and fair-skinned, managed to escape to Algeria disguised as an Arab labourer. Eventually he reached Britain by way of Portugal. Many soldiers from the 10th Brigade also escaped to Britain, and the unit was re-formed in Berwickshire.

When the 1st Polish Armoured Division was formed in February 1942 in preparation for the liberation of Europe, Sikorski appointed Maczek as its first commander. On July 31 1944 it landed in France and, under the command of the 2nd

Canadian Corps, went into action south of Caen. In May 1945, at the end of the north-west Europe campaign, Maczek was promoted Lieutenant-General and appointed Commander of 1st Polish Army Corps, with headquarters in Scotland.

After demobilisation he settled in Edinburgh and worked on the staff of the Polish Resettlement Corps. Unable and unwilling to return to his native land while it was ruled by Communists, Maczek resented the breezy indifference of Field Marshal Montgomery, who in 1959 declared that he would be "delighted" if Russian troops remained in Poland, as long as they abandoned Germany. Maczek received no pension from Britain or Poland, and during the 1960s he worked as a part-time barman at the Learmouth Hotel in Edinburgh, which was run by one of his former sergeants. Old Polish comrades patronising the establishment would click their heels and bow before ordering their meals.

For Maczek's 80th birthday, in 1972, Prince Bernhard of the Netherlands and the Brabant Symphony Orchestra flew over to a celebration at the Connaught Rooms in Great Queen Street, London. On his 100th birthday a group of veterans gathered outside his Edinburgh home. "I haven't forgotten you," he assured them. President Lech Walesa marked the occasion by promoting Maczek to full general and conferring upon him the Order of the White Eagle, Poland's highest award, normally only given to heads of state. Unfortunately Maczek was too frail to travel to Poland. In addition to his Polish decorations and honours from the countries in which he had campaigned Maczek was awarded the DSO in 1944 and appointed honorary CB the next year.

In 1961 he published his memoirs, *From Horse-drawn Wagon to Tank*, which mentioned some of his encounters with his superiors. Montgomery, he recalled, asked him if "Poles among themselves, at home, spoke German or Russian". Maczek married, in 1928, Zofia Kurys; they had a son and two daughters.

BRIGADIER
ANTHONY WINGFIELD

Brigadier Anthony Wingfield (who died on March 1 1995, aged 87) was awarded the MC and an immediate DSO in the Western Desert, and was assistant stud and racing manager, later manager, to the Queen from 1957 to 1963.

Wingfield won his MC in an action north-west of Saunnu in North Africa on January 23 1942. After an initial retreat, Rommel counter-attacked with 90 tanks and mechanised infantry: 2nd Armoured Brigade was ordered to stop them in a night attack led by the 10th Hussars, of which Wingfield commanded the leading squadron. The Hussars were promptly attacked by 12 German tanks from the left, while enemy anti-tank guns opened fire at short range on the right. Using smoke to cover his position, Wingfield extricated his squadron and overran several anti-tank guns, killing their crews.

The Hussars then saw off the enemy tanks, scoring several hits. Later Wingfield returned in his own tank to collect the crews and the wounded of his disabled vehicles: "No praise can be too high for this officer's courage, leadership and devotion to duty," noted his citation.

The DSO was awarded for Wingfield's conduct near El Hamma on March 26 1943. Immediately after the brilliant, but costly, success in the Battle of the Mareth Line the Eighth Army pressed on to El Hamma. "As night fell," ran the citation, "Lieutenant-Colonel Wingfield found the echelons held up by a defile, with the enemy on his right and left. He deployed his forces in pitch darkness to protect the echelons and succeeded in getting the whole of his force through the defile without loss.

"When the advance continued at midnight, the echelons came under fire. Lieutenant-Colonel Wingfield handled his forces in such a manner that no casualties were incurred, and a large number of prisoners were collected."

At first light the 15th Panzer Division launched an attack on the rear of the British division, and Wingfield moved his regiment at high speed to frustrate the Germans. He personally reconnoitred positions in advance of his squadrons, under fire all the time. The enemy tanks withdrew as soon as the 10th Hussars arrived.

Wingfield went on to command 2nd Armoured Brigade in the North-West Europe campaign, from Normandy to the Elbe.

The son of Major-General Maurice Wingfield,

Anthony Desmond Rex Wingfield was born in Dublin on February 20 1908. The family derived from Wingfield Castle in Suffolk. Sir Richard Wingfield was Marshal of Ireland under Mountjoy, and was created Viscount Powerscourt in 1743; Anthony was a grandson of the 7th Viscount. After Eton and Sandhurst he was commissioned into the 10th Hussars in 1928.

He served in Egypt and India, and in 1936 returned to Britain for a mechanisation course at Bovington. Though mechanised, cavalry officers were still allowed to draw two chargers from the Remount Depot at Melton Mowbray. Wingfield had success on one of these, May Spring, and also hunted with the Heythrop and the Quorn in the later 1930s. He hoped to ride in the Grand Military, but could not afford a suitable mount; however, he did acquire Lady Pamela, with which he won several victories.

In 1939 he was made Intelligence Officer of 2nd Brigade. He was sent on an air photo interpretation course, and appointed local security officer, in which capacity he took action against transmissions of weather reports by amateurs as well as a pro-Nazi teacher who tried to obtain copies of British training manuals from troops. His time at the Staff College, Camberley, began with a huge cocktail party. A few days later one of the wives developed chickenpox, and everybody was put into quarantine.

Wingfield was then posted to York as Brigade Major, 1st Armoured Brigade, where he met Enoch Powell, then a lieutenant in the Intelligence Corps. On a divisional exercise Wingfield occupied a luxury farmstead, which he discovered was owned by an Army major who had beaten him at Eton and who was determined that his property should not be appropriated by the military. Recalling the strong wrist of the absent owner, who had been captain of racquets, Wingfield took the opportunity to park his tanks in the yard and allowed them to turn on the ornamental lawn.

In 1941, still on the Staff, he was posted to Egypt but was then allowed to rejoin the 10th Hussars and command a squadron. He was overjoyed, though he knew that their guns were vastly outranged by the German 50 mm and 75 mm weapons. During the desert campaign Wingfield had several narrow escapes from death. He was posted temporarily to the Middle East Training Centre in Palestine but returned to the 10th Hussars as second-in-command in time for El Alamein. During the battle he had no sleep for 36 hours and inadequate food and drink. At one point he drove his jeep over an anti-personnel mine: his passenger died, but he was unscathed. Eventually he was wounded, but stayed at his post. In the concluding stages of the battle the 10th Hussars shot up a German tank, and captured the commander of the opposing forces.

After Alamein, Wingfield saw almost continuous action. In April 1943 the 10th were transferred from the Eighth Army to the First for the final destruction of the Axis forces in North Africa. Wingfield noted the contrast between the smartly dressed First Army and the officers of the 10th Hussars, who were by then sporting corduroy trousers and coloured scarves, their trucks and lorries full of chickens and pigs acquired en route. General Alexander collared one of Wingfield's officers: "What are you doing here? I thought you never left White's." Wingfield told Alexander that the man had been awarded an MC in France and had twice been wounded in the desert.

On June 4 1943 Etonian Hussars arranged a boat race against Harrovians: the boats were telegraph poles, which the eights straddled, but there were no prizes for the winners. Outside Benghazi the Hussars "rested" in temperatures of up to 120°F; putting a hand on a tank at midday resulted in blistered fingers. They were then moved towards the coast, where they were visited by King George VI (code-named General Lion). Wingfield was posted back to Cairo as GSO1 (Armoured Fighting Vehicles). He was by now exhausted: often ill, his hair falling out and his eyesight failing.

After recovering he was posted back to Britain as second-in-command of 34th Tank Brigade. On July 2 1944 he landed in France. In Holland he was given command of 22nd Armoured Brigade and charged with clearing west Holland and relieving Antwerp. Subsequently the brigade crossed the Elbe, and took 500 prisoners a day. At the end of the war it remained in the Kiel area, disarming Germans coming down from Norway and Denmark. Wingfield hoped to capture Martin Bormann, Hitler's designated successor, but failed, although the brigade did pick up Max Schmeling, the former world heavyweight boxing champion.

Wingfield was next posted to the War Office in the Royal Armoured Corps directorate before becoming a GSO1 instructor at the Staff College, Camberley, for two years. He then moved to Co Westmeath, where he combined farming with point-to-pointing and race judging. He was a senior steward of the National Hunt Steeplechasing Committee in Ireland for two terms (a total of six years). As a steward he was strict but fair; he was never heard to speak ill of anyone and was esteemed for his kindly nature, excellent horsemanship and dash in the field.

Wingfield was secretary of the Meath Hunt for 12 years. He also ran a small stud farm and owned a useful horse, Persian War. In 1957 he returned to England to take up his post as assistant stud and racing manager to the Queen. Those who served with him recalled his intelligence and courage. A cultured man with a quick sense of humour, he was never rattled. He married, in 1935, Juliet ("Judy") Stanley, who predeceased him; they had a daughter.

LIEUTENANT-COLONEL
BRIAN GAIT

Lieutenant-Colonel Brian Gait (who died on March 12 1995, aged 63) won a Distinguished Conduct Medal while serving with the Black Watch in Korea in 1952, and a DSO while commanding the 2nd Regiment, Royal Military Police, in Belfast in 1975. His DSO was the first to be awarded to an officer in the RMP.

Brian Arthur Gait was born in Liverpool on August 12 1931, and educated locally. Enlisting as a private in the Black Watch at 18, within three years he had risen to sergeant; his youthful appearance earned him the sobriquet "Boy Gait".

On the night of November 16 1952 the Black Watch was holding a key feature known as the Hook, which dominated the invasion route to South Korea; Gait was in command of a patrol on a spur known as "Ronson". When the Chinese delivered their night attack Gait inflicted heavy casualties with his own weapon and – when there were sufficient numbers to justify it – called on artillery fire. His own patrol suffered five casualties from an enemy shell, and he himself was badly shaken by the blast, but he remained calm and efficient, requesting assistance by wireless and rendering first aid. On November 18, Gait's platoon commander became a casualty, and soon after taking command Gait was ordered to carry out an immediate counter-attack to clear the enemy from the feature.

"He swept forward with his men through heavy enemy shell and mortar fire," recorded the citation, "killing and chasing the enemy until he reached the line of the lateral trench across the Hook. There his men were pinned down by fire from several light machine-guns and showers of grenades from the high ground. Sergeant Gait, without thought for his own safety, proceeded to organise the defence of the ground retaken. He got in touch with a neighbouring platoon commander and by co-ordinating their actions and by intelligent anticipation of enemy outflanking attacks was able to stabilise the situation. Later in the night he and his remaining men succeeded in preventing the third enemy attack from penetrating the trench line, and single-handed he beat off one enemy probe which came in round the flank."

The citation stressed that when in close contact with the enemy Gait showed himself to be a fearless, inspiring and highly efficient leader.

After Korea the Black Watch moved on to Kenya, where it was responsible for the Rift Valley and part of the Aberdare mountain range, hunting Mau Mau terrorists who used it as a base. Gait was noted for his skill and determination in tracking down terrorists.

On his return to Britain he was posted as an instructor at Sandhurst and then commissioned into the King's Regiment, formed in 1958 by the amalgamation of the Manchester and the King's (Liverpool) Regiments. Gait then transferred to the Corps of Military Police, becoming Deputy Assistant Provost Marshal (Operations) in Northern Ireland in 1969. In 1972 he was appointed to command his second regiment, the Royal Military Police, after which he was awarded a DSO.

"He consistently displayed exceptional leadership qualities", the citation noted, "and not a day passed when he did not visit his troops on the ground, joining them on patrol irrespective of the hour." Gait's RSM recalled that on Christmas Day he would accompany his CO, driven by Corporals Greenhill and Greenoak as shotgun, and visit every man from 2 RMP on duty. The tour would start at 0600 hrs from RHQ and end at 1700 hrs.

Gait liked to be at the sharp end, to the extent that he became personally involved in a gun battle in north Belfast, where he shot and wounded one of the gunmen in the groin. He later visited the wounded man in the secure wing of Musgrave Park Hospital.

After his retirement from the Army he became an Army careers officer in Liverpool; in his final retirement he was president of the RMP Association of North Wales. Brian Gait married, in 1958, Freda Yates; they had three daughters.

BRIGADIER
LORD LOVAT

Brigadier the 17th Lord Lovat, the 24th Chief of the Clan Fraser (who died on March 16 1995, aged 83), was a legendary Commando leader in the Second World War. A daring, charismatic and sometimes contro-versial figure, Lovat played an important part in the raids on Lofoten and Dieppe – as well as in the D-Day landings, during which he was severely wounded.

He was in command of 1st Special Service Brigade, a force containing five Commando groups, which landed at Ouistreham on June 6 1944. The men washed, shaved, and cleaned their boots aboard ship – and under fire – before going ashore. They then fought their way six miles inland to the Orne bridges, which had recently been captured and were being held against a German counter-attack. Accompanied as usual by his piper, Lovat marched across the Orne and took up position to repulse the advancing Panzers. He was subsequently wounded, and as he was being carried off the field on a stretcher sent a message to his men: "I can rely on you not to take one step back." Nor did they. Lovat's role in the proceedings was featured in the epic film *The Longest Day* (1962), in which he was portrayed by Peter Lawford. "Shimi" Lovat was not averse to the publicity.

He had joined the newly-formed Commandos in 1941, when he took part in the raid on the Lofoten Islands off Norway. The object was to destroy the fish-oil processing station there, from which Germany was obtaining glycerine for the manufacture of explosives. Lovat's Commandos sank 12 ships, destroyed 18 factories and burned some 800,000 gallons of petrol and oil. They also brought back an Enigma machine which proved vital to the Ultra deciphering operation.

Before leaving for England, with Norwegian volunteers and German prisoners aboard, Lovat sent an insulting telegram to Hitler from the local post office. After this came similar raids on Spitsbergen and Vaagso, which had the effect of making Hitler wastefully retain 300,000 troops in Norway against a possible Allied invasion. Lovat went on to enjoy a rare triumph amid the otherwise disastrous Dieppe raid of 1942, when his Commandos fought through heavy opposition to reach and destroy a large German battery behind Varengeville. He had been training 4 Commando in Ayrshire for a year, and believed he had turned them from "a rabble in arms" into a highly effective force expert in street-fighting and rock-climbing.

When he arrived at Combined Operations Head-quarters in London he found, he said, "a fair proportion of drones among the inmates". The Canadian commander, Gen "Ham" Roberts, was "a nice fellow but thick", while Mountbatten, who had overall responsibility, had been "lucky at sea". After Lovat and his force had completed training at Lulworth Cove (on a kinsman's estate in Dorset), he called together all ranks before they moved to boat stations, and told them that, though they were the finest in the Army, casualties might be high and no man was to lie down unless hit. He himself made a remarkable sight: the only Commando not "blacked up" for the landing, he wore under his battle-dress a sweater emblazoned with his name, and carried his favourite Winchester sporting rifle.

Lovat had expected the Germans to be waiting for them, but in the event the Commandos sustained only light casualties when negotiating the barbed wire defences, and then proceeding to the battery. Once they had reached the objective the men charged through their own smoke screen, their eyes smarting, and took the enemy by surprise; many of the Germans did not have time to put on their trousers before taking up positions and spraying the Commandos with machine-gun fire. As soon as the target had been taken a flight of Messerschmitts went over, whom Lovat reassured with a friendly wave. By the time the Commandos had returned to the beach Lovat was bubbling with excitement. "Went straight in, cut them to shreds," he said before wading out to a landing craft.

On his return to London, Lovat reported to Mountbatten and then, penniless and filthy, made his way to the Guards' Club, where an elderly servant gave him a precious bar of soap. After bathing Lovat fell asleep in the library, wrapped in towels. He was awarded the DSO to add to his earlier MC (for a reconnaissance raid on Boulogne), and his part in the Dieppe raid became celebrated as a classic Commando exercise. Lovat later discovered that the Gestapo had offered 100,000 Deutschmarks for his capture, dead or alive.

Simon Christopher Joseph Fraser was born on July 9 1911, the elder son of the 16th Lord Lovat, a celebrated all-round sportsman who, in the South African War, had raised and commanded the Lovat Scouts, a regiment of his own clansmen. The Lords Lovat have the rare distinction of being Highland chiefs as well as members of the old Scots peerage. As chiefs of the Clan Fraser, they are known by their Gaelic title of MacShimi, and they have plenty of Celtic blood in their veins from maternal ancestors of Highland stock; but in the male line, they are Norman-French, not having migrated from the Lowlands to the hills of Inverness until the 14th century. The Jacobite 11th Lord Lovat, known as "the Old Fox" and familiar as the mountainous grinning septuagenarian painted by Hogarth, became in 1747 the last peer to be beheaded in the Tower of London. He died a Catholic, and in 1815 the peerage and the chieftainship passed to the present Catholic branch of the Frasers.

The Master of Lovat, as he was styled until succeeding his father in 1933, was educated at Ampleforth, where he showed a precocious interest in practical war games. Under his enthusiastic guidance, contestants would advance upon each other across a cornfield and endeavour to hit each other's backsides with pellets as they crawled along. In the event this proved less of a test of the range of the weapons than the thickness of the trousers. After a period working on a coffee and cattle ranch in South America – an experience which gave rise to his love of the pampas and an abiding delight in cowboy films – he went up to Magdalen College, Oxford, where he occupied rooms that had been prepared for the Prince of Wales. He was a member of the Oxford University Cavalry Squadron and on coming down joined the Scots Guards, with whom he served from 1932 to 1937. While with them he served in Egypt and also fought in the Army Fencing Championships.

Finding regimental life rather dull, he left the Army in 1937 but on the outbreak of war two years later joined the Lovat Scouts. After more frustrations during the "Phoney War" Lovat became involved in the formation of the various irregular forces out of which the Commandos grew. He was promoted lieutenant-colonel in 1942 and brigadier in 1943. As well as the DSO and MC, he was awarded the Croix de Guerre with palm, the Legion d'Honneur and the Norway Liberation Cross.

In 1945 Lovat was appointed Under-Secretary for Foreign Affairs in Churchill's caretaker Government – a period of office which was brief and not particularly distinguished. He then withdrew to his family seat of Beaufort Castle in Invernessshire, where he devoted himself to forestry and bred shorthorn Aberdeen Angus and Highland cattle, which he also judged at shows all over the world. An inveterate traveller and sportsman, Lovat went on many safaris to South Africa, and also travelled to South America, Mexico and the Rockies, the Canadian lakes and southern Texas. For 35 years he was chairman of the Shikar Club, the illustrious big-game fraternity. As a boy he had acquired the quick observant eye of the Highlander, and was never happier than when on the hill or by the river.

A supremely conscientious clan chief, Lovat regularly visited Commonwealth countries on clan business, and welcomed overseas clan members to Beaufort. Athletic, good-looking and with consider-able presence, he was a natural leader, though he possessed a formidably autocratic streak. Winston Churchill described him as "the handsomest man who ever cut a throat". As his lively memoirs, *March Past* (1978), show, he had no grey areas between like and dislike, but he could be an outstandingly loyal friend. In many ways "Shimi" Lovat epitomised the old fighting Highland chief, but he was also erudite, intelligent, humorous and shrewd. He did much good public work for his beloved Scotland and it was strange that he never received any official recognition of this.

He married, in 1938, Rosie Delves Broughton, only daughter of the notorious Sir "Jock" Delves Broughton, the baronet acquitted of the sensational murder in Kenya of his second wife's lover, the 22nd Earl of Erroll, in 1941. They had four sons and two daughters. In March 1994 he lost two of his sons: Andrew, the youngest, was gored to death by a buffalo in Tanzania, aged 42; a fortnight later Simon, the eldest, suffered a heart attack while riding out with a local hunt, aged 54. His grandson Simon, the Master of Lovat, born in 1977, succeeded to the peerage and the chieftainship.

LIEUTENANT-COLONEL MAHMOOD KHAN DURRANI, GC

Lieutenant-Colonel Mahmood Khan Durrani (who died on August 20 1995, aged 81) was awarded the George Cross after he undermined Japanese efforts to infiltrate India with members of the "Indian National Army" while in a prison camp during the Second World War.

Mahmood Khan Durrani was born on July 1 1914 into the old royal family of Kabul. As an under-graduate he came to the attention of the Nawab Bahadur of Bahawalpur, who was seeking men of good family, education and impressive stature for his bodyguard; and, after basic training with the Nawab's forces, he was sent to the Army Signals School at Poona. In 1941 Durrani was a captain in the 1st Bahawalpur Infantry, India State Forces, which was assigned to airfield defence in northern Malaya. When the airfields were bombed, and the few undamaged aircraft withdrawn, Durrani, with a small party, tried to make his way back through Japanese occupied territory to link up with other members of his regiment.

Since a general retreat was under way, this proved impossible. Durrani managed to avoid the Japanese, keeping his party undetected and hiding in the jungle for three months – though they nearly starved to death in the process. Eventually he was betrayed and sent to a Japanese prison camp in Singapore. Conditions were appalling but Durrani managed to persuade the Japanese that if he was allowed to attend to their welfare, the prisoners would be more likely to join the Indian National Army. The INA, comprising 10,000 former Indian Army soldiers who had been captured by the Japanese and 20,000 civilian volunteers, presented a considerable threat after the Japanese had occupied Burma.

Although he himself declined to join the INA he expressed great interest in helping the Japanese to "liberate" India. In truth, his observations of Japanese behaviour in Malaya had left him in no doubt as to what "liberation" would mean. He persuaded the Japanese that he could organise a school to train agents to land submarines and engage in sabotage in India. Durrani chose his "saboteurs" carefully; they were, in fact, briefed to warn the British about Japanese plans, offer them help, and convey intelligence. Eventually the suspicions of Subhas Chandra Bose, the chief recruiter for the INA, were aroused, and Durrani was arrested by the Japanese, who demanded the names of his accomplices.

When Durrani resisted he was subjected to systematic torture. He was made to kneel on a stone floor while an overhead electric heater, burning day and night, turned the cell into an oven. Through lengthy interrogations he was kept conscious by the application to his legs of lit cigarettes. When he refused to talk, Durrani was handed over to the INA, who tortured him further, frequently beating him and allowing him only small and virtually inedible portions of burned food.

By the end of the war Durrani's health had been permanently impaired; but at first he was regarded with suspicion by the British Army, on account of his INA link. When his full achievements were realised, he was awarded the GC. In the event, the INA's military record was one of dismal failure; it won no battles, and had 750 killed, with 5,000 desertions. The rest died of disease or were captured. Durrani was informed of his award at lunch with Field Marshal Sir Claude Auchinleck in 1946, and had the medal pinned on his chest by Field Marshal Lord Wavell. Some years later he gave it to his friend the Nawab of Bahalpur for safekeeping and to display as an honour to the state of Punjab; but it disappeared after the Nawab's death and was recovered in 1999 when it appeared for auction at Spinks in London. The medal appeared to have been sold by a dealer in Rawalpindi in 1976; once documentary proof of the loan was produced, Spinks agreed to sell it to the Imperial War Museum.

Durrani attended the Royal Garden Party in 1962, and frequently returned to Britain for liver treatment; on his last visit, in 1994, he went with the VC and GC Association to take tea with the Prince of Wales at Highgrove. Some 6ft 4in tall and a man of exceptional courage, stamina and loyalty, Durrani bore no rancour about the past. His book *The Sixth Column*, published in 1955, tells his story with modesty and tolerance, calmly describing the appalling horrors he witnessed and endured. Cultured and widely read, Durrani was a poet of merit who detested racism, stressing that ideas of national superiority were based on ignorance of the achievements of other peoples. He was married, and had three sons and a daughter.

LIEUTENANT-COLONEL VICTOR WILDISH

Lieutenant-Colonel Victor Wildish (who died on November 1 1995, aged 79) was awarded an MC during operations in Waziristan, on the North-West Frontier, while serving with the 1st Battalion, 10th Baluch Regiment, in 1938. The notorious Fakir of Ipi was engaged in one of his periodic incitements to tribesmen to make trouble for the government forces in the area. His supporters planted bombs on roads and parade grounds and regularly sniped at troops and posts.

By the end of May 1938 the Fakir, who convinced his followers that his prayers would give them immunity from enemy bullets, had established a *lashkar* (a large body of armed tribesmen) in the Tochi Valley. Despite the presence of two British brigades in the area, the number of attacks increased at a pace which demanded drastic action.

On June 2 a column formed by the Razmak and Jhelum brigades advanced towards Mami Rogha. The terrain was rugged, and progress slow. As the column neared its objective it was met with heavy fire, and had great difficulty in locating the snipers in dense scrub. Once the enemy stronghold had been identified, A Company was ordered to clear it, and Wildish led the attack with outstanding speed and determination. The report on the operation stated that A Company "attacked with great spirit and, after a precipitous climb through thick scrub, were very soon in occupation of their objective. Two of the company were killed and three wounded . . . The column then advanced and eventually succeeded in dispersing the *lashkar*. The Fakir subsequently fled into Afghanistan."

The son of a mercantile marine engineer, Victor Oswald Frederick Wildish was born at Kisimu, Uganda, on May 31 1916, and educated at Bedford and Sandhurst. After being commissioned in 1936 he was posted to India, where he was at first attached to the South Staffordshire Regiment and then gazetted to the 10th Baluch.

Wildish was engaged in further operations on the North-West Frontier until 1941. He was then appointed GSO3 (Operations) at HQ 21 Indian Corps in Paiforce, the army based in Persia and Iraq to block any drive German forces might make towards seizing the Middle East oilfields. In the event the Germans were too heavily occupied in Russia to make the attempt, and Paiforce was charged with safeguarding arms and equipment worth £5 million which were being carried from the Persian Gulf to be handed over to the Red Army on the Russian border. The journey, over 1,000 miles of scorching sand and freezing mountains, was an epic achievement.

In 1942 Wildish went to the Staff College at Haifa before being posted the next year as an instructor to the Middle East training centre at Gaza. In 1944 he returned to his battalion as second-in-command for jungle warfare training; but the Far Eastern war ended before he was able to put the lessons to use. At intervals up to 1946 he was acting CO of his battalion, and in 1947 he returned to the staff as Deputy Assistant Adjutant General at HQ Secunderabad.

After Partition in 1947 Wildish returned to Britain, and joined the Royal Artillery. From 1948 to 1950 he commanded 155 Battery, 60th Heavy Anti-Aircraft Regiment in Belfast, and from 1950 to 1952 he was Brigade Major, RA, in 89 AGRA at Colchester. From 1952 to 1954 he commanded 109

Battery, 40th Field Regiment at Dortmund, after which he returned to the staff at DAAG (Plans) at GHQ, Middle East Land Forces in Nicosia. This period saw the beginning of the Eoka troubles.

In 1957 Wildish returned to command 35th Light Anti-Aircraft Regiment, near Bremen. The regiment raised and trained a ski team which competed at the Army ski meetings in 1958, where it won the downhill, slalom and cross-country events, and as the champion unit ski team won the Princess Marina Duchess of Kent Cup. Wildish's next posting was as SO1, RA, Allied Forces Northern Europe, and his final appointment was AA and QMG at HQ Rhine Area until 1962.

After retiring Wildish was deputy secretary for the Charities Aid Foundation and then worked for EMI. Subsequently he and his wife ran an antiques business near Windsor.

Victor Wildish was a natural leader and a man of great charisma, who seemed to have no fear. Cool and analytical, he set a high standard in anything he did and raised the units he commanded to peak efficiency. Tall, lean, always smartly dressed, he was strict and outspoken but never pompous. In younger days he had rowed at Bedford and Sandhurst and had stroked for Sandhurst VIII at Henley in 1935; in India he hunted and shot, notably in the Himalayas. His sense of humour was notorious, as were his escapades. One stormy night at Latakia in Syria he swam across the harbour and back for a bet, accompanied by a boatful of fellow officers. He then challenged anyone to hang upside down from the mess tent-pole for longer than he could for "double or quits". There were no takers.

On another occasion, when a battery commander in Belfast, he scorned the traditional practice of sliding down the stairs on a tea tray as too tame, and decided instead to go down headfirst on an upturned table. The result was a dislocated jaw. Less well-known than his exploits were his many kindnesses, which he took great care to conceal. Wildish's main interest apart from the Army was exploring countryside. With keen powers of observation, he built up a store of detailed knowledge of animals and birds, not only in Europe but also in India and Africa. He was an expert fisherman.

Victor Wildish married, in 1944, Audrey Bryning; they had a daughter.

BRIGADIER
BILL BRADFORD

Brigadier Bill Bradford (who died on March 4 1996, aged 83) was awarded an immediate DSO when commanding the 5th Battalion, the Black Watch, in France in 1944, and an immediate Bar at Goch, on the Rhine, in 1945. Earlier he had been awarded an MC in North Africa and an MBE for an epic escape from France in 1940.

The first DSO was won at St Julien Le Faucon on August 18 1944 when his battalion was ordered to capture a high wooded feature on a moonless night.

As it was moving up to the start line the command post received a direct hit, knocking out many of the key personnel and wounding Bradford. He refused to be evacuated and led the battalion to its objective against determined opposition, personally bringing forward the tanks through shellfire and up a steep incline so that they could support the infantry. For the next 24 hours, while enemy infantry made determined attacks on his position, Bradford, although in great pain, insisted on remaining with his men, repelling all attacks and carrying out local operations to clear the forward defence line.

Not until the enemy withdrew did he consent to leave and receive proper medical attention. The citation stressed that the loss of key personnel before the fighting began had thrown much extra work on Bradford, whose leadership and skill were outstanding.

The Bar to the DSO was won on the night of February 20-21 1945 when his battalion was given the task of capturing Goch. The tactical plan involved capturing two farms to the south of the town before moving north to take two more farms. After a difficult approach march on bad tracks, the first farm was overwhelmed in an attack perfectly co-ordinated with the preliminary artillery strike. The capture of the second farm involved fierce close-quarter fighting for the rest of the night. Bradford, ignoring the heavy artillery and machine-gun fire that swept the area, was continuously in the forefront of the battle encouraging his men.

During the attack on the third farm Bradford's wireless received a direct hit, which wounded the operator; undaunted, Bradford went forward in person to direct the attack. Dawn found the battalion still locked in the struggle for the second and third farms, with the fourth unequivocally in the enemy's hands and the German self-propelled guns doing much damage. But by 10am the whole area had been secured and all counter-attacks beaten off.

Berenger Colborne Bradford was born on October 15 1912 and educated at Eton and Sandhurst. He was the fourth generation of his family to be at Eton; much of his childhood was spent at Jane Austen's family home at Chawton, Hampshire. Bradford was commissioned into the Black Watch in 1932, and posted to the 1st Battalion in India.

On the outbreak of war he was adjutant. When the 51st Highland Division was trapped at St Valéry in 1940 Bradford was taken prisoner but managed to slip away on the long march to a camp in Germany. He tried but failed to find a boat on the coast; so walked south while living on raw vegetables and scraps. He swam the Loire, crossed the Pyrenees and reached the Spanish border. Having failed in two attempts to cross the frontier, Bradford was arrested by the Vichy police and interned in harsh conditions at Marseilles. He escaped again, stowed away on a ship to Algiers, borrowed some money from an American and bought a 14ft boat which was scarcely seaworthy. With a Communist and a Jew, who were as anxious as he to escape from the Germans, but who also had no experience of sailing at sea, Bradford succeeded in covering the 500 miles to Gibraltar, nearly capsizing several times on the way.

For his astonishing escape, which had occupied a year, Bradford was appointed MBE. Back home, he joined the newly constituted 51st Highland Division just before it sailed for North Africa; he then fought at Alamein and through the rest of the desert campaign, being awarded the MC in North Africa when serving as Brigade Major of 154 Brigade. Later he fought in Sicily, and in July 1944 took command of the 5th Battalion, the Black Watch, in Normandy.

After the war Bradford held various staff appointments before being given command of 16th (Welsh) Battalion, TA, the Parachute Regiment; he did all his qualifying jumps in one day. Subsequently he served on the staff of 16th Airborne Division before commanding the 2nd Battalion, the Black Watch, from 1953 to 1956 and taking them from BAOR to British Guyana. From 1957 to 1959 he commanded 153 Highland Brigade, Territorial Army, at Dundee.

After retiring from the Army, the magnificiently moustached Bradford turned his energies to revitalising the family estates in Aberdeenshire, which involved extensive forestry conservation and the establishment of a successful mixed farm. He was a member of the Queen's Body Guard for Scotland, Royal Company of Archers. A first-class shot and an expert fisherman, he continued with both pursuits to the end of his life, disregarding the handicap of Parkinson's Disease which had been diagnosed in 1960. One of his subalterns said that Bradford was "a hard taskmaster but absolutely fair, and the battalion was very professional and happy under his leadership.

He was always fun at a party and never happier than when seeing people enjoying themselves. It was a great privilege to have served under one of the finest commanding officers of the Black Watch."

Bill Bradford married Susan Vaughan-Lee in 1951; they had three sons and a daughter. The youngest son was second-in-command of the 1st Battalion, the Black Watch, at the time of his death.

———

LIEUTENANT-COLONEL JACK CHURCHILL

Lieutenant-Colonel Jack Churchill (who died on March 8 1996, aged 89) was probably the most dramatically impressive Commando leader of the Second World War. His exploits – charging up beaches dressed only in a kilt while brandishing a dirk, killing with a bow and arrow, and playing the bagpipes at moments of extreme peril – won him the admiration and devotion of those under his command; they nicknamed him "Mad Jack".

Churchill believed that an assault leader should have a reputation which would at once demoralise the enemy and convince his own men that nothing was impossible. He was awarded two DSOs and an MC, and mentioned in despatches. Romantic and sensitive, he was an avid reader of history and poetry, knowledgeable about castles and trees, and compassionate to animals, even to insects.

John Malcolm Thorpe Fleming Churchill was

born in Surrey on September 16 1906. His father, Alex Churchill, was on leave from the Far East, where he was Director of Public Works in Hong Kong and Ceylon. After education at the Dragon School, Oxford, King William's College, Isle of Man, and Sandhurst, Churchill was commissioned in 1926 into the Manchester Regiment and gazetted to the 2nd Battalion, which he joined in Rangoon.

Returning from a signals course at Poona, he rode a Zenith motorcycle 1,500 miles across India, at one point crashing into a water buffalo. In Burma, he took the Zenith over railway bridges by stepping on the sleepers (there was nothing in between them) and pushing the bike along the rails. Churchill moved from Rangoon to Maymyo, where he was engaged in "flag marches"; this meant moving up and down the Irrawaddy by boat, visiting the villages and deterring those who might be contemplating murder or dacoity. At Maymyo he learned to play the bagpipes, tutored by the Pipe Major of the Cameron Highlanders, and became an outstanding performer.

But when the regiment returned to Britain in 1936, he became bored with military life at the depot in Ashton-under-Lyne and retired after only 10 years in the Army. Churchill went on a grand tour of Europe, accompanied by his great friend Rex King-Clark; took minor parts as an archer in films; played the bagpipes as an entertainer; and represented Great Britain at archery in the 1939 World Championships.

On the outbreak of war in 1939, he was recalled to the colours and went to France, taking with him his bow and arrows which he used on patrols against the Germans in front of the Maginot Line. The weapon was silent, accurate to 200 yards and lethal. After the Germans attacked in France, Churchill was awarded the MC in the retreat at the Battle of l'Epinette (near Béthune) where his company was trapped by German forces. He fought back with two machine-guns (and his bow) until ammunition was exhausted, then extricated the remains of the company through the German lines at night and reported back to Brigade HQ. Later he was wounded, and carried a bullet in his shoulder all his life.

After returning to England, he joined the Commandos. In 1941, he was second-in-command of a mixed force from 2 and 3 Commandos which raided Vaagso, in Norway. The aim was to blow up local fish oil factories, sink shipping, gather intelligence, eliminate the garrison and bring home volunteers for the Free Norwegian Forces. Before landing, Churchill decided to look the part. He wore silver buttons he had acquired in France, carried his bow and arrows and armed himself with a broad-hilted claymore, and led the landing force ashore with his bagpipes. Although he was again wounded, the operation forced the Germans to concentrate large forces in the area.

After recovering, Churchill was appointed lieutenant-colonel commanding 2 Commando, which he took through Sicily (leading with his bagpipes to Messina) and then to the landings at Salerno. They captured the village of Pigoletti with its garrison of 42 men as well as an 81mm mortar and its crew. In further fighting along the Pigoletti Ridge, he was recommended for the VC but eventually received the DSO. His action had saved the Salerno beachhead at a critical time.

Churchill's next assignment was in the Adriatic, where he was appointed to command a force comprising 43 Royal Marine Commando plus one company from the Highland Light Infantry and eight 25lb guns. They landed on the island of Brac, then attacked and captured the Vidova Gora (2,500 ft high), the approaches of which were heavily mined. Playing his pipes, Churchill led 40 Commando in a night attack which reached the top of the objective where he was wounded and captured.

"You have treated us well," he wrote to the German commander after only 48 hours in captivity. "If, after the war, you are ever in England and Scotland, come and have dinner with my wife and myself"; he added his telephone number. The German was one Captain Hans Thornerr; and later the note saved Thornerr's life when the Yugoslavs wanted to have him shot as a war criminal. The Germans thought, wrongly, that Churchill must be a relation of the Prime Minister.

Eventually he was imprisoned in Sachsenhausen Camp, near Berlin, where he was chained to the floor for the first month and found himself in company with such VIPs as Kurt von Schusnigg, the former Chancellor of Austria, Friedrich von Thyssen and Hjalmar Schacht, Hitler's Economics Minister. Churchill tunnelled out of the camp with an RAF officer, but was recaptured and transferred to a PoW camp in Austria. When the floodlights failed one night he escaped and, living on stolen vegetables, walked across the Alps near the Brenner Pass. He then made contact with an American reconnaissance column in the Po Valley.

Churchill was appointed second-in-command of 3 Commando Brigade, which was in India preparing for the invasion of Japan; but the war ended – much to his regret, as he wanted to be killed in battle and buried in the Union flag. He took a parachute course, making his first jump on his 40th birthday, and commanded 5th (Scottish) Parachute Battalion, thus becoming the only officer to command both a Commando and a Parachute battalion. Churchill had always wanted to serve with a Scottish regiment, and so transferred to the Seaforth Highlanders, becoming a company commander.

In 1948 he was appointed second-in-command of the Highland Light Infantry, then serving in Jerusalem. Terrorism was widespread and on April 13 1948, Arabs ambushed a Jewish convoy of doctors en route for the Hadassah Hospital, near the city. Churchill, having ordered reinforcements for his small force, walked alone towards the ambush, smiling and carrying a blackthorn stick. "People are less likely to shoot you if you smile at them," he said. So it proved.

He then managed to evacuate some of the Jews, but many thought that Haganah (the Jewish army) would save them and did not require his services. As one of the HLI had now been killed by Arab fire, he withdrew; and 77 Jews were then slaughtered.

Later Churchill assisted in the evacuation of 500 patients and staff from the hospital.

Back in Britain, he was for two years second-in-command of the Army Apprentices School at Chepstow before serving a two-year stint as Chief Instructor, Land/Air Warfare School in Australia. In 1954, Churchill joined the War Office Selection Board at Barton Stacey. During this period he rode a surf board a mile and a half up river on the Severn bore. His last post was as the first commandant of the Outward Bound School.

After retirement, Churchill devoted himself to his hobby of buying and refurbishing steamboats on the Thames; he acquired 11, which made journeys from Richmond to Oxford. He was a keen maker of radio-controlled model boats, which he sold at a profit. He also took part in motor-cycling speed trials. When not engaged in military operations Jack Churchill was a quiet, unassuming man, though not above astonishing strangers for the fun of it. In his last job he would sometimes stand up on a train journey from London to his home, open the window and hurl out his briefcase, then calmly resume his seat. Fellow passengers looked on aghast, unaware that he had flung the briefcase into his own back garden.

Jack Churchill married, in 1941, Rosamund Denny; they had two sons.

MAJOR-GENERAL
BRIAN DAUNT

Major-General Brian Daunt (who died on March 18 1996, aged 96) was always at the centre of battle and often to be seen engaging enemy infantry with a tommy-gun; he was awarded a DSO in Italy while commanding the Royal Devon Yeomanry (142 Field Regiment, RA) in support of the attack on Cava di Tirreni in 1943.

The Germans were fighting back with all the weapons they had, and the town was full of debris and dust when Daunt assumed command. Apparently fearless, as well as lucky, he walked without hesitation among minefields during the advance.

Soon after the attack on Cava di Tirreni, Naples fell to the Allies and a bridgehead was established across the river Volturno, which was held against counter-attacks by German tanks and machine-guns. The next assignment was the Garigliano crossing, where, in addition to his own unit, Daunt commanded six guns from an American unit. After this gruelling battle the regiment came under the command of the American 88th Infantry Division whose general subsequently wrote to thank Daunt for his "splendid support", noting that the division had been particularly appreciative of "the effective firepower so capably delivered by your weapons".

In the ensuing battle of Monte Cassino, Daunt was constantly out in front, often with the infantry that his regiment was supporting; they were said to have been the first artillery to cross the Rapido.

Subsequently the 1st Canadian Corps awarded the Royal Devon Yeomanry the right to wear the Maple Leaf in recognition of the support it had given them.

The regiment then saw continuous action on the drive up through Italy which culminated in the Battle of Florence, where they supported the New Zealanders. In September 1944 Daunt, who had now commanded the regiment for 23 months, was promoted to become Commander, RA, in 1st Armoured Division. In 1945 he was mentioned in despatches.

A doctor's son, Brian Daunt was born on March 16 1900, and educated at Tonbridge and Woolwich before being commissioned into the Royal Artillery. From 1921 to 1930 he served on the North-West Frontier in the 3rd (Peshawar) Mountain Battery, Royal Artillery, where he acquired an appreciation of the countryside and a particular understanding of mules. This was very useful later when he had 500 under his control. He soon observed that, properly loaded and treated, mules were thoroughly co-operative.

At his first pay parade he noted with interest that although the Indian soldiers signed for 15 rupees (by pressing their right thumbs on to a pad of indelible ink and then on to the pay sheets) they received only five rupees or even three. On inquiring of the pay *havildar* (sergeant) as to what happened to the remainder he was blandly assured that it was stopped against the man's possible needs in the future: for his wedding, a death in the family, or the purchase of a house or land. Although Daunt was well aware that in the British Army a small sum was deducted each week to provide money for when a man went on leave, or for "barrack room damages", this seemed a blatant case of fraud, and he had it changed, although not without difficulty.

During leaves Daunt made endless excursions into the Himalayas and was estimated to have walked 10,000 miles, trekking, stalking and shooting, during which he shot red bear and other game. On one occasion a black bear attacked his *shikari*, who was carrying Daunt's rifle slung over his shoulder. Daunt managed to distract the bear, but not before it had removed a piece of the man's face with a blow from its claw. The bear then looked at him, gave a terrifying growl, and shambled off. "Armed only with a stick I went even faster up the hill than I had come down it," Daunt recalled.

He bathed the *shikari's* wounds with permanganate of potash, but the man refused to go to hospital, preferring his own village where the treatment was a plaster of bear's fat and cow dung. Daunt waited anxiously for him to die of gangrene, but three weeks later he returned ready for duty with "nasty-looking but healthy scars".

In 1929 Daunt was visited at Landi Kotal by "Snaffles" (the artist C J Payne) who stayed with the mountain battery for a week and, in between pig-sticking, polo and shooting, drew numerous sketches. The following year when Daunt was on leave in England, Snaffles wished to finish certain sketches and asked Daunt to pose for him. The first was on Leith Hill (with Daunt sucking a pipe which he did not smoke), much to the interest of a Bank Holiday crowd. The second task was to finish off a sketch of a member of the Peshawar Vale Hunt who had taken an involuntary header into a river. Daunt had to stand on his head in an armchair waving his legs in the air until they were in the right position, which he held for 20 minutes. "Thus," he said, "does one achieve immortality."

After the war Daunt's appointments included Commandant, Coast Artillery School, and GOC, Malta, from 1953-56. He retired from the Army in 1957 and became Controller, Home Department, British Red Cross Society, from 1957 to 1966. He was Colonel Commandant, RA, from 1960 to 1965.

Brian Daunt was a perfectionist but also tolerant. An excellent horseman and polo player, he rowed and boxed for Tonbridge and was attracted by dangerous sports. For his treks on the Frontier he learned the languages and dialects of the hill tribes and enough of medicine to cure many of their ailments. He also wrote playlets, one of which, on psychological warfare, Montgomery had specially flown from Malta to Paris to use in a demonstration.

He was appointed CBE in 1953 and CB in 1956. At the age of 93 he travelled to Delhi with his wife, a talented artist and musician, who gave a recital with a Celtic harp to enthusiastic Indian audiences; they made an outstandingly good-looking couple. He married Margaret Balfour in 1938. They had a son, who died at an early age through an accident, and two daughters.

BRIGADIER
"ROSCOE" HARVEY

Brigadier "Roscoe" Harvey (who died on March 28 1996, aged 95) was an exceptionally gallant cavalry officer and a prominent figure on the Turf. As an Army officer he won three DSOs; as stewards' secretary to the Jockey Club, he meted out justice to numerous crooks and dopers.

Harvey acquired the nickname "Roscoe" when riding in an Irish steeplechase, aged 21. A mere two pounds overweight, he was unfavourably compared by a senior officer to Roscoe "Fatty" Arbuckle, the American actor. "I was glad he wasn't two stone lighter or I might have had a serious rival," remarked the jockey Sir Gordon Richards.

Harvey was short-sighted and wore thick round spectacles. In his twenties he had a bad fall in the National Hunt Chase at Cheltenham, when his spectacles broke and left splinters deep behind his eyes. His first DSO was awarded immediately when he was commanding the 10th Hussars in North Africa in May 1942. When Harvey's own tank was destroyed, he walked about the battlefield shouting: "Don't give a yard! Please do not give one yard!"

"An important element in a commander is the ability to make his troops feel less inclined to incur his displeasure than to face the enemy," observed General Sir Cecil "Monkey" Blacker. "The sight of Roscoe's Sherman tank following close behind, with his red hat poking out of the turret – he always refused to wear a tin hat, though we had to – was a considerable deterrent to any desire to linger." Though aggressive in battle, Harvey was of an essentially kindly disposition, and preferred to deploy a quiet word rather than wave a big stick.

As commander of 29th Armoured Brigade – "the Bulls" – for the D-Day invasion of Normandy, he kept an open door to all ranks. "And if for some reason I don't want to see them," he said, "I'll tell them to f--- off." Harvey remained on generally good terms with Montgomery, despite his willingness to think aloud. "I'll tell you something," Harvey said on one occasion, "being a master of hounds is a damn sight more difficult than being a general." Imbued with a true cavalier spirit, Harvey once inadvertently drove the wrong way up the fast lane of the M4, and also survived breaking his neck in a point-to-point.

Charles Barnet Cameron Harvey was born in Sarawak in July 1900. His father worked for the Borneo Company and was a close friend of the White Rajah Charles Brooke. He died soon after Charles's birth, and his widow returned with the family to England, where she rode to hounds with the Beaufort. At 11 Charles went to Downside, where he excelled at games and scraped through the School Certificate. He did not do well in the Sandhurst entrance and obtained a place via a competitive interview, in which the subject of foxhunting featured large.

From Sandhurst Harvey was commissioned into the 10th Hussars ("the Shiny 10th") in 1920, and joined them on the Curragh. Harvey had his first ride as an amateur jockey under Rules in 1920, in the National Hunt Chase at Cheltenham; he fell off at the last when lying fourth. He later had better luck at Cheltenham, where Golden Miller won the Gold Cup five times running.

In the 1920s a cavalry officer could have two months' hunting leave a year, and as many long weekends as he wished, provided they were for hunting. Harvey made full use of this, and ventured into show jumping. He came close to winning the King George V Cup at the Royal International Horse Show, only losing in the final jump-off. In 1928 Harvey rode Commonside in the Grand National, but they fell at the Canal Turn. The same thing happened the next day when Harvey rode the same horse in the Foxhunters', but this time he clambered back on to his mount and finished third.

In 1929 he went with the regiment to Egypt, where he rode with great success. He was then posted to Meerut in India, where he excelled at polo, pig-sticking and tent-pegging. He reached the final round of the Kadir Cup, the blue riband of pig-sticking. In 1936 the regiment returned to England for mechanisation. Harvey was sent on a course at Bovington. His report read: "This officer shows absolutely no aptitude for mechanisation whatso-ever." Harvey was otherwise occupied, hunting with the Berkeley. "The hounds were a wonderful pack," he recalled. "We had a hell of a hound called Whipcord, who had only half a tail, because it had been bitten off by a rat."

In May 1940, Harvey embarked for France as second-in-command. The battle for France was already lost; most of the Hussars' two-pounder guns were still in their crates, lashed to the sides of the Crusader tanks (which did not have armour to stop a rifle bullet). None the less, the regiment fought several brisk actions before being evacuated from Brest on June 17. When the 11th Armoured Division was formed, Harvey was given command of the 23rd Hussars, and then succeeded to the command of his own regiment. On arriving in the Middle East in November 1941 he formed his own opinion of the situation. "Everybody talked about Montgomery restoring the morale of the Eighth Army," he said. "It was a load of cock. The morale was tremendous, long before he arrived." Harvey also took exception to allegations that British armoured troops were badly trained.

The 10th fought several actions but their tanks were out-gunned by the Germans. In October 1942 at Alamein, Harvey was second-in-command to General "Pip" Roberts in the 22nd Armoured Brigade, before being promoted to command the 4th Light Armoured Brigade. For the final stages of the North African campaign, Harvey was appointed commander of the 8th Armoured Brigade, which was in the New Zealand Corps under General Bernard Freyberg VC. By the time of the German surrender in North Africa, Harvey had collected two DSOs and had twice been mentioned in despatches.

In June 1944 Harvey took the 11th Armoured Division into France, where it fought its way over the Orne and through the blockage. In spite of heavy casualties, his active, vigorous leadership kept morale high. The division took part in the push for Amiens, which they reached by driving past columns of German troops who were so surprised to see British tanks that few offered much resistance. As they moved towards Antwerp, Harvey was up with the leading tanks, sometimes taking chances which scared the life out of his contemporaries. The next December, Harvey's brigade was sent to the Ardennes, where the Germans had made an unexpected and successful counter-attack. When the Germans had been driven back, 29th Brigade returned to Antwerp and pushed on to Holland.

During one brisk skirmish Harvey was lightly wounded in the groin. Shortly afterwards he received a signal from a fellow officer: "Lucky it was a cold day." In a 48-hour push over boggy ground, in the face of determined resistance, the brigade inflicted many casualties and took 700 prisoners. Harvey was recommended for a third DSO. 29th Brigade were the first into Belsen, where they made the SS guards pick up and bury the corpses. They were then ordered to reach Lübeck before the Russians.

At the end of the war, 11th Armoured Division was allotted Schleswig-Holstein, and while General Roberts was at home on leave, Harvey became divisional commander. Two of his officers captured William Joyce ("Lord Haw-Haw") and Heinrich Himmler. In spite of Montgomery's order that there should be "no racing", Harvey organised small meetings which were described as "horse trials". He was not discovered.

At the age of 46 he decided to retire from the

Army, although later he became Colonel of the 10th Hussars. For the next 22 years he served as stewards' secretary to the Jockey Club ("because I couldn't do anything else"); and in retirement, in the Cotswolds, he bred and owned some excellent National Hunt horses, perhaps most notably Burnt Oak which won the Grand Military in 1987. He served on the British Board of Boxing Control for three years. In 1994, Harvey took the salute from his wheelchair at the VJ-Day parade at Stow-on-the-Wold.

Roscoe Harvey was twice married, first to Biddy Mylne; secondly to Betty Stoddard, who died in 1980.

———————

BRIGADIER
THE REVEREND "JOHN" HARRIS

Brigadier the Reverend "John" Harris (who died on May 4 1996, aged 99) took part in the cavalry charge at Cambrai in November 1917.

Although the British achieved a breakthrough with tanks at the start of the battle, the Germans successfully counter-attacked and drove them back. Field Marshal Haig had kept a large force of cavalry in reserve to exploit the expected success of the tanks; and even though the initial advantage was lost, Harris's regiment, the 2nd Lancers (Gardner's Horse, Indian Army), was ordered to charge the German position. But as they advanced on a shallow valley, the Lancers came under German machine-gun fire from right and left. There were 100 casualties, including their colonel, before they came to a halt in a wired sunken road after 3,000 yards.

Charles Edwin Laurence Harris, known as John, was born on May 10 1896, a descendant of Sir Lachlan Maclean of Douart and nephew of Major-General James Harris – "China Jim" of Indian Mutiny fame. He was educated at St Paul's and began his career working for the Anglo–Mexican oil company at Tampico. On the outbreak of the First World War he returned to England in an oil tanker, and enlisted in the Artists Rifles.

In May 1915 Harris went to France, where he was employed on guard duties at St Omer. He was then posted back to England prior to being sent to India for officer training at Wellington in the Nilgiri Hills. After being commissioned he spent several months with 113 Infantry in Dargai Fort on the North-West Frontier and was then dispatched to France where he joined the 2nd Lancers at Athies on the Somme.

The 2nd Lancers had been raised by a former Highland officer in 1809 as an Irregular regiment, and was originally paid strictly according to merit. It attracted first-class recruits, who were dressed in silver embroidered emerald green coats and red pyjamas (breeches) and carried curved sabres, long matchlocks, shields and lances. They fought with tremendous success in the Burma Campaign of 1824 to 1826, marching 2,000 miles without losing a man.

When the regiment arrived in France in 1916, they still carried sabres and lances, in addition to more modern weapons. Dressed in cotton drill they camped in the snow at Orléans, and later one of their

number won a Victoria Cross. Harris's initial duties
were to clear a road through three German trenches
and 10 belts of wire. This task was completed just in
time for the attack on November 20 when the tanks
and infantry went through first and the cavalry
followed. Harris remembered especially the Scots
Greys whose horses were dyed a reddish brown
colour with potassium permanganate for camouflage
purposes. His own regiment had charged after a
German counter-attack, which had shelled them
with high explosives and gas, but was subsequently
ordered to withdraw under cover of darkness.

The regiment next served as infantry in the front-
line trenches before being reunited with its horses
and sent to Palestine. After an unpleasant sojourn in
the Jordan Valley, Harris took part in the final stages
of Allenby's successful Palestine Campaign. He was
then in Syria and Palestine before completing the
nine-month course at the Cavalry School, Saugor,
then returning to be adjutant at Poona.

Harris shot a tiger and a bear in the jungle of the
Central Provinces, won the Salmon Cup for pig-
sticking at Gujerat, and was in the final of the
Gujerat Cup; the regimental polo team, of which he
was a member, won the Open and Junior tourna-
ments in Bombay. He then spent two years as an
instructor at Sandhurst before himself becoming a
student at Staff College, Quetta, where the future
Field Marshal Sir Claude Auchinleck was chief
instructor. Harris then returned to his regiment at
Meerut and Ferozopore, captaining the polo team
which won the Meerut Polo tournament and the

Indian Cavalry Polo tournament at Lahore.

His next two postings were as GSO2 at HQ Meerut District for a year and HQ Simla and Delhi for a second year. Here he served under Brigadier Lord Gort, who would be Commander-in-Chief in France at the beginning of the Second World War. This was followed by three years as a cavalry instructor at the Staff College, Quetta, where he served under the future Field Marshal Lord Montgomery.

When war broke out in 1939, Harris was on leave in Devon, but he promptly returned to India by troopship, completing his journey with a nine-day march to Sialkot. He was posted for a three-month course in mechanised training at Ahmedmagar and returned to Sialkot to start the mechanisation of his regiment. In June he became a GSO2 (Operations), at Simla in the summer and Delhi in the winter and, in June 1941, took command of the 2nd Lancers with orders to reconstitute it as an Indian armoured car regiment and take it to Mena camp in Egypt. Three months later Harris led the regiment up to Deir-Ez-Zor on the Euphrates, where its role was to maintain internal security and defend Syria.

After six months they returned to Egypt where he was appointed commander of the Desert Brigade (called for deception purposes 8th Division, which would have been at least three times as large). It moved up the Gazala line but was badly cut up at Bir Hacheim when the British armour proved no match for the Germans, though Harris was mentioned in despatches. The 2nd Lancers were then withdrawn and sent to north Syria to combat any possible thrust by the German Army towards the oil fields of the Middle East.

When that danger receded, Harris was successively commander of 23rd Lorried Infantry Brigade of Gurkhas and Deputy Director of Military Training at Delhi, which at the time was concentrating on training for jungle warfare. A year later he joined General Slim's 14th Army HQ in Western Bengal, but after contracting pneumonia and malaria simultaneously, he was evacuated to England on a cargo ship carrying onions.

Harris left the Army in 1946, entered Ridley Hall, Cambridge, and after 18 months was ordained. His clerical duties began with a curacy at Dorchester, where he became chaplain to the prison. Two years later he was given the living of Burbage, Wiltshire, and in 1965 he retired finally to Kent where (despite having both hips replaced) he was for 16 years chairman of the local Conservative Association. He still took occasional services, keenly supporting the retention of the Book of Common Prayer.

Harris's ambition was to be photographed on horseback in uniform on his 100th birthday. A horse had been acquired for the purpose but, sadly, he was pipped at the post six days before the event.

He married first, in 1919, Audrey White, who died in 1961, and secondly, in 1962, Margot Gibson. He had three daughters.

MAJOR
DAVID FLOYER

Major David Floyer (who died on July 15 1996, aged 73) was awarded an MC when fighting against Nationalist rebels in Indonesia in 1946.

After the capitulation of Japan in August 1945, Achmed Sukarno, the collaborationist leader of the Nationalist puppet government, had launched his 12,000-strong army into a campaign of murder and intimidation against the Dutch and other civilians. Many of these were still in the camps where they had been interned by the Japanese. British and Indian troops were flown in and restored order after much bloody fighting.

Floyer witnessed the murder of his brigade commander, Brigadier A W Mallaby, during "peace" negotiations with the treacherous rebel leader – a fate he himself only narrowly escaped by diving through a window into a canal and swimming to safety.

Soon afterwards, Floyer's company was pinned down by superior numbers and was in danger of being overrun and massacred. During the night he crept to within 100 yards of the enemy position to guide his gunners to put mortar shells directly on target. While doing so he was in great danger, both from the enemy and his own mortars. But the manoeuvre proved successful, and by morning the enemy had been forced to withdraw.

David Cornish Floyer was born on July 18 1922 in British Columbia into an old Exeter family which traced its pedigree back to the Domesday survey of 1086.

He was educated at Bedford School. The day after leaving young David joined the Army, and was commissioned into the Royal Corps of Signals; he then transferred to the Royal Engineers.

In 1942 Floyer was posted to Lahore, and joined the Bengal Sappers and Miners. He served in Waziristan, where there was always potential trouble, and which was being supplied with German and Italian money and weapons. He made several incursions into tribal territory in Chitral on the North-West Frontier.

In 1945 Floyer joined 71 Forward Company, 23rd Division, ready to take part in Operation Zipper, the invasion of Malaya, but the Japanese surrender made the operation unnecessary. After taking part in the re-occupation of Malaya, Floyer was posted to Java. When he took over as OC 71 Forward Company in Bandung, he was believed to be the youngest major in the Indian army.

He returned to Britain in 1946, served for a further year with Central Mediterranean Forces in Padua, and was demobilised in 1947. After leaving the Army Floyer took a degree in Civil Engineering at McGill University, Montreal, and then returned to England for legal studies. He was called to the Bar by Lincoln's Inn.

In 1954 he joined the Burmah Oil Company, becoming its chief representative in Pakistan and Australia, where he was instrumental in securing Burmah's control of the Cooper Basin and gas fields on the North-West Shelf.

In 1976 Floyer returned to England to practice at the Bar, before retiring to Devon, where for 10 years he was governor of a school for the blind and partially-sighted children.

A keen sportsman, he played rugby for Bedford School and Rosslyn Park, and when at McGill re-introduced the game to Canada. He organised an annual match between McGill and Harvard which is still played. He also boxed for the Army at welter-weight and was an accomplished oarsman.

Floyer's main passion, though, was sailing, and he helmed dinghies and yachts all over the world. Widely read, he took delight in debate and was fascinated by conceptual developments in the field of Chaos Theory.

David Floyer was twice married and left three children.

———————

LIEUTENANT-COLONEL
COLIN MITCHELL

Lieutenant-Colonel Colin Mitchell (who died on July 20 1996, aged 70) fought with distinction in a number of campaigns, most famously in Aden. But the crusade in which he most desired success and to which he brought all his flair for publicity, the campaign to Save the Argylls at the end of the 1960s, fell short of complete victory.

In 1967 "Mad Mitch", as he was affectionately

known, cut through the British policy of neutral peacekeeping in Aden by leading his Argyll and Sutherland Highlanders to retake the terrorist-dominated Crater district of the city. On June 20 British forces had been repulsed from the district with the loss of 22 lives. Mitchell determined to reoccupy it, though he had been warned that 500 well-armed police mutineers and terrorists had taken up positions there and were prepared to fight. On the night of July 3 he ordered Pipe Major Kenneth Robinson to sound the regimental charge, 'Monymusk'.

As Mitchell recalled: "It is the most thrilling sound in the world to go into action with the pipes playing. It stirs the blood and reminds one of the heritage of Scotland and the regiment. Best of all it frightens the enemy to death." A burst of machine-gun fire rattled out from the edge of the town, but the Pipe Major played on undeterred while his comrades flung themselves to the ground. None of them knew how much resistance would be encountered; as it turned out, the only man to be shot dead that night was an Arab who had been challenged and had made to run away.

The Treasury building, containing the entire currency reserve for southern Arabia, was taken from the police mutineers by negotiation. By the end of the night it was clear to Mitchell that his determination to push on into the Crater area had utterly demoralised the enemy. He sensed success in the air: "To me that single moment in Crater was worth all my quarter century of soldiering." At dawn on July 4 the pipes and drums sounded again from a rooftop overlooking Crater. The Argylls kept the peace there for five months by terrifying the rebels. "They know that if they start trouble we'll blow their bloody heads off," was Mitchell's characteristic comment.

Of his style of leadership he said: "I took flamboyant risks in order to demonstrate to my own officers and NCOs that we led from the front." Not one British soldier was lost in the operation. The feeling of relief in Britain was, in Mitchell's opinion, best expressed in a leading article in *The Daily Telegraph*: "British troops have shown the combination of skill, tact and cool courage for which they are unequalled . . . A dangerous and humiliating state of drift, which the British Government permitted to continue for a fortnight, has been ended."

But Mitchell's troubles were just beginning. He rubbed the GOC up the wrong way and annoyed the Ministry of Defence. He also proved a thorn in the flesh of the Labour Government – which at that time was anxious to withdraw from the remaining outposts of the Empire – by capturing the imagination of the British newspaper-reading public. In return Mitchell was denied the expected DSO, and given to understand he would not be promoted brigadier. With the very future of his regiment under threat, he decided it was time to leave the Army.

Mitchell went on to become the Conservative MP for West Aberdeenshire from 1970 to 1974, but did not seek re-election.

Colin Campbell Mitchell was born in south-west London on November 17 1925, the eldest son of Lieutenant-Colonel Colin Mitchell, MC, also of the

Argylls. When accompanying his father to the Presbyterian church in West Croydon on Sundays he wore the kilt. Young Colin was educated at Streatham Grammar School and Whitgift, where he was a voracious reader as well as being captain of swimming and a useful rugby footballer. He joined the Army in 1943, after a spell in the Home Guard, and was commissioned into the Argyll and Sutherland Highlanders; he then joined the 8th Battalion in Italy, just in time for the final campaign.

Mitchell saw fierce fighting on the route up through San Patrizio, Bastia and Consandolo; and as the battalion advanced through the Argenta Gap he was wounded, though not seriously. As this wound was not entered in his records, he did not qualify for the 1939-45 Star, but only for the Italy Star. Mitchell was then posted to Palestine and had an extremely lucky escape when on his way to lunch at the King David Hotel in Jerusalem; it was blown up just before he arrived. By now Mitchell was with the 1st Argylls, with whom he learned to fly and operate from gliders.

In Palestine he had several narrow escapes from death, but was eventually wounded by one of his own Bren–gunners, when he was doing some personal reconnaissance and was mistaken for a terrorist. The Australian surgeon who operated on him predicted: "You'll have a lot of arthritis in those ankles, and I fear you're going to be pretty short-tempered in your old age." In Palestine Mitchell learned the importance of maintaining friendly and close relations with the press. He also made friends among both Arabs and Jews, and met the future

Israeli Defence Minister General Moshe Dayan, who later became one of his heroes.

After recovering from his wounds, Mitchell became aide de camp to Lieutenant-General Sir Gordon Macmillan, GOC Scottish Command. When the Korean War broke out in 1950, he was allowed to rejoin his regiment. He took part in the first advance northwards during which he had some bloody close-quarter fighting before reaching Taechon, near the Manchurian border. But when the Chinese crossed the Yalu river in vast numbers, the regiment was forced to take part in the general retreat. They held what became known as Frostbite Ridge, where shaving brushes froze solid in the time it took to lift them from boiling water to the chin; Mitchell recalled that even anti-freeze froze. When the thaw came, they moved to a new position on the ridge, only to find that their new trench was swarming with black rats, as this was an old battlefield.

On being relieved and withdrawn in 1951 they had just begun advancing again. After Korea Mitchell was posted home, but at the end of 1957 he returned to the 1st Battalion of the Argylls as a company commander in Cyprus. The Eoka terrorist campaign was then in full swing, but the Argylls faced greater danger from forest fires than from enemy snipers. Some of these conflagrations were started by villagers who knew they would then be paid half-a-crown a day to fight them; others were lit by terrorists to engulf British troops. In windy conditions fires raced along at 30 mph.

Mitchell returned with the regiment to the British

Army of the Rhine, and then applied successfully to serve with the King's African Rifles in Kenya. He was soon engaged in restoring order in Zanzibar, where there was fierce fighting between Arabs and Africans, with accompanying atrocities, as a result of a general election. Several thousand rioters were arrested, and the disorder ended in two days. Keeping the peace in the Northern Frontier District was a lengthier process, as cross-border raids with Uganda were a traditional occupation. The frontiers with Sudan, Ethiopia and Somalia were scarcely more peaceful.

During the latter part of his time in Kenya, Mitchell was brigade major to Miles Fitzalan-Howard (later the 17th Duke of Norfolk), whose appreciation of the need to press on with the Africanisation of the King's African Rifles did much to smooth its ultimate conversion into the Kenya Army. Mitchell had an extraordinary experience when flying in a helicopter less than 20 ft above the ground, looking for Somali guerrillas. He encountered a herd of elephants, all of which scattered, except for the bull, which, rearing up, nearly caught the helicopter with its tusks.

When the Argylls were preparing to join the Borneo campaign, Mitchell was sent for, and after evading an attempt by the MoD to send him to the Joint Services Staff College at Latimer, engaged in a series of jungle operations and battles. Officially this was not a war, as the British Government did not wish for out-and-out hostilities with Indonesia, but those on the ground thought otherwise. After six months of jungle warfare, the regiment was sent to recuperate in Singapore, and Mitchell was posted back to Whitehall as a staff officer to the Chief of Defence Staff, at that time Earl Mountbatten of Burma. He found Mountbatten an exacting taskmaster, who sent most of his papers back to him covered with scathing comments in green ink.

When the proposals to cut the strength of the Army were being debated in the 1960s, Mitchell felt that the Services were being asked to achieve the impossible with limited resources. He therefore began writing articles on the subject (passed reluctantly by the censors) which were published in the Royal United Services Institute journal, as well as in *Punch* and other papers. Then in 1968 he learned that his own regiment was due to be disbanded in 1972.

Meanwhile the Argylls were sent to Aden, where Britain was establishing a strong military base to make up for the loss of bases in the Canal Zone and Kenya. However subversive elements, financed by Egypt and Russia, helped to convince both the Ministry of Defence and the Labour Government that Britain should withdraw from the area and that Aden should become independent as soon as possible. Mitchell had scant respect for his political or Service superiors.

Subsequently he wrote of the GOC: "General Tower, for some reason I can never understand, always wanted to talk about infantry tactics as if he understood what it was like to be a fighting infantry-man." Tower was, of course, an ex-gunner, but a very experienced soldier. But in Mitchell's view his voice carried "a note of veiled sarcasm which I was to hear often". Although Mitchell and his Argylls handled the military situation with skill and courage, Mitchell's forthright attitude, readiness to spout for the benefit of the media and contempt for authority, both military and civilian, did little for his career. He was mentioned in despatches, but the omission of a DSO caused considerable public indignation.

At the time, however, Mitchell was more concerned with the fact that his beloved Argylls, whose fighting record was unsurpassed, were to be abolished in the Army cuts, as being the junior Highland regiment. Mitchell disputed the "junior" claim, but, realising that he could fight for their survival better outside the regiment than within it, resigned in 1968. In his efforts to gain support for the "Thin Red Line" of the Argylls, Mitchell recruited Margaret Duchess of Argyll, to the cause. In later life Mitchell probably regarded the Save the Argylls campaign as his greatest achievement. But, though the regiment was given a reprieve from disbandment or amalgamation in 1971, it was reduced to a single company.

A week after resigning from the Army, Mitchell landed in Vietnam as a war correspondent for the *Daily Express*. During his four years as MP for Aberdeenshire, from 1970, he was parliamentary private secretary to the Secretary of State for Scotland, and served on the Select Committee on the Armed Services. He sought, unsuccessfully, parliamentary candidatures for Carshalton in 1976 and Bournemouth in 1977 while taking up the first of a series of consultancy posts; in 1976 he advised the Rhodesian Prime Minister Ian Smith on dealing with African terrorists; in 1983, he advised the Mujahideen in Afghanistan on how to attack Russian positions; and in 1986 he went to Pakistan and the North-West Frontier Province. He was given the Freedom of the City of London in 1979.

Colin Mitchell was a brave, clear-headed, loyal and intensely patriotic man. He had a gift for publicity, but was impatient of opposition and incompetence. This is apparent in his lucid and absorbing account of his experiences in *Having Been a Soldier* (1969). Mitchell's experience in Afghanistan led him to set up the Halo Trust (Hazardous Areas Life Support Organisation) to clear mines and allow refugees to return to their homes. In 1991, when he led a British operation to clear thousands of mines left behind in the 13-year-long civil war in Cambodia, he observed that the charity was being starved of cash by the Overseas Development Administration. "They're all bureaucrats," he complained. "They can't make a decision. They don't seem to understand that 250 people a month are being injured by these mines." The ODA responded by saying that their funds for that year were already committed and that they were trying to raise money for the project from the UN. Mitchell had heard such excuses before.

He married Susan Phillips in 1956. They had two sons and a daughter.

COLONEL
MURRAY DE KLEE

Colonel Murray de Klee (who died on December 21 1996, aged 68) fought in eight active service theatres after the end of the Second World War; mentioned in despatches twice, he was awarded the Croix de Guerre and showed such coolness in action that he was nicknamed "The Iron Duke".

Murray Peter de Klee, the son of Lieutenant-Colonel F B de Klee, who commanded the Royal Horse Guards (The Blues), was born on January 3 1928 and educated at Wellington; he enlisted in the Scots Guards in 1945. After being commissioned he went to Malaya in 1948 with the 2nd Battalion on anti-terrorist duties at the start of the Emergency. Almost immediately he had two narrow escapes from death.

The first was when, leading a patrol through the jungle, he encountered two bandits who opened fire and fled. Although wounded in the head, de Klee gave chase and caught one of the attackers; he was a notorious bandit, Pan Poh, who was carrying a packet of letters destined for other bandits in the north of the peninsula. A remarkable feature of de Klee's wound was that it was caused by a bullet hitting the foresight of his rifle, propelling the foresight into his forehead, from where it slid around his skull.

Then, on June 11 1950, de Klee and three others were ambushed by 16 bandits in the Kanchang Pass. Two of the party were killed in the crossfire. De Klee returned fire until a bullet struck his hand and he lost his revolver. The jeep in which they were travelling spun off the road, and its occupants were thrown clear. De Klee and his driver were closely inspected by their attackers, but as they were covered in the blood of their comrades they were assumed to be dead and left where they were.

In 1956 de Klee served in Cyprus and, having joined the Guards Independent Parachute Company, was chosen to select and lead a detachment of pathfinders down the Suez Canal in order to establish the strength of the enemy forces prior to the main Anglo-French invasion. Parachuting with members of the French Foreign Legion they landed just south of Port Said, to find their dropping zone occupied by Egyptians. Two of de Klee's detachment were wounded before they were out of their parachute harnesses. Nevertheless, de Klee penetrated 15 kilometres behind enemy lines, and was still engaged in his reconnaissance when the invasion was halted. He was mentioned in despatches and awarded a Croix de Guerre.

In 1965 he served in Borneo, and the next year was chosen to form and command G Squadron (drawn mainly from the Brigade of Guards) in 22nd Special Air Service Regiment. Characteristically he insisted on completing the gruelling SAS selection course himself. The squadron was deployed in Aden in 1968, and Malaya the next year. De Klee returned to take command of the 1st Battalion, Scots Guards, and commanded the Queen's Birthday Parade in 1969 when the crowd gave a standing ovation as the participants left the Horse Guards.

His next assignment was to take the 1st Battalion to West Belfast in 1970, a period of marked escalation of terrorist violence in which "internment" was introduced and the security forces arrested all known terrorists whenever the opportunity arose. Three years later de Klee, as Assistant Adjutant-General for London District, was responsible for the military manoeuvres required for the wedding of Princess Anne. In 1974 he was appointed OBE, and the next year became Lieutenant-Colonel commanding the Scots Guards. After various staff appointments, including two years in Saudi Arabia as defence attaché, he retired from the Army in 1983.

De Klee returned to his home at Auchnacraig on the Isle of Mull, where he spent 13 years improving the pedigree herd of Highland cattle which had been built up by his parents after the war. He became a non-active member of the Royal Company of Archers, the Queen's Bodyguard for Scotland.

Murray de Klee was a first-class athlete who had represented Wellington, won the Pan-Malayan high hurdles in 1950, and the Steward's Medal at the Oban Games in 1951. He was also a good skier, a fine shot and an accomplished horseman and polo player. With all this went great modesty, a delightful sense of humour and absolute integrity. He was also an authority on deer, and took an active role in the re-introduction of the sea eagle to Scotland. The latter involved diplomatic skills and a conflict between his outlook as an ornithologist and his interests as a sheep farmer. Local farmers were naturally opposed to the reappearance of a predator which took their lambs, but de Klee, who had lost more lambs than anyone else, was able to mollify them.

De Klee's athletic prowess and rugged good looks induced Launder Gilliat Productions to write to him in 1951 suggesting that he play the part of Geordie in the film version of the novel by David Walker.

He married, in 1955, Angela Stormonth-Darling; they had three sons and a daughter.

——————

CAPTAIN
DESMOND LYNCH

Captain Desmond Lynch (who died on December 30 1996, aged 75) was awarded a Distinguished Conduct Medal in North Africa when a sergeant in the Irish Guards; many thought a VC would have been more appropriate.

Lynch was the platoon sergeant in the leading company when it met with heavy fire during an attack on April 27 1943. The company commander and two platoon commanders were wounded or killed, and the company sergeant-major killed. Lynch laid his wounded platoon commander in a slit-trench, saluted, asked "Leave to carry on, sir?" then took charge of what was left of the company. As the advance continued he organised it to con-tinue the assault and gain its objective. During the next three days, the force was continually attacked with the company holding a ridge under shell and mortar fire when infantry attacks were not in progress.

Lynch remained in command except for a brief period, and he presented an outstanding figure. His soldierly appearance, calmness and bravery in the most difficult circumstances created a great impression upon the men. At 10 am on April 28, enemy 88 mm guns opened up on the west of the ridge with unexpected violence. There were casualties, and some of the men were badly shaken.

Lynch, who was at Force HQ at the time, ran without hesitation up through the heavy fire to his company, held the men steady in their positions, and moved a Bren gun forward at great personal risk to meet the first infantry assault. He gave the first fire order. The initial German assault was beaten back thanks to Lynch, whose example showed that the fiercest fire could be endured and that determined attack could be broken by small-arms fire. Even when half blinded by a blast he continued to encourage his rapidly dwindling company.

Lynch later became a legendary regimental sergeant-major at Eaton Hall and Mons Officer Cadet School. A general recalled: "It was a terrifying experience to be inspected by him. He was a powerful towering figure, immaculately smart, and with a pronounced Irish accent that could be detected even in his words of command. I can remember the explosion, almost nuclear in its pro-portions, when a cadet asked him whether it was in order for officers to carry umbrellas when in uniform." An officer who served with him in the Irish Guards remembered: "He had a reputation for ferocity unequalled in the Micks. All I can say is, thank God Sergeant Lynch was on our side."

Desmond Thomas Lynch, was born in Dublin on January 1 1921, the son of Tom Lynch, who had served in the First World War and was president of the British Legion of the Republic of Ireland. At 16 he joined the Irish Guards, and in 1938 served in Egypt and Palestine. In 1941 he became an instructor at the Royal Military College of Science. His next posting was back with the Irish Guards.

Before the action which won him the DCM, Lynch had led his platoon to attack an enemy observation post from which he had brought back an artillery officer and two sergeant–majors as prisoners; the remainder, if not killed, having prudently dispersed. After being captured the officer put his head against a Bren carrier, and wept copiously. Asked why he was so distressed, the German said he was sorrowing for his dead companions. Lynch urged him to be a man and be philosophic but, as Lynch had killed most of them himself, the man took little comfort.

Lynch was wounded twice in the North African campaign, but recovered to take part in the landing at Anzio and the ensuing Italian campaign. At Carroceto, where two companies were overwhelmed by German parachute troops, he was wounded again and taken prisoner. Initially he was put in a hospital in Rome and cared for by nuns. But on recovery he was transferred to Stalag 7A in Germany.

After the war Lynch served in Europe and West Africa, and then became the first drill sergeant at the

All Arms Wing at Caterham, moving on to Pirbright (where the Lynch Room commemorates him). From 1951 to 1954 he was, by special request, RSM at the Indian Ministry Academy at Dehra Dun. The following year he began his tour of duty at Eaton Hall, where he showed considerable tact by ensuring that the adjutant, who had to drive in from a distance on a road notable for traffic delays, was never late for his own parades. This Lynch accomplished by having the clock strike the hour when the adjutant had arrived.

In 1958 Eaton Hall was amalgamated with Mons Officer Cadet School at Aldershot, and Lynch became the RSM there for the next three years. He was appointed MBE in 1960. The next year he was commissioned and posted to the Commonwealth Brigade at Taiping and Malacca in Malaya, where he stayed till 1963. Then, after a three-year home posting, he returned east as adjutant of the Singapore Guard Regiment. His last posting before retiring in 1973 was to the Ministry of Defence in London as a staff captain. "Retirement" for Lynch meant first a posting to the Joint Services Mountain Training Centre at Tywin, and then to RMA Sandhurst, as assistant adjutant and security officer.

Although popular, Lynch was no respecter of rank or status in enforcing regulations. The speed limit in the grounds was 25 mph, and offenders were liable to have their cars banned from the grounds for 14 days. Protests (even from affronted senior officers) were useless; these were the orders of the commandant. The commandant's wife once incurred the penalty herself with no remission.

On retirement from Sandhurst Lynch moved to Boston, Lincolnshire, where he was again engaged in security, but also involved himself in community affairs, victim support, emergency planning and prison visiting. At 6ft 3in, Desmond Lynch was an impressive figure, but he was sociable, interested in others and endowed with a pleasant sense of humour. Although regarded with awe by many, he never appeared to take himself as seriously as they did. Nevertheless he was deeply grateful for the tributes paid to him, especially for the establishment of the D T Lynch Room.

Lynch appeared in two films about the Army, *Unpublished Story* (1940) and *They Were Not Divided* (1949). The impression left on anyone who knew Lynch was that here was an exceptional man, utterly sincere, outstandingly brave, a leader by example and someone whom it was a privilege to have known.

John Keegan writes: I shall always remember Desmond Lynch, as will anyone who served on the Sandhurst staff in his time. Desmond was unforgettable. His great height, breadth of shoulder, set of feature and immaculate turnout in the civilian clothes he wore after a lifetime in uniform singled him out even in a community where large and perfectly attired men were commonplace. Yet it was Desmond the man, his strength of character and largeness of personality which commanded attention.

The post of security officer is a junior one in Sandhurst's elaborate hierarchy. A lesser man might have become a headquarters functionary. Almost on arrival Desmond became a Sandhurst figurehead. Loyalty was the principle by which he had lived his life, and he transferred it from the institutions he had formerly served to Sandhurst in formidable intensity.

A fund of Desmond stories arose, including his genuine puzzlement that his warning of local roadworks causing "delays for up to two weeks" was in any way ambiguous. His dedication to the security of Sandhurst was given on a 24-hour basis. Legend had it that he had escaped from German captivity by strangling his guard, and no one doubted his readiness, if not positive eagerness, to repeat the process on any IRA terrorist unwise enough to cross his path. Yet Desmond was not simply the ferocious warrior. He was also dedicated to "standards", not just standards of drill, turnout and manners but of moral principle.

It was impossible to conceive of Desmond committing deceit or dishonesty or of tolerating either in others. Despite that, he was curiously sensitive, quite ready to condemn the rigidity of the pre-war Guards discipline by which he had been raised for its unfairness, even cruelty, to weaker spirits than his own. He also had a strong sense of responsibility towards those for whom life had gone wrong. In retirement he became a prison visitor with a particular commitment to those serving life sentences. He established a compassionate friendship with a man who had murdered his wife, and in his regular telephone calls to me he never failed to report on how the prisoner was coping with his sentence and private anguish. Desmond, the man of war, was also a man of love. It was the conflict between those two strands of his character that made him so unusual and won him such wide affection.

———

DRUM MAJOR
PHILIP BUSS

Drum Major Philip Buss (who died on May 18 1997, aged 72) blew a series of defiant bugle calls when the Gloucestershire Regiment was fighting desperately against hordes of Chinese in the Battle of the Imjin River in Korea on April 25 1951.

The Glosters, one of three British regiments in 29th Brigade (along with the Royal Northumberland Fusiliers and the Royal Ulster Rifles) were thinly deployed, with a Belgian battalion over a seven and a half mile front along the Imjin River, which was too shallow to be an effective obstacle. The brigade was vastly outnumbered by fanatical Chinese troops who seemed indifferent to enormous casualties, and though every regiment fought with dogged courage in an impossible situation, eventually the Glosters found themselves isolated with no hope of relief or withdrawal.

In the early hours, it became obvious that the enemy were preparing for a final, overwhelming attack. The Glosters were now down to three rounds of ammunition per man, and had not eaten for 48 hours. The adjutant, Anthony Farrar-Hockley (then a captain but later a major-general) decided to defy and confuse the enemy by playing bugle calls as if preparing for an attack. Drum Major Buss, a talented musician as well as an experienced infantryman, produced a bugle from his knapsack and asked what he should play.

Farrar-Hockley told him to begin with *Reveille*, to continue with *Fire Call* and to work through a normal day's calls up to *Retreat*, but not to play that. Although the whole ridge was swept by enemy machine-gun and mortar fire, Buss climbed out of his trench and, standing in the open, started his calls. There was a cheer from the Glosters, who astonishingly managed to counter-attack and recover some lost ground, which they held until they were finally overwhelmed by vastly superior numbers and firepower.

The Chinese had 10,000 casualties in this battle against 1,000 in 29th Brigade; but the heroic stand by the Glosters and their companions had destroyed the Chinese spring offensives, and prevented them reaching the South Korean capital. Only 169 of the original 850 Glosters mustered for roll call after the battle; the rest were killed, wounded, or taken prisoner in isolated positions.

Philip Buss (Drummie to his comrades) was born on April 2 1925, the son of a naval engineer in the submarine service. His great-great grandfather was a country lawyer, celebrated for his walking feats: he would walk to London from Mayfield in Sussex (48 miles) in one day; transact his business at Doctors' Commons the next day; and walk back on the third. From Dover Grammar School young Philip went to

Reading University to read Agriculture. But after two years he decided to join the Army, enlisting in the Queen's West Surrey Regiment, with whom he served in the North-West Europe campaign and was subsequently stationed in Berlin.

Buss then joined the Gloucestershire Regiment, with which he served in Jamaica and later in Korea. After release from captivity in 1953, he continued with the Glosters in Aden, Bahrain, Kenya (against the Mau Mau) and Cyprus. He transferred to the Royal Army Education Corps before retiring, and then returned to Reading University, where he qualified as a teacher.

Buss could play any brass or woodwind instrument on sight. By the time he retired he had been senior Drum Major in the British Army, and he later became a popular and greatly respected music teacher at Archers Court School, Dover, for 20 years. He composed a march for the Glosters, built up a brass band in Kent, and conducted many others. In early life he had been a keen cricketer; later he became a Conservative member of Dover council and chairman of the District Council for many years, as well as a Kent county councillor.

Philip Buss married, in 1954, Sheila Perry; they had two sons and three daughters.

CAPTAIN
BERNARD HARFIELD

Captain Bernard Harfield (whose death was recorded on November 20 1997, aged 84) had the unusual distinction of winning an immediate MC while serving in the Army Dental Corps in the Second World War.

In March 1945, when the Allies were planning to cross the Rhine, Harfield (serving with 174 Field Ambulance) learned that the assault troops of 153 Infantry Brigade were short of medical officers. He volunteered to take command of one of the two casualty evacuation points (CEPs) on the night of March 23-24. With his section, and carrying light medical equipment, he crossed the river and rapidly established himself on the east bank.

During the night, his stock of stretchers and blankets for casualties was exhausted. Harfield re-crossed the river in the face of fierce shell and mortar fire. He contacted the officer in charge of the casualty disembarkation point, and made sure that there would be no failure in replenishment of these and other medical stores. Soon after Harfield's return to the CEP, a Bren carrier, which had just been disembarked from a landing craft about 200 yards away, received a direct hit from a shell.

Despite continued shelling, and disregarding the danger of mines, Harfield immediately ran out with a stretcher party to the wrecked carrier, and gave first aid to its four badly-wounded crew. He had them carried into the comparative safety of the trenches.

Bitter enemy resistance continued until March 25, and the enemy were often able to direct accurate shell and mortar fire on the crossing point just next to the CEP. Nevertheless, Harfield continued his work. His citation paid tribute to his "coolness, complete disregard for his own safety and his unfailing cheerfulness".

Bernard Harfield (formerly Hirschfield) was born unexpectedly early on December 27 1912 in Cardiff, where his parents were on holiday. He was educated at King Edward's Camp Hill School for Boys, Birmingham, and Birmingham University, qualifying in 1936 as a dental surgeon, like his father.

He joined the Army in 1940, and was posted to the re-constituted 51st Highland Division, under Lieutenant-Colonel Macklin (who had been a member of Shackleton's expedition to the South Pole). His early military training took place in Scotland, and gave him a life-long love of that country. During the desert campaign, Harfield saw action with the Black Watch from El Alamein to Tripoli, and after the invasion of Sicily he became a Town Major and treated General Montgomery. (Both would have been incredulous at the idea that Monty would pin a medal for gallantry on his chest 18 months later.)

Harfield landed with the Black Watch on D-Day, and served throughout the North-West Europe campaign into Germany. After the war, he developed a thriving dental practice in Birmingham. He loved the turf and at one time owned two racehorses. He was also a keen golfer until well into his eighties.

Ben Harfield was twice married. By his first marriage (dissolved amicably in 1957) he had a son and a daughter. From his second marriage he had a son.

───────

MAJOR-GENERAL
JACK IRVINE

Major-General Jack Irvine (who died on July 16 1997, aged 83) received the Act of Gallantry award for his part in an operation on a man's leg under water during the Italian campaign in April 1944.

A train loaded with petrol had derailed, crashed through a bridge and landed on its side in freezing water, where it was gradually sinking with the driver trapped underneath. After giving him morphia, Irvine, a major in the Royal Army Medical Corps, found that the driver was pinned below the knee by the regulator bar in mud and gravel some two feet under water. Attempts to release the injured man by cutting the regulator bar with hacksaws failed because of the cramped and submerged position. It was dark and, as the train had been hauling petrol cisterns, no naked lights could be used.

Irvine had to crouch in water up to his neck, and support the victim's head above water for two and a half hours while amputation was performed. Soon after the operation had been completed the train blew up. To recover from his ordeal in the water, Irvine ran six miles back to his camp, drank some whisky and then went to bed.

John Irvine was born on May 31 1914 and educated at Glasgow High School and Glasgow University. On graduating he was immediately commissioned into the Royal Army Medical Corps. He began his military career at sea, as a medical officer on ships sailing from Glasgow to the Middle East which made a long detour around the Cape to avoid German attacks. Before the war was over he had been sunk three times, captured and escaped twice, and parachuted out of damaged aircraft twice; ships on which he travelled had so many dangerous encounters that he was affectionately nicknamed "the menace to British shipping".

In 1941 Irvine took part in the Greek campaign for which Wavell dispatched a British force from the desert to help Greece; but it was outgunned by the German Panzers and forced to evacuate to Crete and onwards. Soon afterwards Irvine was on a hospital ship evacuating casualties from the Western Desert via Tobruk, and in June and July 1942 he served in the desert following the disastrous Gazala battle when Rommel pushed the British Army back to Alamein.

After the October-November battle at Alamein, when Rommel was forced to retreat, Irvine commanded the 8th Ambulance Train until the end of the North African campaign. He was appointed Deputy Assistant Director of Medical Services for the Sicilian Campaign, and continued as a staff officer through the Italian Campaign and into Yugoslavia. He was mentioned in despatches.

From 1947 to 1949 Irvine was with British troops in Austria. He then commanded a field ambulance in

Korea, where he was awarded an MBE (Military). From 1954 to 1956 he served in Malaya, during the worst period of the Emergency, and was again mentioned in despatches. Subsequently, he served in Germany, commanded a military hospital in Accra, and returned to Germany in 1962. He became Deputy Director of Medical Services at HQ BAOR in 1968 and in 1973 Director of Medical Services. He was Honorary Surgeon to the Queen from 1972 to 1975, when he retired from the Army.

Jack Irvine was a first-class staff officer with a clear brain and notable organising skills; he was also a cool, courageous leader at the sharp end of a battle. In earlier days he had been a fine rugby player and, but for the war, looked set for an international career. He won the Army doubles tennis championship at the age of 52.

His memory was phenomenal. Years after the war, he remembered old soldiers and their ailments long after they themselves had forgotten them. He recalled the telephone numbers of all the 28 houses he had lived in during his military career. Everyone he met was important to him. He was extremely sociable, a good dancer and singer, and had a terrific sense of humour. He recalled seeing in War Office notes that after one of his sinkings he was laconically described as "disembarked at sea". Fortunately he was an expert swimmer.

Irvine married, in 1941, Mary McNicol Cossar, whom he had first met when he was five, decided to marry when he was 12, and married at the age of 26, on graduating. They had a daughter.

GENERAL
SIR JOHN HACKETT

General Sir John Hackett (who died on September 9 1997, aged 86) was a brilliant soldier and an outstanding scholar; he was wounded three times in the Second World War, and awarded an MC and two DSOs.

At 33, he survived the disastrous Battle of Arnhem, an experience which left him deeply sceptical of staff planners. The strategists, he would complain, had set up a kind of "airborne picnic", to which the enemy were added as an afterthought, like salt and pepper. Always a radical thinker, Hackett exercised an important influence in the defence review that led to the abolition of National Service in 1959. He went on to be Commander-in-Chief, British Army of the Rhine, and Commander, Northern Army Group in Nato, from 1966 to 1968.

Slim, dapper, energetic and friendly, "Shan" Hackett could converse fluently in nine languages. After retiring from the Army in 1968 he was for seven years Principal of King's College, London. He also became a best-selling author and a television personality. Among his hobbies in *Who's Who* he listed "the pursuit of exactitude, called by some pedantry".

Of Irish ancestry, and the only boy among five children, John Winthrop Hackett was born in Australia on November 5 1910, the son of Sir John Winthrop Hackett, who owned two newspapers in Western Australia and founded the University of

Perth. After education at Geelong Grammar School, Hackett studied painting at the London Central Art School, before going on to New College, Oxford, to read Greats. He had hoped to become a don but as his degree was not quite good enough he joined the Army, and was commissioned in the 8th King's Royal Irish Hussars.

"I never went into the Army," Hackett would insist, "I joined my great-grandfather's regiment. There's no such thing as the British Army – there are only regiments. That's the great source of strength in the British endeavour: it's a family thing." Hackett kept up his academic studies as a junior officer, working principally on the medieval period and producing a thesis on Saladin and the Third Crusade. In 1936 he was posted to Palestine, where he was mentioned in despatches for his part in anti-terrorist operations. Seconded to the Transjordan Frontier Force in 1937, he was twice more mentioned in despatches.

He was wounded in the Syrian campaign against the Vichy French in 1941, and again in the Western Desert in 1942, when he was GSO1 Raiding Forces, Middle East Land Force. In the latter appointment he gave much help and encouragement to unorthodox units such as the SAS, the Long Range Desert Group, and Popski's Private Army. In 1943 Hackett raised and commanded 4th Parachute Brigade, winning a fourth mention in despatches while serving with them in Italy.

The next year he jumped with the regiment at Arnhem, carrying with him visiting cards and a walking stick. On his unexpected arrival, six German soldiers tried to surrender to him; Hackett told them somewhat irritably to wait until he had found the stick which he had dropped on landing. Soon afterwards he was badly wounded by shell splinters and taken to a local hospital, where a German surgeon pronounced that it would be a waste of time to operate.

Hackett's life was saved by a brilliant South African surgeon; and as he was recovering the Dutch underground smuggled him out past the German guards and put him in the home of a family who lived only 40 yards from a German military police billet. Hackett's protectors nursed him back to health – he passed the time by reading the New Testament in Greek – until he was able to escape to British lines. His safe arrival was announced to the courageous and devoted family who had looked after him in a coded message: "The grey goose has gone."

After 1945 Hackett commanded the Transjordan Frontier Force before moving, in 1956, to the British Army of the Rhine, where he commanded 7th Armoured Division, the "Desert Rats", with whom he had served in the desert. From 1958 to 1961, he was Commandant of the Royal Military College of Science at Shrivenham, before becoming GOC-in-C, Northern Ireland. From 1963 he was Deputy Chief of the Imperial General Staff, then Deputy Chief of the General Staff, Ministry of Defence.

At King's College, London, Hackett astonished the students by recognising them and knowing their names very soon after his arrival. He joined them in a National Union of Students march over grants and even suggested that cannabis might be legalised and taxed heavily to fund university research. After retiring as Principal in 1975 he became visiting Professor of Classics at King's College. He wrote a moving account of his experiences in the Arnhem battle and his convalescence with the Dutch family, in *I Was a Stranger* (1977), a title taken from St Matthew's Gospel. Although the book describes a grim and traumatic period, it is often enlivened by shafts of whimsical humour.

When Hackett arrived back in Britain and went to the bank to collect his pay, an official told him that he could not have any because he was posted as "wounded and missing". Until the War Office agreed that he was neither dead nor missing, nothing more than his wife's married allowance was due. "Then with a friendly goodbye," his account concludes, "the official turned elsewhere." Hackett wrote an imaginative work entitled *The Third World War* (1982) which sold three million copies in 10 languages. Subsequent events showed that he had been prescient, for the novel predicted the disintegration of the Soviet Union and paid special attention to the strategic importance of oil in the Middle East.

During the Falklands War Hackett frequently appeared on television as an expert commentator. In 1983 he wrote a television series on the British Army, 'The Profession of Arms'. He also edited *Warfare in the Ancient World* (1989). He became an honorary livery man of the Worshipful Company of Dyers in 1975, and a Freeman of the City of London in 1976. He was President of the English Association and the Classical Association; and a member of the Lord Chancellor's Committee on Reform of the Law of Contempt. In 1972 he was elected an honorary fellow of New College, Oxford.

Hackett was appointed MBE in 1938, CBE in 1953, CB in 1958, KCB in 1962 and GCB in 1967. He was ADC (General) to HM The Queen in 1967 and 1968, and Deputy Lieutenant, Gloucestershire, in 1982. Other appointments included Colonel Commandant, REME, from 1961 to 1966; Honorary Colonel of 10th Battalion the Parachute Regiment, TA, from 1965 to 1967, and of the 10th Volunteer Battalion, the Parachute Regiment from 1967 to 1973. He was also Honorary Colonel of the Oxford University OTC from 1967 to 1978. In 1985 Hackett won the Chesney Gold Medal awarded by the Royal United Services Institute.

He relished his longevity. "Life begins at 70," he once remarked. "You have had your lot, and every day after it is one for free, to use and to be enjoyed." Shan Hackett married, in 1942, Margaret Frena, the Austrian widow of a German; they had a daughter and two adopted step-daughters.

COLONEL
MARK DILLON

Colonel Mark Dillon (who died on October 17 1997, aged 101) was the last surviving Tank Corps officer to have fought at the Battle of Cambrai in

1917 when the use of tanks in large numbers for the first time had a devastating effect. Dillon, who was wounded three times and twice mentioned in despatches during the First World War, won an MC for diverting a tank attack which was heading for a well dug-in German artillery position.

There was no radio communication between the tanks and no transport available to help him to contact the lumbering vehicles, which were already under small arms fire, so he ran as fast as he could. He had to zig-zag across the road, as a sniper had picked him out as a target. Somewhat incongruously, he was still carrying his officers' cane "swagger stick", and when a German bullet hit it he was slightly wounded in the hand by the splinters.

Undeterred, the 19-year-old Dillon pressed on until he reached the leading tank, leapt on to the back, climbed up to the top and banged on the metal plate to attract the commander's attention. Luckily, the commander realised it was a friend, not an enemy, opened up, heard Dillon's frantic message and slewed the vehicle round. No tank was lost.

Norman Margrave Dillon was born on July 27 1896 and educated at Haileybury. He began training as a mining engineer in the Seaham Colliery, where the coalface was three miles under the sea. With another apprentice he walked the four miles from the pit shaft, mostly in a stooping position, carrying an oil lamp which easily went out and could not be relit underground. A "day" meant rising at 3 am, coming up at noon and going to the office in the afternoon. The foremen, who resented the presence of Dillon and his companion, often led them through the most difficult ways, but soon found that the two youngsters, well trained at sports, had more stamina than their tormentors. However, Dillon hated the dirt, grease and smells.

When war broke out he promptly volunteered for the Northumberland Fusiliers, and was immediately commissioned into the 14th Battalion. "I was totally ignorant of military procedure," he recalled. At first he saluted bemedalled NCOs under the impression that they were officers. Foot-drill seemed to be the only thing that mattered, and no heed had been taken of the lessons of the Boer War. The battlefield tactics seemed unchanged since the Crimea.

Most of the men were in their oldest civilian clothes, as the promised uniform did not arrive for months. Dillon bought himself a four-cylinder Rudge motorcycle for £4, but he had to repair it himself as no one else could. Petrol was bought in cans from grocers' shops. Senior officers were unbelievably unhelpful and incompetent. Officers had to buy their own revolvers: "I bought mine from the traveller of a London firm of tailors," Dillon said. His pay was 5s 3d (26p) a day, most of which went on messing costs, as there were no rations for officers in the early days. He was appalled by the badly cooked food provided for the men.

Dillon landed in France on September 15 1915 and marched 25 miles to reach the battlefield of Loos in time to bury the dead, who lay in neat rows, cut down by machine-gun fire in front of the uncut barbed wire. At first, some of his men thought the corpses were merely asleep. He was sent to make contact with the Guards Brigade, who had already been in action very effectively, and whose HQ was under fire; he found them dining calmly off a clean cloth on a table with Fortnum and Mason's ham and port.

Dillon's unit was now employed building trenches and laying duckboards. He volunteered for one raid on enemy trenches, and subsequently concluded that trench-raiding was a waste of good men and achieved nothing. While returning from No Man's Land he felt in greater danger from his own side than the enemy. When he was issued with a steel helmet, Dillon thought it a joke, but he put it on. At that moment a shell exploded overhead and made a great dent in it.

He moved on to mining and counter-mining, in which his previous training proved useful. He was extremely critical of the way the tanks were used over the worst ground conditions on the Somme, and when he had the chance, volunteered for the 2nd Battalion, Heavy Branch Machine Gun Corps, the cover-name for the tanks. As one of the few who could read a map, he was appointed reconnaissance officer.

In February 1917, Dillon was wounded in the face and evacuated. This at least gave him a delightful convalescence in Park Street, Mayfair, where Lady Mountgarret had turned her house into a hospital. "It was wonderfully run," Dillon remembered. "But it was shut down later, because of her evasion of the rationing regulations."

Dillon recalled that at Cambrai the 474 tanks sent into action crossed wide ditches after bundles of brushwood had been dropped into them. This technique had been used by cavalry for centuries before tanks were invented. The attack was a great success at first, but after numerous breakdowns and a German counter-attack it failed to produce the hoped-for conclusive victory.

In 1918 Dillon and his fellow commanders were supplied with horses. "I cannot think why," he commented later. "They were frightful brutes, many being vicious or unmanageable animals which their owners had been only too glad to sell to the Army. One 'bolter' mounted by an expert Australian horse-man went seven miles before it could be stopped."

After the decisive battle of August 8 1918, Dillon was wounded again, this time in the legs and back. By the time he had recovered, the war was over and he transferred (nominally) to the Munster Fusiliers, which seemed to offer the best prospects for promotion. However the Munsters were disbanded on the partition of Ireland, and he was then gazetted to the King's Liverpool. In spite of having served through the war Dillon was still a lieutenant with the acting rank of captain, and had to attend a crammer to pass his promotion examination. He was still officially in the Northumberland Fusiliers, though he never joined either of his other regiments as he was on a tank course or instructing at Bovington all the time.

One of his pupils was T E Lawrence, then calling himself Private Shaw, who relieved his boredom by taking notes on Dillon's lectures in Arabic. In 1925

Dillon was at last promoted captain again, and posted to India. He soon became the owner of a horse called Sweep, on which he hunted jackal with the Peshawar Vale Hounds and rode in point-to-points. Later, out with the Delhi Hounds, he was ridden into a tree by another rider and swept off by a bough; the fall damaged his spine so badly that medical experts were surprised he was still alive.

However, he recovered and took up shooting crocodiles; one of his kills contained a huge bullet which was estimated to date from 70 years before. Stalking crocs up rivers brought him into contact with tribes who spoke no Urdu and used no coinage. In India Dillon owned a succession of ancient cars, most of which he kept going by his own mechanical ingenuity. One was a Rolls-Royce with wooden wheels; as Rolls-Royces were usually the prerogative of VIPs, he was the subject of much professional teasing and jealousy. In 1934 he was posted back to England. While on the gunnery range at Redesdale, he was intrigued to receive a box of shells from Woolwich Arsenal labelled thus: "These shells must on no account be stood on their noses. To simplify matters tops of cases have been labelled bottom."

In 1935 he married Margaret Munro Ellis, nicknamed Jimmie. As his own nickname was Dora (after the music-hall star Dora Dillon) the names caused some bizarre misunderstandings. Soon afterwards Dillon was posted to Mersah Matruh in Egypt, where the dust storms were so bad that he was sometimes lost in the camp between the mess tent and his own in daylight.

On the outbreak of war in 1939 he was posted to the War Office to assess new weapons, including searchlights of intense power mounted on tanks to blind the enemy; though effective they were never used. Most of the other inventions were not even practical. His next posting was to Catterick, training officers and men for the Royal Armoured Corps. But although his own interests were in training recruits to drive tanks, fire guns and understand engines, senior officers nagged him about the poor standard of saluting among the more bolshie-minded soldiers. He therefore told these men that saluting was of vital importance in the Soviet Army; on his next big parade he was told by a visiting officer that he had never seen such a high standard of saluting, even in the Brigade of Guards.

After a period as president of a War Office selection board, near Tadcaster, he was posted to a similar appointment in Cairo. He then commanded HQ, the Canal Area, at Fayid, containing some 80,000 men, half of them PoWs.

In 1947 Dillon retired to farm near Durham, where he lived in an old hall infested with rats and mice. He made a success of dairy farming, then changed to poultry and pigs. After giving up farming, Dillon took an active part in local government. As a hobby he repaired antique furniture and made high-quality reproductions. He loved all types of vehicles, whether tanks, cars or motorcycles, and had a genius for keeping them going. Mark Dillon was remembered for his care for the welfare of his men and their wives and families. He unofficially improved their food and living conditions, sometimes incurring severe reprimands for his unorthodox methods; but he shrugged these off.

His wife, whose courage and stamina matched his own, died in 1968.

CORPORAL
TED MATTHEWS

Corporal Ted Matthews (who died in Sydney on December 9 1997, aged 101) was the last survivor of the Australian and New Zealand troops who landed at Gallipoli on April 25 1915, the first day of that disastrous invasion. Ever afterwards, Matthews warned against romanticising the campaign, describing it starkly as an example of the futility of war.

He seemed rather pleased that in nearly eight months he fired only one or two shots at the Turks – or rather, at one Turk – "and I hope I missed the poor bugger". Matthews was lucky: as a promising young signaller, splashing ashore at the beach, he was hit by shrapnel and saved by his pocket-book, a present from his mother. When two of his friends were killed together in their dug-out, one on either side of Matthews, he was left unharmed.

Matthews was at Gallipoli from first to last, which meant he was evacuated less than eight months after the landing. The evacuation was the most successful enterprise of the campaign: thanks to unmanned guns rigged to fire automatically and camouflage the retreat, not a soldier perished. In later years, Matthews studied the Gallipoli campaign, and came to the conclusion that Winston Churchill's strategy was probably right; he blamed the "fool British" who failed in the planning and the execution. Australian generals, he thought, would have carried out Churchill's strategy to cut Turkey out of the war, link up with Russia, and thus exert a profound effect on the policies of the Balkan nations.

The Gallipoli landing came early in the life of Australia as a nation, and the Australians still keep Anzac Day (Anzac being an acronym for Australian and New Zealand Army Corps) as a holiday each April 25, in tribute to the living and dead of all wars involving Australia. In the Australian calendar it remains the nearest thing to a national day.

Ted Matthews's longevity made him a symbol of Anzac Day. A handful of other Gallipoli survivors remained of the 50,000 Australians who served there; Matthews, though, was the last of the originals. He had, in fact, been among the very first of some 15,000 Australians and New Zealanders who, amid the shambles of the first day, had been landed at the wrong beach, and were faced by an enemy firing from steep hills above them.

In an interview just before his 100th birthday, Matthews described how many men had been drowned with their heavy gear in deep water. On the narrow beach there was no cover. "Nobody knew what was going on. Blokes were shot all around me. They were screaming out. Blood came spurting out everywhere. It was terrible." "Dig in" was the imperative at Gallipoli, and Matthews, who knew better than most, maintained that this was how Australian soldiers came to be called "Diggers".

After Gallipoli, he went on to France, and, as a corporal, was with the Australians who won fame by taking Villers-Bretonneux in 1918. He remembered marching for 19 hours beforehand.

Ted Matthews was born in Sydney on November 11 1896. He was a 17-year-old carpenter when he joined the Army following the propaganda about German atrocities, and went to Gallipoli with the 1st Division Signals. After the war he went back to carpentry, but had a hard time in the Great Depression. He established a travelling library, using a motorcycle and sidecar, and made soft drinks. He tried to enlist for the Second World War, but at 43 was too old. Straight-backed, intelligent, articulate, independent, uncomplaining, with a dry humour, Matthews represented the cream of the Australian working class.

At Gallipoli he wondered what God was up to, but abandoned the question as too deep. Told on his 100th birthday that a message was coming from the Queen, he found it a little droll: "I can't believe that the Queen actually sits down and says, 'Oh, I must drop a line to Ted Matthews today'." He outlived two wives, Stella (née Broderick) and Freda (née Corlett). There were two daughters from the first marriage. After the death of his second wife, Matthews lived for 17 years with one of his daughters in Florida, returning to Sydney in 1994 so as not to be a burden.

MAJOR
GEOFFREY BRAIN

Major Geoffrey Brain (who died on January 20 1998, aged 84) was for 34 years regimental secretary of the secret regiment "Phantom"; it was disbanded in 1945, but Brain organised an annual reunion and ensured that its records were preserved.

Phantom, officially known as GHQ Reconnaissance Regiment, was created in 1940 as a highly mobile unit whose task was to inform the Higher Command where the "bomb line" was. In the fluid conditions of modern battle, ground troops are usually spread over a large area, making it all too easy for air forces or artillery to destroy units by "friendly fire". However, the main purpose of Phantom soon became to inform the Commander-in-Chief of the state of affairs on the battlefield by direct radio communication with his HQ, rather than by relaying it through the normal channels, which were much slower.

Phantom members travelled by any means possible – some were attached to the SAS and became parachutists – and had often to transmit from extremely dangerous locations. Phantom proved itself very useful in France and Belgium in 1940, and was thereafter built up by Lieutenant-Colonel G F "Hoppy" Hopkinson, later to become a General before being killed in Italy. Hopkinson recruited an extraordinary variety of talented young men who had an instinct for reaching the centre of any trouble spots and were adept at barging into the offices and conferences of their seniors.

The regiment boasted many who would achieve public distinction after the war. Among those eligible for its reunions were two Privy Counsellors, three professors, a Law Lord, an ambassador, a Commissioner of the Metropolitan Police, the Master of a Cambridge college and the actor David Niven. Hopkinson trained them relentlessly in Morse Code and other necessary skills, sometimes making them stay up all night and never allowing them to take shelter, even under the heaviest shell fire. "Slit trenches," he would firmly assert, "make cowards."

Geoffrey Brain was born at Kingswood, Surrey, on May 25 1913, but spent most of his early years in Hampshire. After education at Taunton's School, Southampton, he joined Lloyds Bank in 1929, and the Royal Wiltshire Yeomanry in 1936. Soon after the outbreak of war, Brain was on parade with his cavalry squadron awaiting an inspection when a Spitfire dived on them, causing havoc. Although he was by then a highly skilled horseman, Brain decided there and then that there was no place for the horse in modern warfare.

He therefore transferred to the Wiltshire Regiment, and trained with the Home Guard Auxiliary Unit to operate behind enemy lines in the event of an invasion. One day, Brain was told to report to Boodle's club, in St James's, where he was informed that he had been selected for a secret unit known as Phantom. Although other Phantom squadrons were dispatched to Greece and North Africa, Brain stayed in Britain and was attached to the Canadian Army in preparation for the D-Day landings. He landed in Normandy in June 1944 with 4th Canadian Armoured Division, whom he was soon supplying with information about the fighting in the Orne Valley. Subsequently, he was attached to the 1st Polish Armoured Division under General Maczek, and was with them when they played a vital part in the trapping of two German armies in the Falaise "pocket", leading to the capture of 50,000 prisoners.

Brain stayed with the Poles for the drive through Europe, apart from a brief attachment to the American First Army in the Ardennes. He was receiving a mess tin of food as their building was hit by a shell. When the dust settled, the Americans were surprised to see Brain removing dusty chunks from his mess tin and licking them to see if they were glass or meat. If it was meat, he ate it.

He was temporarily attached to the 3rd Canadian Infantry Division for the Rhine crossing, but returned to the Poles for the liberation of concentration camps and the capture of Wilhelmshaven. At the end of the campaign he was mentioned in despatches and awarded the Polish Cross of Valour, a distinction much prized by the brave Poles.

Although tempted to stay in the Army after the war, Brain decided to return to banking. He eventually became staff manager at Lloyds Bank's head office in London. He maintained his links with the TA, commanding A Company of the Wiltshires in Salisbury. He was a school governor, and treasurer of the Devon Long-haired Sheep Breeders' Society. Brain was also a creative gardener, a connoisseur of wine and very knowledgeable about antiques, especially English china and mahogany.

He had the knack of making everyone he met feel that he was genuinely glad to see them – which he usually was – though he did not tolerate anything but the highest standards. Geoffrey Brain married first, in 1939, Betty Langton, who died in 1985. He was survived by his second wife, Iris, whom he married in 1986, and by a son of his first marriage.

MAJOR
KENNETH BALFOUR

Major Kenneth Balfour (who died on January 25 1998, aged 88) gave a remarkable eye-witness account of a battle against German tanks in a Dutch village in September 1944. He was awarded a Military Cross for his part; but his own account gives an idea of what lay behind the reserved language of the citation for the MC, which noted merely that he had served with distinction as a troop leader, particularly during the fighting to keep open the Nijmegen-Eindhoven road. He had prevented the road being cut, and thus saved many military vehicles from destruction.

Balfour told the story less formally: "Having lost my squadron owing to illness during the pre-invasion period, when we landed in Normandy, I found myself relegated to commanding HQ squadron, which was a very dull occupation. So I asked to be posted to a Sabre Squadron, as troop leader. As there was no vacancy, I therefore some-what surreptitiously joined my old friend Anthony Goodall's troop in the capacity of a troop corporal, one of the nicest things about a family regiment being that you can get away with this kind of thing.

"The troop corporal normally leads the troop in a Dingo armoured scout car, and it was in that position that on September 22 the troop was warily making its way through the village of Eerde when it came under fire. Anthony signalled to me to let him through and almost immediately his armoured car was wrecked by a Bazooka team hidden in a ditch. By this time I could see quite a lot of Germans, who were firing bullets and armour-piercing shells at us, resulting in the loss of two more armoured cars.

"I, with the remaining Dingo, raced back a mile to the main Eindhoven-Arnhem road, to give warning and prepare for the impending attack. On arrival I found the traffic at a standstill, the road having already been cut by the enemy to the north. Luckily our immediate stretch of road contained the windfall of four 3.7in anti-aircraft guns, nicely to hand on transporters.

Despite my knowing nothing about artillery, it was not difficult to make a plan whereby the guns could give massive support to our little force, which now numbered nearly 100 men. For further strength, I had been able to whistle up three tanks from Divisional HQ, just as the enemy debouched from the woodland round the village.

"It all seemed very simple to me: tanks to lead the

infantry on the flanks, and the 3.7s to fire straight down the middle, which they did with tremendous success. I saw them pick off two enemy tanks before I had gone a hundred yards. It took nearly an hour to regain Eerde. On arrival, and flat on my stomach, there was a fair old wail of rattles, sizzles and hissings, but the opposition was no longer very resolute, and a lone Tiger, with a damaged track, seemed more anxious to find its way out of the place than to stick around.

"Suddenly, peace and quiet was established, but we had lost 12 officers, a further 10 other ranks, and 20 wounded. The enemy had suffered similarly, but we identified only two officers. At last light I rejoined the squadron, knowing that I had been lucky, or maybe privileged, to be in the right place at the right time, with the right wireless sets."

Balfour returned to Eerde just before first light next morning, and was relieved to find the village free of Germans. "But just as I was finishing my second mug of tea," he remembered, "I got the fright of my life when, on looking back behind me, I saw perching in the semi-darkness a swarm of dour-looking men, hung with picks, spades and rifles." They were Argyll and Sutherland Highlanders, who proceeded to dig themselves in.

Balfour was recalled soon afterwards, a few hours before the Germans began a serious attack. Later that day the US 101st Airborne took Eerde.

Kenneth George Francis Balfour, the son of Lieutenant-Colonel K R Balfour, was born on June 14 1909 and educated at Eton and Harvard, where he read English Literature. Intending to become a journalist, he spent several months in Spain during the Civil War, sending reports back to the *Morning Post* in London. He was also commissioned into the reserve of his father's regiment, the 1st Royal Dragoon Guards, which he joined in Palestine at the outbreak of war. He served in Egypt, Sudan and Abyssinia. In the Western Desert, he spent a time with the Long Range Desert Group, and took part in the battles of Tobruk and Alamein.

Going on to Italy and North-West Europe, he finally took part in the liberation of Denmark. In addition to his MC, Balfour was twice mentioned in despatches, and throughout the war he acted as regimental photographer.

After the war, Balfour bought a newsagent's shop in Chalfont St Peter, Buckinghamshire. It flourished and the business expanded, eventually comprising 136 shops. Balfour was twice Mayor of Marlow and gave the Balfour Gardens to the town. Eager to explore the world, he travelled extensively in Uganda, and up the Niger to Timbuktu. At 52, he climbed the Matterhorn (14,691 ft) but on reaching the top was disappointed to find that conditions were not suitable for photography; so he climbed it again the next day.

Balfour's wife Heather, a physio-therapist, died in 1985.

———

MAJOR
ALAN BUSH

Major Alan Bush (who died on March 3 1998, aged 83) was awarded an immediate MC at Arnhem during which he was wounded, taken prisoner, escaped, and rejoined his battalion. Given command of another battalion, he was wounded again, then finally succeeded in leading the remnants of his force back across the Rhine to safety.

Bush was wounded on the first day of the airborne operation, September 17 1944, and became separated from his unit. Next day he attempted to rejoin it but was taken prisoner. With great resourcefulness he managed to escape, and rejoined what was left of the division, which was still in action. On September 22, he was given command of the 1st Parachute Brigade sector. So successful was his skill at organisation, that its front was never broken.

On September 25, while leading a counter–attack, Bush was again wounded, but he continued to lead his men until the operation was completed. "Throughout, at great risk to himself," the citation for his MC recorded, "he constantly visited his men in every forward position, and his personal example was at all times heartening and inspiring."

Alan Bush was born the youngest of nine children on July 18 1914 in Westmorland. He was educated at Heversham Grammar School and Queen's College, Oxford, where he read English and History, and was awarded a Rugby Blue in 1934. After leaving Oxford he taught at Mill Hill School until the outbreak of war, when he enlisted in the Coldstream Guards before being commissioned into the Border Regiment. In spring 1941 he volunteered to join the recently formed Parachute Brigade, in which he was posted to the 3rd Battalion.

When the First Army landed in North Africa in November 1942 Bush parachuted into Bone with the 3rd Battalion, which subsequently fought as infantry during the remainder of the campaign. His principal memories were not so much of the fighting, in which the battalion distinguished itself, as of the cold relentless rain, the hostility of the local Arabs and the unfriendliness of the French.

In July 1943 he was parachuted into Sicily in a disastrous airborne assault which dropped many of the gliders and parachutists into the sea or into the wrong dropping zone (as happened to him). After the Sicilian campaign, he landed with his battalion at Taranto in southern Italy and fought his way up the coast.

He then returned to England to prepare for the North-West Europe campaign. Eventually, after three months and 23 false starts, 1st Airborne saw action at Arnhem, the "Bridge Too Far" operation in which the lightly armed British Airborne Division found itself confronted by two Panzer divisions, four divisional battle groups and an infantry division. The outcome was that more than 1,000 British were killed, many more were isolated or wounded and taken prisoner, and some 2,000 of the original 10,000 managed, with great difficulty, to make their way back across the Rhine when the order was given to do so. But the Germans disclosed that their own casualties had been 3,300 killed and wounded.

It took Bush a long time to recover from his wounds, which, added to injuries sustained in North Africa, gave him severe problems for the rest of his life, though he made light of them. After demobilisation he returned to Mill Hill, where he became a housemaster. In 1958 Bush was appointed Head Master of Merchiston Castle School, Edinburgh, from which he retired 10 years later. His foresight over financial investments during the sixties ensured the school flourished. After his retirement from Merchiston, Bush continued teaching for a while at Campbell College, Belfast.

Alan Bush was an inspiring leader, English teacher and rugby coach. He was a useful cricketer, an ardent letter writer, an excellent communicator at all levels; he was also a capable poet and author, and, above all, a man who in spite of the pain he suffered in his later years, managed to make others feel that life was fun. To his pupils he communicated the fact that English was something to be enjoyed, not merely a subject to be studied. He was also a talented musician with an excellent ear, able to play on a piano almost any tune he had heard.

Alan Bush was survived by his wife, Kate, two sons and a daughter.

BRIGADIER
"BIRDIE" SMITH

Brigadier "Birdie" Smith (who died on March 7 1998, aged 74) was awarded an immediate DSO during the Second World War for his part in taking a German-occupied village in Italy; two decades later, after a helicopter crash in the jungle in Borneo, he had his right arm amputated with an army clasp knife without an anaesthetic, a process which took an hour and which he bore in silence without flinching.

In 1944 Smith was commanding C Company of the 2nd Battalion, 7th Gurkha Rifles, in Italy. On the night of September 3, it was given the task of capturing the heavily fortified village of Tavoleto. The Germans launched a pre-emptive attack, but were beaten off. C Company went on the attack, and when intense Spandau machine-gun fire checked their advance, Smith ran forward and, in spite of being wounded in the leg, killed all the occupants of the first Spandau post with a combination of grenades and tommy-gun fire.

By this time the company had sustained 35 casualties. Smith pressed on with the remainder, taking every building in turn and also disposing of the Germans occupying trenches. By 4 am the remains of C Company, now down to 28, had cleared the village of the enemy. The Germans then began the expected counter-attack with a mortar barrage, but Smith had deployed his remaining men so skilfully in the buildings that were still standing that the counter-attack failed. Smith was awarded an immediate DSO.

Eric David Smith was born in Fife on August 19 1923 and educated at All Hallows School, Dorset, before joining the Army in 1941. After attending the Officer Cadet Training Unit at Bangalore, he was commissioned in 1942 and gazetted to the 7th Gurkha Rifles. From Italy he was posted to Greece, where his regiment helped to prevent a Communist takeover after the German withdrawal.

Subsequent postings included attendance at the Staff College, Camberley, a tour in Malaya, where his regiment was engaged in counter-terrorist operations during the Emergency, and service in Cyprus during the Eoka troubles. In 1962 President Sukarno of Indonesia decided that the three Borneo states of Brunei, Sarawak and Sabah were ripe for a takeover by Indonesian troops. The 2nd/7th Gurkhas were sent to Borneo to persuade him otherwise.

Smith, serving as second in command of the 2nd/7th, set off by helicopter to visit one of the forward companies. As they approached their destination, the helicopter crashed into the jungle. His fellow passengers, the battalion medical officer and six Gurkha riflemen, managed to escape from the wreckage unhurt, but Smith was trapped by his arm. A strong smell of hot oil indicated that there was a danger of fire. The medical officer, Captain Pat Crawford, with the company commander, who had now arrived on the scene, decided that immediate amputation was essential.

Since there were no instruments and no anaesthetics, Crawford had to use a clasp knife for the purpose. The hour-long operation was made even more hazardous by the fact that the helicopter was upside down and awkwardly balanced; Smith was conscious throughout and did not utter a word. Crawford was awarded the George Medal for his action.

Subsequently, Smith wrote of the incident: "I sensed that the Gurkha soldiers of B Company were now grouped around the wreckage. Bravest of the brave, how often had I seen their courage when wounded in battle. Now I had to try to live up to their standards, to show that I was worthy to be one of their officers."

Despite the loss of his arm, Smith went on to command 1st/2nd Gurkhas in Borneo, and then in Hong Kong. On his return to Britain, he served at the War Office and, finally, was Brigadier commanding the Gurkha recruiting bases in Nepal. In 1978 Smith retired from the Army.

He became bursar and then chairman of the governors of St John's School, Sidmouth, and was chairman of the local branch of the Royal British Legion and of Sidmouth Town Council. He was Colonel of the 7th Gurkhas from 1975 to 1982, and the author of *Britain's Brigade of Gurkhas* (1973). Birdie Smith, who had acquired his nickname from his rather beaky nose, was devoted to his Gurkha soldiers, who returned his feelings in full measure; but he was a realistic idealist.

After Partition in 1947, six regiments of the Gurkhas were incorporated in the Indian Army and

four in the British. Some Gurkhas who had been
domiciled in India tried to enlist in the British
Gurkhas, thus posing a delicate diplomatic problem.
Smith, at this time commanding a recruiting camp in
Calcutta, found a practical solution by setting
physical standards which could rarely be met by
anyone not domiciled in the hills.

Birdie Smith was appointed CBE in 1978. He
married, in 1947, Jill Waycott and they had two
daughters.

MAJOR
PETER LEWIS

Major Peter Lewis (who died on July 10 1998, aged
71) was, as a sergeant-major in the Grenadier Guards,
renowned for combining a forbidding appearance
and high standards with a sense of humour and a
preference for improving subordinates by encouragement rather than criticism.

Lewis excelled because he enjoyed the theatre of
soldiering, the spectacle, the tragedies and the
comedies of Army life. He was as steady in other less
predictable situations as he was on the parade
ground. When serving with the 1st Battalion in
Sharjah in 1968 he was asked on Forces Radio:
"What do you dislike most about Sharjah, Mr
Lewis?" He replied crisply: "Long hair and short
shorts" – a reference to the RAF, who shared the
Coldstreams' barracks. The RAF was not over-

pleased, and invited him on a flight over the Persian Gulf, largely conducted upside down. Lewis endured it without comment. After he had landed the station com-mander asked him if he had enjoyed the flight. Ramrod straight, Lewis looked him in the eye: "Very much, sir. Do your aeroplanes ever fly the right way up?"

After being commissioned in 1969, Lewis was posted to Londonderry, where British troops were at first received ecstatically by the local Roman Catholic population. When he returned in 1973 with the 2nd Battalion, on a four months tour of the Ardoyne and Shankill, the situation was very different. Although the IRA shot dead 50 British soldiers that year, no Grenadier was among them, a fact partly attributed to Lewis's contribution to the maintenance of alertness and morale. After the tour he was awarded the MBE.

Stories about Lewis were legion. Once, irritated by young officers in the next room talking loudly late into the night and disturbing his efforts to sleep, Lewis put his loudspeaker against the wall and delivered Beethoven's Fifth Symphony at full volume. An eyeball to eyeball confrontation was followed by a mutual understanding.

Surprisingly he was sent to Edinburgh to train the Royal Company of Archers for their annual parade before the Queen. Realising there were murmurings about him, as the Archers included many former Scots Guardsmen, he decided to tackle the matter head on, and addressed them thus: "Many of you gentlemen will be wondering why it is that the

Army has sent a sergeant-major from the 1st or Grenadier Guards rather than one from the 3rd or Scots Fusilier Guards. The answer, gentlemen, is simple. We are the best." The parade was a great success, but only after a senior Scots Guards general had been given a brisk refresher course on sword drill at the back of Holyrood, away from critical eyes.

In 1977 Lewis was appointed head of security at De Beers. He introduced modern training methods, and organised the department into an efficient force that was the envy of many companies in the City. However, he remained in close touch with Grenadier comrades and was always ready to partake in any venture. He was asked to train six actors to march like Guardsmen for an opera at the Coliseum, a task he found by no means easy. At the dress rehearsal, when the "soldiers" were required to turn to their left and march off, all did – except one who turned to the right, whereupon a voice bellowed from the pit: "Where the hell do you think you're going? Covent Garden?" On the night it went brilliantly, and Lewis treated all six to dinner.

Peter Arnold Lewis was born on April 6 1927 at Tattenhall, Cheshire. He was educated at Ludford School at Crewe, joined the Grenadiers in 1945, and was posted to Palestine with the 3rd Battalion. He served in Egypt, Cyprus, Malaysia and Germany, earning high commendation. Always immaculate, often with a rose in his buttonhole, Lewis led by example – to all ranks. Devotion to his regiment and his family, was the mainspring of his life.

A new march was played at the 1998 Trooping the

Colour, entitled *The Sergeant Major*. It was written by the Director of Music in honour of Peter Lewis. He was survived by his wife, two sons and a daughter.

GENERAL
SIR KENNETH DARLING

General Sir Kenneth Darling (who died on October 31 1998, aged 89) was renowned for expressing his forceful opinions in vocabulary which left no room for misunderstanding. "The only Eoka terrorist I am interested in is a dead one," he said in 1958, on taking command in Cyprus.

Darling served as GOC, Cyprus, from October 1958 to the beginning of 1960. His troops suffered a severe trial from the terrorist methods of the insurgents. Eoka had attempted to assassinate Darling's predecessor in Cyprus, Major-General D A "Joe" Kendrew, and Darling's first act was to launch Operation New Broom to screen 5,000 inhabitants of three villages in an attempt to round up Eoka suspects.

He then urged all British personnel to improve their marksmanship, "including the butcher, baker and candlestick-maker". Darling questioned the need for male British civilians to be made special constables before being permitted firearms. "Eoka seem to have plenty of arms, so why not provide everybody with some weapon for his own protection?"

In Britain, the *Daily Mirror* ran a campaign criticising the management of the Cyprus crisis. "Sir Hugh Foot, Governor of Cyprus, is losing control to the military," the tabloid declared while quoting Darling as saying: "I have got these Eoka bastards on the run. I am going to beat them." The *Mirror* doubted this optimism. Julian Amery, the Under-Secretary for War, commented that nothing could be better calculated to spur on Eoka to kill more British soldiers. "What is worse," he added, "the *Mirror* article goes on to insinuate that the Army commander's plans are doomed to failure. It is intolerable that our troops should be stabbed in the back by such devilish and defeatist propaganda."

Shortly after this controversy, British troops killed the most wanted Eoka leader, Kyriakos Matsis, aged 32, by tossing two hand grenades into his hiding place when he refused to surrender. Darling telephoned Foot. "I have good news," he said. "We've got Matsis." There was controversy about the exercise of excessive force by British troops. But within three months of his posting to Cyprus, Darling's tactics had secured a Christmas truce from Eoka.

Darling's role was then complicated by changing political circumstances. An amnesty made provision for the return of the Greek Cypriot leader Archbishop Makarios, and in 1959 Darling found himself at a cocktail party in Nicosia talking to two Eoka leaders whom his men had hunted a few months before in the anti-terrorist sweep; they were now ministers in the transitional cabinet. He refused to talk politics to reporters who asked if a civil war were now likely in Cyprus. "I can only say that today we have men coming into high positions here who for years have expressed their political opinions by violence and shooting. I would be surprised if they had forgotten all their earlier methods overnight."

By the time he left Cyprus, Darling was said to have gained the respect of Cypriot nationalist leaders. There was certainly nothing blimpish about his attitude. Those serving under him were sure that whatever decisions he reached would be the right ones. Ken Darling was a born leader, popular with those under his command. A short, slight man he bubbled with energy. He had a marked sense of humour, which he often needed when people accidentally telephoned his number and received the brisk answer, "Darling".

Kenneth Thomas Darling was born on September 17 1909, the son of G K Darling, CIE. As a boy he acquired the nickname Katie, a play on his initials. He was educated at Eton and Sandhurst and commissioned in the Royal Fusiliers in 1929. During the Second World War he served with the airborne forces, commanded 12th Parachute Battalion on the Rhine Crossing and was awarded the DSO in 1945.

In 1946 he commanded 5th Parachute Brigade, in 1948 the Airborne Forces Depot in Aldershot and, in 1950, 16 Parachute Brigade. One of the brigade's duties under his command was to guard a new road being constructed to link the garrison at Suez to a water purification plant outside the port. Three houses had to be blown up to prevent their use by snipers and bomb-throwers threatening the installations.

Before being posted to Cyprus Darling served in 1957 as Deputy Director of Staff Duties at the War Office. Afterwards he became Director of Infantry, from 1960 to 1962, then went to Germany as General Officer Commanding, 1st British Corps. In this post he made use of closed circuit television in Signals exercises. "It will absolutely revolutionise the system of control at a commander's head-quarters," he said from his command caravan. Darling proceeded next to GOC-in-C Southern Command, United Kingdom, where he opined: "The strategic reserve is like a supermarket. The customer can obtain a variety of skills, from those of a general to a bulldozer driver."

From 1967 to his retirement in 1969 he was Commander-in-Chief, Allied Forces Northern Europe. Darling was Colonel of the Royal Fusiliers (City of London Regiment) from 1963 and, after its amalgamation in 1968, Colonel of the Royal Regiment of Fusiliers, until 1974. He was also Colonel Commandant of the Parachute Regiment from 1965 to 1967. During the Falklands war Darling blamed the press for giving away strategic information. "Had the Argentine junta a liaison officer in the Ministry of Defence," he said, "it could hardly have obtained more information about our operations."

Ken Darling was appointed CBE in 1959 and KCB in 1963. In 1968 he was appointed ADC General to the Queen. He married, in 1941, Pamela Denison-Pender, who died in 1990.

CHEF CAPORAL
JAMES WORDEN

James Worden (whose death was recorded on January 27 1999 aged 75) served for seven years in the French Foreign Legion; he saw action against the "Fell" rebel forces in Algeria in the 1960s and later became the historian of the Legion's British association.

In his entertaining and fluently written auto-biography, *Wayward Legionnaire* (1988), Worden stated that his reason for joining the Legion in 1959 was not to seek adventure but to find the anonymity and refuge denoted by the force's motto, *Legio Patria Nostra* (the Legion is our homeland). Aged 36, Worden had already fought with the RAF in the Second World War, and had to pretend to be younger than he was to be accepted at the Legion's recruitment depot at Marseilles.

Many of the other recruits were Germans, some of them SS veterans. British volunteers had the highest desertion rate of any nation represented in the Legion, and new English recruits received tough treatment from the instructors at the Legion's Algerian base, Sidi-el-Abbes. Tuition in French was accompanied by kicks to the backside as an aide-memoire; push-ups were done clapping hands between each repetition, while wearing a rucksack laden with rocks. Worden completed his training successfully, somewhat to his surprise, since he was both older than the other recruits and a dedicated smoker.

His survival was due in large part to his ability to

bend rules and regulations. Almost his first act on joining the Legion was surreptitiously to swap his over-large fatigues for those of the adjutant. He became an expert scrounger and fixer, and was able to supplement his sparse existence with winnings at poker. After one marathon session of 20 hours, he rose from the table having won more than £2,600. The greater part of it was subsequently blown in the regimental bordello.

Having deliberately failed a radio mechanics' course to ensure he was posted to a combat unit, Worden then served for almost three years with the 3rd Infantry Regiment. Much time was spent hunting down pockets of the Algerian Army of National Liberation, or the "Fell", based in the Aures mountains. The legionnaires' patrols usually lasted 10 days, sleeping rough and moving fast. They rarely took prisoners, and once they scented the Fell they would drop their packs and close in for the kill at a run. Worden narrowly survived when surprised once by two rebels during his morning visit to the bushes. He was saved, he said, by the sudden burst of wind the fright brought on, the volume of which startled the intruders.

Conditions in the mountains were harsh but, Worden recalled, "after struggling for five hours to reach the crest, there is no feeling in the world equal to that of looking down to see all the other silly bastards that still have a further 80-metre climb to reach you. By the time they do arrive, you have fully recovered and immediately offer a light for their cigarette." On one patrol, Worden was joined on night sentry duty by a sleepless and talkative legionnaire, whom he did not recognise. When Worden looked for the man the next day, there was no sign of him. He told his sergeant about the encounter, and was told that the soldier belonged to a unit that had been wiped out a year earlier in that very place.

In 1963, aged 40, Worden − who had been decorated several times − survived the brutal NCO selection course, completing a 20-kilometre forced march with a broken ankle before fainting. He passed second out of his group of 40, and later became a *caporal chef*, roughly equivalent to a very senior British Army sergeant. He then qualified as a parachutist and joined the Legion's crack 2nd Parachute Regiment − the 1st was disbanded after supporting the attempted coup against de Gaulle in 1961. Worden enjoyed his time as a para, being one of the select band who have opened a bottle of beer and drunk its contents between exit and landing. But his career in the Legion was brought to an abrupt end in 1965, by a jump that ended in a collision with a stone farmhouse. He was invalided out.

James William Worden was born at Bermondsey, south London, on April 1 1923 and went to school locally. At 17, he lied about his age so as to be accepted for war service by the RAFVR. He claimed to have trained as a wireless operator and air gunner, and later became a bomber pilot. He served with 114 Squadron in the Western Desert and Europe, flying 94 missions. He then had a variety of jobs in construction before joining the Legion.

After leaving it, Worden eventually returned to

Bermondsey and, in 1984, became secretary-general of the Foreign Legion Association of Great Britain, helping ex-legionnaires to find their feet. In 1996 he became the association's historian, and two years later was presented with a citation recognising his work by the Legion's senior officer, General de Division Christian Piquemal. "To those," Worden wrote, "who have a son, a brother, a sweetheart in the Legion, I say: 'Do not fear for his well-being. Be proud you know a man who is serving alongside men. Life in the Legion is hard, but life is hard anyway'."

Four legionnaires carried the coffin at his funeral. He never married.

MAJOR
BILL DAVIDSON

Major Bill Davidson (who died on November 17 1998, aged 81) was awarded an MC while serving with the Queen's Own Cameron Highlanders during the bitter fighting around Kohima and in the subsequent drive to open up the road to Imphal in Burma. Between April and June 1944, the Japanese made a desperate attempt to break through the British defences in India.

During that period, Davidson was in continuous command of B Company, and although wounded insisted on remaining with them – "setting," as his citation proclaimed, "a magnificent example throughout the battle". Between November 15 1944 and February 15 1945, the 1st Camerons fought one major and several minor actions, and in every case B Company, under Davidson, distinguished itself.

On the night of January 3 1945, the battalion was ordered to form a bridgehead across the Mu River to the south of Yeu. Wading neck-deep through the strong current, Davidson's men established a small lodgement with minimum loss, enabling the remainder of 5th Brigade to cross without inter-ference, thus outflanking and finally capturing Yeu. "This officer's conduct throughout has deserved the highest praise," Davidson's citation concluded. When wounded in the shoulder by a shell splinter at Kohima, Davidson had stood in the open, stripped to the waist in pouring rain, with shells dropping close by, and had a dressing put on – all the while continuing to give orders to his platoon until the situation clarified. The shell splinter was later removed under anaesthetic by the medical officer.

During the Burma campaign, the Cameron Highlanders had been forbidden to play their pipes when in contact with the Japanese, as this might give away the identity of the unit to the enemy. However, in the final stages, Davidson decided to ignore this instruction. He ordered his piper, David Laidlaw, to play the regimental marches 'The Cameron Men' and 'Black Donald's War March' as the company attacked and briskly disposed of the enemy. (David Laidlaw was a relation of the Daniel Laidlaw who had been awarded a VC at the Battle of Loos in 1915, when he had continued to play though wounded and with a number of Germans shooting at him.)

Everyone who encountered Davidson in Burma was convinced that an immediate DSO would have been a more appropriate award than an MC for his exploits.

William Dunkeld Davidson was born on December 10 1916 and educated at the Royal High School, Edinburgh, and Edinburgh University, before joining the legal firm, Mill, Macleod and Rose. He was commissioned into the Queen's Own Cameron Highlanders (79th Foot) in 1940 and posted to the 1st Battalion. He was soon in great demand as a defending officer at courts martial – which are held under English law, even in the case of a Scottish soldier being tried in Scotland. Davidson made a point of taking the oath in Scots form, enjoying the flurry of activity that this imposed on the Captain of the Court, who was not always familiar with it.

In 1942 Davidson sailed for the Far East. Following prolonged training in India he was sent with his regiment into action against the Japanese.

After the war, Davidson returned to the law, became a Writer to the Signet, and a partner of his Edinburgh firm. He was greatly respected for basing his charges on what he thought his client could afford, not on what he thought could be extracted. A keen hill-walker, he became secretary of the Scottish Rights of Way Society. He was also a very active secretary of the Scottish Committee of Dr Graham's Homes at Kalimpong, near Darjeeling. Dr Graham, a missionary, had set up the homes in the foothills of the Himalayas, to care for illegitimate children of Anglo-Indian parentage who had been abandoned on the streets of Calcutta – a fate which Davidson had observed for himself during his wartime service. The children are cared for, educated and then found careers outside India.

A keen rock-gardener and an expert in the cultivation and propagation of rhododendrons, Davidson and his wife created gardens at Admaddy, Argyllshire, and Langlee, near Jedburgh, which they opened to the public. He married, in 1961, Jocelyn (née Mends), daughter of Captain Robert Mends, RN, who survived him.

MAJOR-GENERAL
SIR CHARLES DUNPHIE

Major-General Sir Charles Dunphie (who died on January 9 1999, aged 96) was awarded a DSO in 1943 when commanding 26th Armoured Brigade, which held the Kasserine Pass in Tunisia after Rommel had routed the inexperienced US 2nd Corps.

In February 1943 Rommel, who had been driven back across North Africa since the Battle of Alamein in October-November 1942 and was now holding the Mareth Line, decided to switch his attention to the First Army which, since landing in North Africa the previous November, was making progress in Tunisia. At the Kasserine Pass, 2,000 Americans, who had no previous experience of Rommel's tactics, were thinly spread over three miles of difficult country where they had negligible air support owing to bad weather. They were utterly outfought by the battle-hardened Panzers.

Dunphie was ordered forward, to come under American command and use 26th Armoured Brigade to help restore the position. He arrived to find a chaotic situation, with no one knowing the location of their own or the enemy's units. When Dunphie himself went forward on a reconnaissance, he ran into a German ambush from which he was lucky to escape. The local American commander refused to believe the Germans had penetrated his position until he suddenly found out for himself.

Dunphie then took his armoured regiments forward to the head of the pass to conduct an organised fighting withdrawal, while his infantry battalions prepared a defensive position in front of Thala, at which 10th and 21st Panzers were aiming. Out-ranged and out-gunned, 26th Armoured Brigade lost many tanks as it fought a delaying action through February 21 and 22. Dunphie's command scout car was the last vehicle to move back into the defensive position, and was closely followed by four German tanks preceded by a captured Valentine.

The German tanks were quickly dispatched at point-blank range by the guns of the 17th/21st Lancers. Fighting continued until 10pm in the dark or in the light shed by burning vehicles. Shelled and machine-gunned all night, but still in their positions with every man capable of fighting at his post, the brigade waited for the inevitable dawn attack, which had to be held off at all costs. But the attack never came; Rommel had decided against continuing the offensive which had seemed potentially disastrous for the Allies. The determination and resolution of 26th Brigade under Dunphie's cool leadership had saved the day.

Charles Anderson Lane Dunphie was born on April 20 1902, the elder son of Sir Alfred Dunphie, a director of Coutts Bank and Queen Alexandra's Comptroller. Hoping for a naval career, young Charles was educated at Osborne and Dartmouth; but when, in a final test, his eyesight was found to be below the required standard for the Navy, he transferred to Woolwich, from which he was commissioned into the Royal Artillery in 1921.

Posted to India in 1924, he enjoyed a full military and sporting life with polo, pig-sticking and shooting. He was awarded his jacket in 1927, and served with Mercer's Troop at Meerut. In 1935 Dunphie attended the Staff College, Camberley. Subsequently, he spent a year in Gibraltar, became a GSO2 in 1st Armoured Division, fought in France in 1940, and was evacuated from Cherbourg. He was mentioned in despatches during the campaign. In 1942 he was appointed to command 20th Armoured Brigade, but was then switched to 26th Armoured Brigade for the North African landings.

After the Kasserine battles, it was decided by Eisenhower and Alexander that certain British officers should be posted to 2nd US Corps to assist the Americans while they found their fighting feet. Dunphie was appointed Chief of Staff to General George Patton, who greeted him with the warning: "I think you ought to know, I don't like Brits."

Patton later became a firm friend, and when award-ing Dunphie the Silver Star he cut the ribbon for it from his own tunic. Dunphie always valued the ribbon more than the Star itself. Later, Dunphie was wounded. After recovery, when Patton had left to plan the Sicily invasion, Dunphie returned to 2nd US Corps to serve with General Omar Bradley, with whom he also developed a warm, mutually respectful relationship.

In late 1943, Dunphie was recalled to England to become Deputy Director, Royal Armoured Corps, and then Director General, Armoured Fighting Vehicles. Determined that the British Army should not have to go to war with tanks which were out-performed by their enemies, he played a large part in the introduction of the Centurion tank, which was to be the backbone of the Royal Armoured Corps in the immediate post-war period.

In 1948 he was offered command of a division, but was also approached by Lieutenant-General Sir Ronald Weeks to join Vickers, which in the 25 years after the war was the holding company of a vast empire that included ship building, aircraft con-struction and engineering and steel. The whole organisation was operated principally by the executive company Vickers-Armstrong, of which Dunphie became managing director in 1952. The following year he also took on Vickers-Armstrong Aircraft, becoming chairman in 1955. He became chairman of Vickers in 1962. Under his leadership, the company built many warships for the Royal Navy, including the first generation of nuclear-powered submarines. Vickers also manufactured torpedoes and tanks, the RAF Swift, Valiant and TSR2, and commercial aircraft such as the Viscount, Vanguard and VC10.

With no engineering qualifications, but possessing a sharp brain, considerable charm and the ability to refine problems to their essentials, Dunphie was able to preside over a team of strong, varied characters and to get on well with them. He was a director of the Westminster Bank, a member of the Court of the Royal Exchange, and a governor of Sherborne School. He was also a keen and able fisherman, a good shot and a strong supporter of family racing, stud and farming interests. Dunphie was appointed CBE in 1942, CB in 1948, and was knighted in 1959; he was a member of the Queen's Bodyguard, the Honourable Corps of Gentlemen-at-Arms, from 1952 to 1962. He was a commander of the US Legion of Merit.

A big man in every sense of the word, Charles Dunphie was an excellent raconteur, with a remarkable memory and a fine sense of humour. He had a zest for life which he imparted to others. He married first, in 1931, Eileen, the daughter of Lieutenant-General Sir Walter Campbell; she died in 1978. They had a son and a daughter. He married secondly, in 1981, Susan, the widow of Colonel Percy Wright.

MAJOR
HERBERT WARBURTON

Major Herbert Warburton (who died on January 29 1999, aged 82) distinguished himself during the Second World War as an Army observation pilot in North Africa, Italy and Burma. After the Operation Torch landings at Algiers in French North Africa in 1942, "Warby" – a nickname which reflected his warm and colourful personality – was quickly in action spotting artillery with 651 Squadron.

It was a perilous occupation, pottering about over enemy positions in a fragile, unarmed, single-engined Auster that seemed more suited to a flying club than to the hazards of war. Derived from the American Taylorcraft, this light monoplane cruised no faster than 100mph, and was restricted to a range of 250 miles. As the First Army made its bold but unsuccessful dash for Tunis, there was a constant demand from Air Observation Post (AOP) crews for tactical information.

Careless of the risk, Warburton circled enemy positions and directed artillery fire. Constantly attacked by enemy fighters, he was also highly vulnerable to ground fire. But Warburton became known as "The Artful Dodger", so canny was he in manoeuvring his Auster until German pilots were forced to break off their attacks for lack of fuel; it was jokingly said that since he was as short as he was broad, the bullets always went over his head. Warburton was awarded the Croix de Guerre in recognition of the operations he had flown in support of the Free French 19 Corps around d'Oum El Abouab, where his courageous observation in the face of enemy fire made possible the destruction of an ammunition dump and artillery battery.

Herbert Bradley Warburton was born at Amersham, Buckinghamshire, on July 26 1916, and educated at Hymers College, Hull. While still at school he learned to fly with the Hull Flying Club. Afterwards he joined the Civil Air Guard and the Blackburn Aircraft Company. On the outbreak of the Second World War, Warburton enlisted in the Royal Artillery, and in 1940 was commissioned as a second lieutenant in the 52nd Anti-Tank Regiment.

He volunteered as an AOP pilot and, after being awarded his Army flying badge in 1942, was posted in the rank of captain to 651 Squadron. The next year, after the end of the Tunisian campaign, Warburton, by now a flight commander, moved to Sicily and Italy. Posted home in 1944, Warburton qualified as a flying instructor at the Central Flying School. The next year he joined 656, a sister AOP squadron, taking part both in its support of the 14th Army in Burma and in Operation Zipper, the liberation of Malaya and Singapore. Following a brief spell as an instructor at the RAF Staff College, Warburton returned to the Far East, where he commanded 656 in the messy attempt to help the Dutch recover their East Indies colonies, much against the wishes of the Indonesian people. He was awarded the DFC in 1947.

Amid the chaos and general sense of frustration, Warburton raised spirits by declaring a weekly "Swiss

Navy Day", when officers were encouraged to wear caps back to front and to drive their jeeps in reverse. While sharing an airfield with a Spitfire squadron, he was piqued by a young RAF pilot who bragged that soldiers flying Austers would stand no chance against a well-handled fighter aircraft. Warburton challenged the young blood to a dogfight, and in a dazzling display of evasive flying made a complete ass of him in front of spectators from the station. That night he ostentatiously wore his spectacles, and fumbled his way to the bar, where the drinks were on the RAF.

On his way home to be demobilised, Warburton served briefly in Palestine with his former squadron, 651. In civilian life, he ran the family shop Warby's Wine Store for a while, but fretted to return to the service. His opportunity came with the outbreak of the Korean War, when he was posted to 1903 AOP Flight. He returned to Malaya in command of 656 Squadron, where his experience and unconventional command – especially with his flight's Austers – contributed crucially to the defeat of jungle guerrillas. He was appointed MBE. At much the same time, his Auster floatplane trials off Singapore, which involved take-off runs of up to a mile, indicated his potential as an experimental pilot.

Much of Warburton's operational success was due to his gift for bringing on new pilots. They might find him forbidding at first, but they soon recognised his incomparable experience, innate kindness and generosity of spirit. Warburton returned home as a major to command 663 AOP Squadron of the Royal Artillery Air Force at Liverpool, before training in

America in 1957 as a helicopter pilot. Subsequently he joined the Joint Experimental Helicopter Unit at Middle Wallop as a trials pilot, flying Whirlwinds and Sycamores, and became a founder member of the Army Air Corps. As part of his work developing Army helicopters, he helped to introduce the troubled Scout helicopter into service.

While second-in-command of the helicopter test squadron at Boscombe Down, he tested an open seated Wallis–Benson auto gyro for altitude, wearing an Irvine jacket, muffler and thick boots. An astonished Boeing 707 pilot called the Wiltshire experimental station and reported he had just passed under a teddy bear flying a curious motorcycle at 11,000 feet. Warburton also undertook high-risk icing trials with the Wessex helicopter at Fort Churchill on Hudson's Bay, and was attached to the Royal Norwegian Air Force to advise on them.

After a spell working on the Lynx helicopter and other projects at Army Aviation HQ, Warburton retired in 1971 as the second-longest serving Army pilot. But there was no break from helicopters. Warburton immediately joined Ferranti Helicopters as flight operations manager at Gatwick, and held similar posts with British Caledonian and British Airways. When he finally retired, his career had embraced 42 fixed-wing and 24 rotary types, involving respectively 4,075 and 2,200 hours flying.

Latterly, Warburton enjoyed trout fishing on the Wiltshire Avon, though his activities were restricted by bronchial problems deriving from his time in the desert. In 1974 he was elected Freeman of the Guild of Air Pilots and Air Navigators, and the next year he received a Ministry of Defence award for his work on the Scout and the invention of the Warby Weight Computer. Warburton was also a Fellow of the Royal Aeronautical Society. In addition to his wartime medals, he was thrice mentioned in despatches. Warby Warburton was survived by his wife Joan.

LIEUTENANT-COLONEL "TISHY" BENSON

Lieutenant-Colonel "Tishy" Benson (who died on March 3 1999, aged 95) was awarded a DSO at Anzio in February 1944 when commanding 78th Field Regiment, RA. During the most critical period, when the Allied hold on the beach-head was still precarious, 78th Field gave continuous and effective support to the infantry. Benson was considered to have been largely responsible for saving what at times appeared to be a critical situation. According to his citation, it was Benson who, from a forward position, co-ordinated the fire of the beach-head artillery on the massed German attacks. "He was apparently a man without fear."

Two years earlier in the Western Desert Benson had been wounded, and had only narrowly escaped capture. He was then second-in-command of 11th Field Regiment, which unexpectedly ran into a German force of some 35 tanks at El Agheila. As they fought desperately in this uneven contest, casualties in men and tanks mounted quickly. Five German tanks, nonetheless, were destroyed in the opening phase, and Benson and a fellow officer, Lieutenant Drage, took over a 25-pounder gun whose crew had all been killed or wounded. The two men continued to fire, though they could neither elevate nor traverse it and the sights had been shot away. As they shot their last round each received a bullet in the leg.

Ordered to withdraw, Benson and Drage crawled towards an ammunition lorry about to move off, but before they reached it, a direct hit sent it up in flames. As a group of enemy tanks breasted the ridge and ran down the line of shattered tanks, spraying them with bullets, Benson and Drage dropped in their tracks. The tanks passed within three yards of them sprawled in the sand, and left them for dead. The two men began to hobble back through enemy lines to where they thought their own troops might be. They encountered a party of Senussi who gave them food and blankets and directions, and as they made their painful way on, wearing the blankets and hoping that any Germans they encountered would assume they were Arabs, they ran into a Rifle Brigade patrol in Bren carriers, on which they were then evacuated. Benson at first refused to have his leg wound treated in the hospital, and carried on until complications made hospital unavoidable.

However, two months later he returned to action as commander of 78th Field Regiment, which he led through the rest of the North African campaign, in Sicily and at Reggio before being sent to support the Anzio landings. Soon after Anzio, Benson was badly wounded and was evacuated to England.

The son of an Army officer John Roxby Erle Benson was born on July 23 1903. He entered Wellington at the same time as Eric Blair (George Orwell), who a year later departed for Eton on a King's Scholarship. From Wellington − where, for reasons now obscure, Benson had acquired the nickname "Tishy" − he went to Woolwich, from which he was commissioned into the Royal Artillery in 1923. Between the wars, he attended the equitation course at Weedon, and served with 94th Field Regiment (Queen's Own Dorset Regiment), TA, as adjutant. He became a battery commander in 11th (HAC) Regiment Royal Horse Artillery in August 1941. He retired from the Army in 1950.

A small, neat man, of elegant appearance, "Tishy" Benson was described by all who knew him as being "brave as a lion". His laconic, laid-back approach disguised great efficiency. He was much admired and liked for his frequent presence in forward and highly dangerous posts, giving constant encouragement. A keen sportsman, Benson enjoyed fishing, shooting, hunting and bridge. He was a successful amateur rider before and after the war, and in 1969 won the Royal Artillery Gold Cup on Solimyth.

Benson had little time for what he considered to be unreasonable orders. Early on in the war, he wrote to the War Office to claim forage allowance for his charger, ignoring an earlier order that the horse should be destroyed. He had a slight drawl and an infectious chuckle, easy for his troops to imitate. Modest and reticent, he disliked talking about his exploits, which included recovering the bodies of two of his officers from a minefield in Italy. He was always friendly and hospitable. Benson was unmarried.

———

MAJOR
JOHN HOWARD

Major John Howard (who died on May 5 1999, aged 86) was awarded a DSO in June 1944 for leading the successful glider-born assault which captured the Pegasus Bridge over the Caen Canal and the Horsa Bridge over the River Orne at Benouville.

Their possession was vital to the second phase of General Montgomery's plan, not only to protect the left flank of the Normandy bridgehead and enable reinforcements to reach the main airborne forces, but also to provide an exit route when the moment for an armoured break-out past Caen should arrive. In addition, the Germans had already wired the bridges for demolition as part of their defensive plan, and it was essential to seize them before the charges could be blown. As they were small, heavily defended targets and there was a strong crosswind, it was an astonishing feat to crash-land the gliders near them, capture the bridges and then defend them against counter-attacks.

Shortly before 11pm on D-Day minus one, June 5 1944, Howard and four platoons of the Oxfordshire and Buckinghamshire Light Infantry, part of 6th Airborne Division, packed themselves into six Horsa gliders ready to be towed across the Channel by Halifax bombers. "It was a hazy moonlit night," Howard later recalled. "At 1,000 ft we opened the glider's doors. The most amazing sight was those wonderful Normandy horses and cattle. They were grazing very quietly, as though nothing was happening, although a lot of bombers were going overhead."

The operation went almost faultlessly. At six minutes past midnight, Howard and his men landed silently 50 yards away from the canal bridge just outside the small hamlet of Benouville near Caen. On arriving at the bridge they took a German pillbox by surprise; the two sentries later told him they had been paralysed with fear when they saw the blackened faces and guns of the assault force. Within 10 minutes both bridges had been captured. They then held the bridges until joined by men from the 7th Battalion of the 5th Parachute Regiment. At 1.30pm on June 6 they were relieved by Commandos led by Lord Lovat, who apologised for being two and a half minutes late.

Howard then moved his men on to take part in the fighting around Escoville, where a sniper's bullet went through his helmet but only grazed his skull. Later he was wounded by shrapnel in his back, although he was not aware of it at the time. Covered in blood, he was thought by his comrades to be dead. Told by a doctor he must be evacuated, he lay on a stretcher, but the medics were extremely busy; Howard became so bored that he got up, recovered his shirt and went back to his unit, which had now lost nearly half its men.

They had devoted much energy to training for the operation, after first being briefed about it on April 16. But they could not predict the appalling weather which caused many other gliders to crash into the Channel, and parachutists to be dropped far from their allotted dropping zones. They were prepared for the eventuality of capture by having silk escape maps sewn into their battledress, tiny com-passes concealed in their buttons and were also given steel files to cut through the bars of prison windows.

Howard later attributed the success of the operation to this training and to the bravery of the glider pilots. "I can't exactly say I wasn't afraid," he said, "but I was very confident. We'd trained ourselves silly for months before. Our glider pilots were wonderful chaps: when they saw on the aerial photos that the only fields near the bridges had been sown with anti-glider poles, or what looked like poles, they said that would be all the better; they'd go in between them and the wings would get torn off, but would take the worst of the shock of landing. You couldn't be too afraid, going over with men like that."

John Howard was born at Camden Town, London, on December 8 1912, the eldest of nine children. His father was a cooper, and as the eldest child, John had to give up some of his time to looking after the younger members of his family; however, he managed to join the Boy Scouts. Despite winning a scholarship which would have taken him on to further education, he left school at 14 to work as a stockbroker's runner, but continued his education by attending evening classes until the firm collapsed in 1931.

As jobs were hard to find, Howard then enlisted in the King's Shropshire Light Infantry, where he was successful at swimming, boxing and cross country running, and rose to the rank of sergeant. At the end of his military engagement in 1938 he joined the City of Oxford police, but in 1939 he was recalled to the KSLI, winning rapid promotion to become acting regimental sergeant-major. He was then selected for officer training, and commissioned into the Oxford and Bucks. He chose that regiment because he had enjoyed his time in Oxford.

When the War Office announced that its 2nd Battalion was to be converted to a glider-born unit, he volunteered, although it meant dropping a rank from captain to lieutenant. However, he was soon promoted to major in command of D company, which was assigned to capture the Benouville bridges. Two months after that mission, when on leave in England, Howard was badly injured when the jeep he was driving was hit by a queue-jumping truck approaching an American convoy. His right hip and both his legs were smashed, and he was invalided out of the Army.

After the war, Howard worked briefly with National Savings, and then for the Ministry of Agriculture, first in Nottingham, and then as Divisional Executive Officer covering Cornwall and the Isles of Scilly. "It's a quiet life", he said, "but it suits me. I have to do quite a bit of travelling around in the open air."

In 1962, Howard's role in the war was made famous in the film *The Longest Day*, in which he was portrayed by the actor Richard Todd. He returned regularly to Benouville on the anniversary of D-Day to lay a wreath at the site where the gliders landed and to host a dinner for his men. He was present in 1995 when a bust representing him was unveiled there.

Reflecting in old age on the events of 1944, Howard remarked: "We were given a job to do on the day, and we did it. We were very proud to do that job and if I held that bridge as long as I did, well, I bloody well did it because it was my job." In addition to his DSO he was also awarded the Croix de Guerre with palm. John Howard was a strong character, always extremely energetic, and a keen gardener. He was in constant demand as a speaker.

He married, in 1939, Joy Bromley, who predeceased him. They had a son and a daughter.

SERGEANT
"TEX" BANWELL

Sergeant "Tex" Banwell (who died on July 28 1999, aged 81) officially impersonated General Montgomery, served in the Western Desert, and was captured during a raid on Crete; he escaped, subsequently took part in the Battle of Arnhem, was wounded and taken prisoner; he escaped again, joined the Dutch resistance, was captured, tortured and put in front of a mock firing squad by the Gestapo before being imprisoned at Auschwitz.

Although weighing less than half his normal

weight when liberated, Banwell parachuted out of aircraft more than 1,000 times "for fun".

Keith Demer Banwell, known as "Tex", was born on October 8 1917 and began his military life with the Coldstream Guards. He then transferred to the 1st Battalion, Royal Hampshire Regiment, which was serving on the North-West Frontier of India at a time of considerable turbulence. In 1938, the battalion moved to Palestine, where they were engaged in counter-terrorist duties. The following year the Hampshires went to Egypt, where they were joined by members of the French Foreign Legion, to whom Banwell became a physical training instructor; the French were tough, but Banwell was tougher.

Soon afterwards, volunteers were required for an unspecified new force. Tex Banwell answered the call and found himself in 52 Middle East Commando. A shortage of shipping, however, hampered seaborne raiding by the Commandos and Banwell found himself captured in a raid on Tobruk; nevertheless, with a friend, he managed to steal a German vehicle and escape. During a subsequent raid on Crete, he was taken prisoner at Heraklion and put under the personal supervision of Max Schmeling, (the world heavyweight boxing champion from 1930 to 1932), who was serving in the German army.

Banwell and a few of his comrades managed to slip away from their captors and acquire an assault landing craft. With the help of some Cretan fishermen they made their getaway, but the craft ran out of fuel and drifted for nine days before reaching the North African coast. The privations of this voyage put Banwell in hospital for 12 weeks. When he had recovered, someone noticed that he bore a resemblance to General Montgomery.

It was decided that he should participate in deception ploys, and so Banwell was sent to Cairo to meet Montgomery, given the appropriate clothing, insignia and general's badges and sent on trips around the Middle East to confuse enemy spies. However, as he was considerably taller than Montgomery, he was told that on no account should he get out of the car. Banwell, finding the assignment boring, requested a return to the infantry. Here he was introduced to parachuting and soon joined what became the 10th Battalion of the Parachute Regiment, with whom he had many successes at regimental boxing and cross-country running.

In September 1944, Banwell flew into Arnhem in a Dakota carrying 15 parachutists, of whom six were killed when the aircraft was hit by enemy fire. Banwell himself landed safely and fought throughout the battle until he was wounded and once more taken prisoner by the Germans. He subsequently escaped by jumping from a moving train as it entered Germany, and linked up with the Dutch Resistance, for whom he became an instructor in weapons and explosives.

He led one of their most successful raids, but while escorting a small party of escaping prisoners was again captured. The Germans considered that as he was living with the Resistance he had forfeited his military status and, after a court martial, sentenced him to death. He was told, however, that if he disclosed the names of his Resistance contacts he would be reprieved. When Banwell refused, he was placed in front of a firing squad, which was given all the orders except the one to fire. He was then sent back to his cell until the following morning, when he was told that this time he really would be shot. The next day the horrific ritual was again enacted, this time with the squad firing blanks. After this, Banwell was taken to the Auschwitz concentration camp where, to make him talk, he was kept in a six foot square cage and starved.

When the camp was eventually liberated by the Russians, Banwell determined to become fully fit again and joined 11 Para (TA) before moving to 10 Para when it was reformed. But on one parachute jump he landed badly, was declared dead and taken to the mortuary. There the attendant noticed a flutter of one eyelid and successfully resuscitated him.

In 1984 Banwell made his 1,000th jump at Arnhem on the 40th anniversary of the battle. He went on to jump again on the 50th anniversary in 1994, at the age of 77. Banwell also became a member of the 10th Battalion cross-country team which won the Eastern Command Cup for six successive years. He was a second Dan black belt at judo, held the record for the 10th Battalion road walk from Birmingham to London, and marched from London to Brighton in ten and a half hours. Banwell also marched from John O'Groats to Land's End in full Army kit, wearing standard issue leather boots with no socks in them, and represented 10 Para in the Westminster to Devizes canoe race five times. His only unfulfilled ambition was to ride in the Grand National.

At the end of his Territorial Army service, Banwell served in the Special Constabulary. He was awarded a BEM in 1969, and in 1992 the Netherlands Silver Cross for his services to the Dutch resistance movement.

Tex Banwell was survived by his wife Ann, and by a son and two daughters from a previous marriage.

MAJOR
EDWARD THOMAS

Major Edward Thomas (who died on August 5 1999, aged 84) was awarded an immediate MC in May 1941 for his conduct in the fierce action at Halfaya Pass in North Africa. The defile between Egypt and Libya at Halfaya, known to the British as "Hellfire", was held by a battalion of British infantry and a few tanks, with 260 Battery, RA, in support.

On May 26 they were attacked by the Germans in great strength. Outnumbered and outgunned, the British inflicted many casualties but sustained heavy losses. As the higher command did not realise the position was untenable, the order to withdraw was delayed. Thomas was sent up to the head of the pass with one gun. Finding all the officers of 260 Battery had been killed or severely wounded, he took command of the battery and arranged the evacuation of the wounded.

When he then encountered 100 leaderless men from the Royal Indian Army Service Corps, he took over their trucks, and drove the survivors of the battle to safety through the enemy lines. This involved going through a camp which the Germans had just established under the impression that all resistance had ceased. This was the first time Thomas had been under enemy fire, and he had no idea that his actions had been in any way out of the ordinary. So when he was summoned to appear before General Erskine, he went in trepidation, fearing that he was going to face a court martial for some inadvertent misdemeanour. His MC came as a great surprise.

Edward Thomas was born on April 15 1915 and educated at Emanuel School, London, before becoming a surveyor. He joined the TA and was commissioned into the Norfolk Yeomanry, which in the war was trained in an anti-tank role. After the Halfaya battle, Thomas was seconded to the Sudan Defence Force and spent the rest of the war in the Sudan and Abyssinia, rising to the temporary rank of Khamakam (Brigadier). He became fluent in Arabic, and administered large areas of Libya from Kufra Oasis.

At the end of the war, he was invited to stay on by both Emperor Haile Selassie and the King of Libya, but decided to return to England and the family property business, which he developed successfully. In middle age, Thomas became a dedicated horseman and a popular joint master of the Hampshire Hunt. At the age of 60, bronchitis prompted him to settle in Spain, where his enthusiasm for life and generosity made him much loved by friends. Edward Thomas was survived by his wife, Ruth, and by their two sons.

MAJOR
JACK PRINGLE

Major Jack Pringle (who died on November 9 1999, aged 84) was one of the very few officers to be awarded an MC for his repeated escapes from prisoner-of-war camps during the Second World War. Having been taken prisoner at Sidi Rezegh in North Africa in 1941, Pringle was held in 11 different camps for the remainder of the war and escaped six times. His most remarkable feat was to escape from the Italian prison fortress of Gavi, in Liguria.

No one had ever escaped from Gavi in the 600 years of its existence, but Pringle discovered a shaft which led to an underground reservoir, and from there he burrowed – with much difficulty – through an outside wall. During his period of incarceration he had managed to make contact with local resistance groups and to send back valuable information in coded letters for the Allied forces. Having escaped, he posed variously as a Greek, as a German deserter and as a Croat, but was eventually recaptured five miles from the Swiss frontier, where he was napping in some bushes.

John Courtright Pringle was born on December 12 1914 in America, where his family were then living. He went to school there and then to Harvard

University, which he left after a month in order to go to Sandhurst. His family had a tradition of producing cavalry officers, and he had been recommended for a place at Sandhurst by the Governor-General of Canada.

It was there that his eventful career began. He recalled being invited to a fancy-dress ball in London, and finding that the theatrical costumier could only dress him up as a potato, all other garments having already been hired out. Duly attired, he presented himself at the house where the dance was being held – only to find out that he had arrived a week early. However, his fortunes prospered at Sandhurst and he was commissioned into the 8th King's Royal Irish Hussars, whom he joined in Cairo.

This posting enabled him to play polo three days a week, and eventually to reach a handicap of seven – an idyllic existence briefly broken by a six-month tour in Palestine dealing with Arab terrorists. In 1939 the expense of living in Cairo and playing regular polo was proving too much for Pringle's precarious finances, so he obtained a temporary secondment to the elite 2nd Nigeria Regiment of the Royal West African Frontier Force at Kano, where the pay was higher and life was less expensive. Since the regiment was in barracks two miles outside Kano Pringle managed to play polo quite cheaply; he also used his time learning Italian from records, in the belief that Britain would soon be at war with Italy.

When the regiment was posted to East Africa, he was transferred to the King's African Rifles, joining the East Africa Armoured Car Regiment, in which he became a squadron leader. The squadron sergeant-major had been the fag of Pringle's uncle at Harrow; he had been a regular officer, but had served a prison sentence for shooting his CO who had discovered that the man had been having an affair with his wife. "He had been an alcoholic but had given it up for the duration," Pringle remembered. "I could not have gotten on without him." One troop leader was a white hunter, another was a charming remittance man.

When war came, Pringle's squadron led 12th Division into Somaliland and Abyssinia, fought in various actions and lost a third of its strength, killed or wounded. Pringle was awarded his first MC, for his leadership. Afterwards he returned to the 8th Hussars. Pringle was then posted to Egypt, and in the advance to relieve Tobruk in November 1941 was involved in the ferocious battles for the Sidi Rezegh airfield. He was then captured by a tank detachment of the Afrika Korps.

Having been taken to Italy in a submarine, he was interned at Brindisi and other Italian prisons, and then sent to Austria and Germany. "Being moved around resulted from being a nuisance," he explained, "or from having escaped." Consequently, Pringle travelled 3,000 miles as a PoW and a further 1,000 miles as an escapee. On one occasion, he disguised himself as a woman and jumped off a moving train, but soon afterwards, when passing some guards, his trouser leg unrolled and slipped below his skirt, leading to his immediate arrest. After more escape attempts he was sent to the punishment prison at Gavi.

Later, after transfer to Innsbruck, he escaped from a train in company with David Stirling, founder of the SAS. When they encountered German police on a motorcycle and sidecar Pringle jabbered away in Italian having told Stirling, who knew no Italian, to whistle *Lili Marlene*. Unfortunately, Stirling remained silent, confessing later that he had been unable to remember the tune on the spur of the moment. They got away with that, but Pringle was later betrayed and captured in a farmhouse. Following more prisons, he was interned in Colditz Castle, from which he was eventually liberated by the American 273rd Regiment.

In 1946, Pringle, whose heart had been affected by his privations, left the Army. He worked for a time as a businessman in South Africa and Portugal, played polo and instructed less experienced players as well as schooling polo ponies. He also lectured to the SAS and rode to hounds. In spite of his affability and iron determination, Jack Pringle was a modest, imaginative man who understood other people's difficulties.

Although his grandfather, Sir John Pringle, had owned 159,000 acres in Jamaica, Pringle was never well off. He became fluent in several languages and enjoyed history. In 1988 he published a book of reminiscences, *Colditz Last Stop*.

In earlier days his name was linked with the Woolworth's heiress Barbara Hutton. Later he married Virginia Nicholson, who had previously been married (as his first wife) to Orson Welles. She and a son predeceased him. Jack Pringle was survived by a daughter and a step-daughter.

COLONEL
BRIAN COOMBE

Colonel Brian Coombe (who died on December 19 1999, aged 78) was awarded a George Medal for his actions in Cyprus in 1955 when he was ambushed by terrorists on a road through mountainous countryside.

Although remote, the road was considered "safe", and Coombe was on the way to visit a detachment when a burst of machine-gun fire suddenly killed his driver. Coombe jumped out, climbed a spur and looked for the attackers, who were in a group below, 30 yards away. He had only two magazines of ammunition for his gun, and after he had fired both the terrorists were still unscathed. The range of his revolver was too short to be effective, but then he remembered that the dead driver had had a Sten gun and ammunition.

As he went down to collect it, the terrorists stayed in their position. Coombe then climbed the hill again, worked round to the back of them and opened fire. Three of the men walked out with their hands up, shouting "Don't shoot", but when he moved forward to take their surrender, a fourth opened up with a machine-gun from a hidden position in a gully. Coombe had no alternative but to shoot the three bogus surrenderers, and then turn on the machine-gunner with his remaining ammunition. He too came out to "surrender", but then dashed to the head of the gully and disappeared.

Only one of the first three terrorists was dead, so

Coombe kept the other two covered. Although he had no ammunition left they assumed he had. One talked English fluently, so Coombe asked him why he was an anti-British terrorist, pointing out that Britain had liberated Greece during the war, and saved it from a Communist takeover later; the man was unmoved. They remained in this tense situation for half an hour until a routine patrol of the Gordons came along the road and took over. The escapee, a notorious Eoka terrorist, was not captured on that occasion but was shot dead in an ambush a year later.

Brian Jackson Coombe was born on July 25 1921, the third son of the managing director of Spear and Jackson, steel manufacturers of Sheffield. He was educated at Wellington and Sheffield University. After the outbreak of war, Coombe was commissioned into the Royal Engineers, and served in North Africa and Italy. During the landings at Salerno in 1943, he was attached to the Americans and was mentioned in despatches for his courage and coolness as beachmaster. He was in a highly vulnerable position directing units to their destinations, and was constantly under fire.

After the war, Coombe took a First Class engineering degree at the Military College of Science, Shrivenham. Then came Cyprus, where the engineers' task was to build camps for the peace-keeping force. From 1968 to 1970 he was Military (and Naval) Attaché in Saigon during the Tet Offensive, when Viet Cong troops fought within the city.

After retiring from the Army in 1975, Coombe became active in good causes, and became director of the Avon County Red Cross (1982-85); he refused to take a salary until he had raised enough money to enable the charity to be self-supporting. Coombe headed the successful campaign against a bypass through the Limpley Stoke Valley, Wiltshire. He also saved the Osborne House Convalescent Home on the Isle of Wight for a time. He would never speak of his own achievements, but could galvanise others into action.

Brian Coombe was survived by his wife, Elizabeth, his daughter (who is married to General Sir Mike Jackson) and two sons.

COLONEL
RAY NIGHTINGALE

Colonel Ray Nightingale (who died on January 17 2000, aged 79) was an outstanding leader in operations against Mau Mau in the 1950s. He served in the Kenya Regiment, the King's African Rifles, the Greenjackets (60th Rifles), and the SAS, whose high standards of physical fitness he was able to meet at the age of 45. In the SAS, his wide experience of counter-terrorist warfare earned him selection as Senior Intelligence Officer, and then Operations Officer. By introducing original and unorthodox ideas, he transformed procedures and training for SAS operations and special missions.

Raymond Clephn Werner Nightingale was born on March 2 1921 at Livingstone in Northern

Rhodesia (now Zambia). His father had left Australia for Africa to fight in the Boer War, and had settled there. Ray was sent to Plumtree School, and always remembered the fear he felt going on the train over the bridge at Victoria Falls. Cecil Rhodes had decreed that the train should pause on the bridge so that passengers could enjoy the view, but Ray, who always thought the bridge was on the point of collapse, would breathe a sigh of relief when it reached the other side. Having been orphaned when he was only four and brought up by his grand-parents, at 16 he felt he should earn his own keep and left school to take up an apprenticeship as an electrician.

On the outbreak of war in 1939, Nightingale joined the Northern Rhodesian Volunteer Defence Force, but, wanting a more active part in the war, drove 1,500 miles to Kenya, where he joined the Kenya Regiment. He was seconded to the King's African Rifles and served in Abyssinia and the Somaliland campaign in 1941. By the end of the war, he was serving as a lieutenant when ill-health forced his discharge.

Nightingale became a marine engineer in Mombasa, but was recalled to the Kenya Regiment at the start of the Emergency in 1953, to earn an MBE and two mentions in despatches. He had an uncanny instinct for locating and eliminating Mau Mau gangs in the forests, and persuaded many of the terrorists to "turn" and assist the security forces. Though prepared to take any risk himself, he was extremely careful with the lives of his men, losing only two (one of them in a motor accident) in 23 months of operations.

Perhaps his most spectacular feat, though, was the capture of a cheetah. On patrol one day, he saw the animal sitting by the side of a path; he cut a forked stick from a tree, stalked it and used the stick to pin its neck to the ground. His men tied up the cheetah, and it became the regimental mascot. Nightingale was a hard taskmaster in the field, but gave his men every encouragement. He insisted they should patrol as if they themselves were Mau Mau – no shaving, smoking or talking – so that they soon looked, and smelled, like creatures of the forest. As a result they considered him infallible.

After four years in Kenya, where his intelligence gathering was said to have had a significant effect in ending the Emergency, Nightingale was seconded to Swaziland to reorganise the police who were trying, not very successfully, to cope with internal troubles. With the approach of Kenyan independence, he transferred to the 2nd Greenjackets in 1965, and in 1969 volunteered for the SAS. During the 1970s the Sultan of Oman's army was engaged in a war in Dhofar, where communist guerrillas, armed and financed through Chinese and Russian sources, were destabilising the region. Nightingale was loaned to the Sultanate as Director of Intelligence; he soon halted the infiltration of spies into Oman and, in one coup, arrested 88 Communists. He was awarded an OBE and the Star of Oman.

After retiring from the Army, Nightingale built up a library of Africana. He was also an accomplished artist and a skilled carpenter. His first wife, Moyra, whom he married in 1946, predeceased him. They had two sons. He was survived by his second wife, Pamela.

CAPTAIN
BILL HALL

Captain Bill Hall (who died on March 21 2000, aged 75) was awarded an immediate MC while commanding a troop of flail tanks at the crossing of the Molem Beek, an anti-tank obstacle near Overloon, Holland, on October 16 1944.

4 Troop, A Squadron, of the Westminster Dragoons, was equipped with Sherman tanks fitted with a revolving drum at the front. Hanging from the drum were heavy chains with a ball that flailed the ground ahead of the tracks, exploding any mines. These tanks were one of the many ingenious devices – popularly known as "The Funnies" – used by 79th Armoured Division, commanded by General Sir Percy Hobart. They had been demonstrated to General Eisenhower, but the Americans decided not to use them and in consequence suffered heavy casualties on Omaha Beach and elsewhere. Forward vision was not always possible from flail tanks, and they needed guidance by radio from the leader, who kept on course using a very accurate gyro-compass. They made an easy target for enemy gunners since in order to explode the mines ahead their speed could

not be much faster than a slow walk.

In appalling weather, over boggy ground and under continuous fire, Hall beat a path up to the bridge over the canal at Overloon, then led his squadron across, though well aware that enemy tanks were waiting on the far side and that his flanks were exposed. His was the first tank to cross the Beek, and in the ensuing battle his troop gave invaluable assistance to Allied armour and infantry. He kept the squadron leader constantly informed of the situation ahead, engaged an enemy anti-tank gun and also knocked out a German mortar position which was inflicting losses on the infantry. He also engaged a Panther tank.

Although constantly under enemy fire, Hall showed complete disregard for danger, and earned the highest praise both from his squadron leader and the commanding officer of the 4th Coldstream Guards. He had to change tanks when his own became a casualty, and the flails in his troop frequently had to be replaced after being damaged, but this did not stop them pressing on and killing 24 enemy and assisting the infantry to take 20 prisoners.

Hall, who was also mentioned twice in despatches, was in the forefront of the action at Broekhuizen the following November when his tank cleared the approaches to the town before being hit by a bazooka, which wounded him. The tank, later recovered by the Dutch authorities, is now on display in the War Museum at Overloon, complete with flails. The Dutch were particularly grateful for the liberation of their town, which lies on the west side of the Maas and was the last pocket in the area to be held by German forces.

William Sydney Hall was born on January 31 1924 and educated at Dolgellau Grammar School before joining the Army. After training at Sandhurst, he was commissioned into the Westminster Dragoons. His troop landed in France on D-Day, after a rough voyage in which he was one of the fortunate ones not to be seasick. He recalled an enormous volume of noise from gunfire as they landed and lined up before the Staffordshire Yeomanry, who were destined for Caen although they did not reach it as had been hoped. Near Pegasus Bridge, Hall's troop had to flail over a minefield, and experienced considerable trouble as parachutes discarded by Allied troops wrapped themselves around the flail chains. He was twice recommended for an MC before he received his award at Overloon.

After the war, Hall opened the very successful Bontddu Hall Hotel, on the Mawddach estuary by Dolgellau, which he ran for 40 years. Each of his three brothers also ran hotels in the area during the same period. Bill Hall was a keen golfer and was captain and later vice-president of the Royal St David's Golf Club, Harlech. He was also a prolific watercolour painter, and held many successful exhibitions. He married, in 1950, Sheila Black, daughter of the film producer Ted Black; they had a daughter.

MAJOR
DENNIS CICLITIRA

Major Dennis Ciclitira (who died on June 9 2000, aged 81) was in charge of the Special Operations Executive's operations on western Crete during the Second World War, and eventually arranged for the German surrender of the island.

Ciclitira arrived just before Christmas 1943, taking over supervision for the area around the town of Canea from Xan Fielding. Liaison with the Cretan Resistance was led by the classicist Tom Dumbabin, who from the spring of 1942 had been supervising the activities of a handful of SOE officers, among them Patrick Leigh Fermor, who were living rough with the *andartes* (guerrillas) in mountain eyries. One of Ciclitira's first important tasks was to help to organise the evacuation of Leigh Fermor after he and Billy Moss had successfully abducted the island's commandant, General Kreipe, from his staff car in April 1944.

In his book *Ill Met By Moonlight* (1950), Moss describes encountering Ciclitira in his cave hideout: "He has grown an impressive beard, which he treats with the affection of a spinster for her favourite cat, and wears an elegant sort of musical comedy costume, complete with wine-coloured cummerbund, turban and the usual trappings." Two of Ciclitira's men had already been killed by the Nazis, but despite their strenuous efforts to catch him, he managed to maintain wireless communications with Cairo and to arrange for Leigh Fermor and his prize to be picked up by motor launch.

When he arrived at the rendezvous he found Moss and Leigh Fermor flashing their torches out to sea in frantic desperation, as neither knew the Morse Code for the pre-arranged signal. Fortunately, Ciclitira did. He left with them on the boat, but subsequently returned to Crete, where he operated under the codename Dionysios.

During January 1945, the German garrison of 12,000 began to withdraw to the western end of the island, taking with them prisoners who included Costa Mitsotakis, later the Prime Minister of Greece but then an agent for the Resistance. The Germans had orders to execute all such captives, but Ciclitira managed to contact the German authorities with a view to making an exchange of prisoners. He went to the meeting with Captain Lassen of the Special Boat Section, who soon became exasperated by the horse-trading and suggested that his commando unit, who were hiding in the mountains, should play the Germans at football, with the winner to take all. This suggestion greatly amused Bishop Xirouhakis of Kydonia, who was mediating at the talks and offered to act as referee in any such match.

In the event, after Ciclitira had travelled by caique to Athens for further discussions, 36 German PoWs were exchanged for 10 Cretan agents, probably saving their lives. On May 8, he received a message to contact General Benthag, the German commander, to make arrangements for a formal surrender. Dressed in suits, he and Mitsotakis – a fluent German speaker – presented themselves at Benthag's headquarters. Preliminary terms were then agreed, but since the general could only surrender to an officer of equal rank, it was decided that he should be flown to the British HQ at Heraklion.

Benthag asked how Ciclitira proposed to contact his senior officer, and was most put out to discover that a transmitter was hidden next door to German HQ, where the volume of radio traffic concealed Ciclitira's own signals from direction-finding cars. The next evening, although the surrender had not been made public, Ciclitira and his comrades sneaked into Canea and invited their German counterparts to a party. The garrison provided them with a jazz band. Next day, Ciclitira joined in the wild celebrations that greeted the liberation.

He had one more service to perform for Crete. SOE had incurred large financial obligations on the island, but in the months that followed rampant inflation rendered the drachma worthless and the stream of gold sovereigns from Cairo dried up. Ciclitira decided to resort to speculation in olive oil, and persuaded the Navy to blockade exports from Canea to Heraklion. Having thus lowered its worth there, and correspondingly raised the price further east, he quickly bought and sold enough oil to raise the sums required.

Dennis John Ciclitira was born on August 11 1918 at the port of Patras in Greece, but grew up in Westcliff-on-Sea, Essex, where he lived all his life. His father, Demosthenes, had emigrated from Greece and set up a successful business importing dried fruit. After Wycliffe School, Ciclitira was sent out to

Greece to learn the family trade. When war came he joined the South Staffordshire Regiment, but his fluency in Greek made him a natural choice for intelligence operations in the Aegean and, in October 1942, he took over as staff officer on SOE's Cretan desk, based in Cairo. There he organised the supply of munitions to those in the field and supervised the evacuation by sea to Egypt of those for whom life in occupied territory became too hazardous.

After the war, Ciclitira returned to England and built his father's firm into a leading importer and distributor. He was chairman of the National Dried Fruit Association from 1958 to 1960, and was widely respected for his forthright dealing and integrity. Of striking looks and imposing physique, Ciclitira enjoyed bathing in the sea off Southend into his eighties. In 1991, he attended the 50th anniversary commemorations of the Battle of Crete, and four years later was honoured by the city of Athens for his wartime exploits. He remained strongly attached to Greece, where he had made lifelong friends (among them Mitsotakis) and was a frequent visitor.

Dennis Ciclitira married while on leave during the Blitz. He liked to recount how a bomb had shattered the window of the room at the Savoy where he was spending his wedding night. Ciclitira is survived by his wife Grace and by a son and daughter.

LIEUTENANT
VIVIAN BULLWINKEL

Lieutenant Vivian Bullwinkel (who died on July 3 2000, aged 84) was the sole survivor of a massacre of young nurses by Japanese soldiers in 1942, a crime which, when it came to light after the war, stirred Australians to a new pitch of anti-Japanese sentiment. A nursing sister, Vivian Bullwinkel was one of 124 women of the Australian Army Nursing Service stationed in Malaya in 1941.

Their units were attached to two brigades of Australia's 8th Division, sent to bolster the British defence. On February 12 1942, with Singapore on the point of capitulation, Vivian Bullwinkel and 64 other nurses were ordered aboard the *Vyner Brooke*, a small island freighter which was crammed with some 300 evacuees – men, women and children – bound for Sumatra or Java. For nearly two days, steaming at night, the *Vyner Brooke* gave Japanese warships and aircraft the slip. Then bombers caught her in daylight halfway down the Bangka Strait between Sumatra and Bangka Island.

Many hours later, Vivian Bullwinkel's group had propelled their boat to Bangka Island where some hundred survivors, including some British Service-men whose ship had also been sunk, were clustered on a beach. There was nothing for it but to surrender; the Japanese controlled the island. While most of the survivors headed inland to give themselves up, the nurses remained on the beach with stretcher cases and the British servicemen to await the Japanese. A contingent arrived purpose-fully. The men were marched around a nearby headland, 40 or 50 shots were heard, and the Japanese returned, cleaning their bayonets.

Next, they ordered the 22 surviving nurses, two of them wounded, together with an aged woman, to march into the sea, line abreast. It was about noon, the sea was tranquil, a light breeze played and palms lined the tropical shore. The nurses wore their grey dresses and Red Cross armbands. They knew what was to happen. Vivian Bullwinkel heard their matron, Irene Drummond, say, as they moved through the water, "Chin up girls. I'm proud of you and I love you all." A nurse said drily: "There are two things I hate in life, the Japs and the sea, and today I've got both." Vivian Bullwinkel saw no tears and heard no lament.

They were almost up to their waists when a machine-gun raked them from behind, back and forth. Vivian Bullwinkel, hit high on the left hip, was knocked over. For a long time, she allowed herself to float with the tide, to all appearances dead like the rest, until she was washed into the shallows. The beach was deserted. The bullet had gone through with no great damage. That night she slept in a large fern in the jungle lining the beach. Looking for water next day, she heard a voice ask, "Where have you been, nurse?"

It was a British soldier, Private Kinsley, who had been among stretcher cases bayoneted on the beach after the nurses were shot. He had been run through twice, but had managed to crawl away. Vivian Bullwinkel nursed him and herself as best she could for more than 10 days, fed by the women of a local village where the men were afraid to help. By then it was clear that the two would have to give themselves up and take their chances. This they did. Kinsley, who had a wife called Elsie and came from East Yorkshire, died a few days later. Vivian Bullwinkel wore a water bottle on her hip to hide the evidence of her wound.

She found herself reunited in prison camp with some other nurses who, after surviving the *Vyner Brooke*, had fallen into less brutal hands. She spent the next three-and-a-half years in a series of prison camps on Bangka Island and in Sumatra. The nurses buried eight of their companions, dead from malnutrition, ill treatment and disease. Yet the story has uplifting elements. The steadfastness of Vivian Bullwinkel and the nurses who died at the beach had an echo in the courage and comradeship that helped sustain those in the camps. Twenty-four of the *Vyner Brooke* nurses survived, and Vivian Bullwinkel gave evidence of war crimes to the Tokyo tribunal. The Japanese officer thought to have ordered the massacre committed suicide; a camp commandant was sentenced to 15 years' imprisonment.

"Bully", as she was known to friends, was 26-years-old when captured; tall, slim, with a gentle face, generous mouth, soft blue eyes and fair hair cut in a sort of Eton crop. Naturally reserved, she could nevertheless find humour sometimes when humour was scarce. Vivian Bullwinkel was born at Kapunda, South Australia, of distant German descent, on December 18 1915. She was educated in the mining city of Broken Hill, where she began her nursing career.

After the war, she rose to the top of her profession, retiring as Matron of the Queen's Memorial Infectious Diseases Hospital, Melbourne. As a Lieutenant-Colonel in the Citizen Military Forces she commanded a nurse-training unit. She played a prominent role in various civil nursing and service organisations. When in London she was invited to meet Queen Mary, who delighted her with a 40-minute conversation and a signed photograph.

Vivian Bullwinkel was appointed MBE in 1973, and an officer of the Order of Australia in 1993. She was also an Associate of the Royal Red Cross, and in 1947 was awarded the Florence Nightingale Medal, given every two years by the International Committee of the Red Cross as the highest distinction a nurse can receive.

In 1977 she married Colonel Frank Statham, of Perth, who died in 1999. In 1993 they had attended the unveiling of a memorial to the nurses who died, which had been erected at her urging on Bangka Island.

COMPANY SERGEANT-MAJOR JOHN KENNEALLY, VC

Company Sergeant-Major John Kenneally (who died on September 27 2000, aged 79) was awarded the Victoria Cross in April 1943 when serving with the 1st Battalion of the Irish Guards in the final assault on Tunis.

In order that the city be taken it was vital that The Bou, a feature which dominated the ground between Medjez el Bab and Tebourba, was captured. A Guards brigade seized a portion of it on April 27, and while a further attack was being prepared, the Irish Guards occupied the western end. They were subjected to frequent German counter-attacks, but it was of the greatest importance that the Irish hold on. Kenneally's citation laconically observed: "They did so."

On April 28, some 100 of the enemy were seen forming up to assault one of the Irish Guards' positions on the ridge. Kenneally decided that this was the moment to attack them himself. Single-handed he charged down the bare hillside, firing his Bren gun from the hip. "This outstanding act of gallantry," stated his citation, "and the dash with which it was executed completely unbalanced the enemy company, which broke up in disorder." Kenneally then returned to the crest of the ridge to harass their retreat further.

Two days later, Kenneally repeated his exploit. Accompanied this time by a sergeant of the Reconnaissance Corps, he again charged an enemy company which was preparing to attack. He inflicted so many casualties that the projected assault was halted in its tracks. Although wounded, Kenneally refused medical treatment and refused to give up his Bren, claiming that he was the only one who understood its use. He continued to fight throughout the remainder of the day.

His deeds proved a turning point in a desperate battle between veteran Afrika Korps troops and the

Irish Guards, an action in which the latter took nearly 90 per cent casualties. His citation recorded that he had "influenced the whole course of the battle", and his courage in breaking up two attacks "was an achievement that can seldom have been equalled".

After the engagement, various awards were published but there was no mention of a medal for Kenneally, although he was promoted to sergeant and told that he was to be commissioned, since the battalion was short of officers. He declined this, as he enjoyed life in the ranks. He had hoped that he might have been awarded a Military Medal, but was philosophical when this was not forthcoming. The announcement of the VC in mid-August came as a tremendous shock to Kenneally. Many in the regiment had been interviewed and had known what was afoot, but it was a very well-kept secret which he was the last to learn.

Kenneally subsequently wrote an autobiography of remarkable frankness in which he revealed that he was neither Irish nor in fact called Kenneally. He was born, he claimed, Leslie Robinson on March 15 1921, the illegitimate son of the 18-year-old daughter of a Blackpool pharmacist. His father, he said, was Neville Blond, then in his twenties but later the chairman of the English Stage Company and husband of Elaine Marks, the Marks & Spencer heiress.

Illegitimacy being considered a great disgrace, Kenneally's mother was sent to stay with friends in Birmingham. She changed her name from Robinson to Jackson, lived with a woman friend and became a dance hostess. Later Kenneally realised that both women were what he called "fairly high-class whores". He recalled that his mother seemed to have plenty of money because his father was paying maintenance after a paternity case had been brought. For his part, Blond later strenuously denied that he was Kenneally's father, although he admitted to having paid the maintenance order. "I was only one of his mother's many friends," he said, "but I happened to have a bob or two, which meant 'Go for that fellow'".

Leslie grew up on a farm in the north of England and was then sent to King Edward's Grammar School in Birmingham. There he excelled at games and was a Scout. On his 18th birthday he joined the Royal Artillery, TA, and at the start of the Second World War was mobilised. He was posted to an anti-aircraft battery in Dollis Hill, north London, but this he found insufficiently exciting. Early in 1941 he fell in with some Irish labourers, who persuaded him to desert and accompany them to Glasgow. They gave him an identity card bearing the name of John Patrick Kenneally, a labourer who had returned to Ireland. The new Kenneally, having fabricated a childhood in Tipperary, then enlisted with the Irish Guards at Manchester; he had already been favourably impressed by the regiment when he had spent a week at their detention centre in Wellington Barracks after overstaying a leave.

The Guards, though rigorous, proved all he had hoped for. "It was a hard school to learn in. Without being over-sentimental, men can love each other. It is born of mutual suffering, hardships shared, dangers encountered. It is a spiritual love and there is nothing sexual about it. It's entirely masculine, even more than brotherly love, and is called comradeship." The regiment landed at Bone, North Africa, in March 1943 and almost immediately proceeded to the front at Medjez el Bab.

Later they fought at Anzio, where Kenneally was again wounded. Subsequently he was stationed in Germany and, after joining the Guards Parachute Battalion, served in Palestine and Transjordan before leaving the Army. After the award of his VC, presented by General Alexander, Kenneally received thousands of letters from all over the world, and in 1945 was praised by Churchill himself. While denouncing Eamon de Valera, the Irish prime minister, for "frolicking" with the Germans, the Prime Minister said that all bitterness for the Irish race "dies in my heart" when he thought of Irish heroes like Kenneally.

The hero was not so pleased by the publicity which surrounded his medal. "It was the worst thing that could have happened to me," he recalled. "I thought 'Now I'm bound to be rumbled', but I never was." He was also less than pleased by the behaviour of Neville Blond when he went to see him. "He told me how proud he was, gave me £10 and showed me the door."

After leaving the Army, Kenneally ran his own garage before retiring to Worcestershire. Six months before he died Kenneally wrote to *The Daily Telegraph* to rebuke Peter Mandelson, the Northern

Ireland Secretary, for saying on RTE, the Southern Irish broadcasting service, that the officers of the Household Division, which includes the Irish Guards, were "chinless wonders."

He married, in 1943, Elsie Francis. They had two sons and a daughter.

LIEUTENANT-COLONEL THOMAS FIRBANK

Lieutenant-Colonel Thomas Firbank (who died on December 1 2000, aged 90) was awarded an MC while serving in Italy with the 1st Airborne Division in 1943, and wrote *I Bought a Mountain*, a best-selling account of life as a hill farmer in Snowdonia.

Firbank published the book in 1940, when he had already joined the Coldstream Guards. He soon volunteered for airborne duties, and in September 1943 he landed in Italy in command of A Troop of the 1st Airborne Cavalry Squadron. A reconnaissance unit, this was given the task of spearheading 4th Parachute Brigade's advance out of Taranto, which had been occupied to draw German forces away from the main Allied invasion at Salerno, on the west coast.

On the evening of the landings, Firbank led his troop through an SAS picket and out into open country. Shortly after dawn, they found Massafra, their first objective, held by the Germans in company strength. After driving these out in a short, sharp engagement, the troop pushed on towards Mottola where, to the south-east of the town, they made contact with a German rearguard holding a ridge with well-sited machine-guns, supported by artillery. Firbank identified a small knoll as the key to the position, then captured it with a spirited left-flanking attack in which Bren guns were fired from the hip.

From this position he was able to give supporting fire to a second flanking attack, by 156 Parachute Battalion, which captured the ridge. Next morning A Troop, having passed through San Basilio, was pinned down by heavy machine-gun and mortar fire from a German position on a ridge just beyond the town. The German force was superior in both numbers and equipment and casualties mounted, but it was essential that Firbank and his men held their ground as a pivot for another flanking attack.

Inspired by his personal leadership, Firbank's men continued to engage the enemy until, in the evening, the flanking movement was successfully carried out. For his conduct in these actions Firbank was awarded an MC. His citation stated that "throughout all these operations, whose swift success was vital for the occupation of Taranto, Captain Firbank's coolness, courage and dash were outstanding and merit the highest praise".

A great nephew of the novelist Ronald Firbank, Thomas Joseph Firbank was born on June 13 1910 on the Heights of Abraham before Quebec, scene of Wolfe's victory which delivered Canada to Britain. Although his parents were only visiting, and returned to England shortly afterwards, Tom Firbank always retained a Canadian passport. He was sent to Stowe, where he was a classmate of David Niven's. After leaving in 1928, he returned to Canada, where he worked for a time as a lumberjack in the Laurentian mountains.

In 1932, being influenced by his mother's Welsh farming background and having come into a small inheritance, he bought Dyffryn Mymbyr farm at Capel Curig, a 2,400-acre sheep farm in the shadow of Snowdon. His life there as a novice sheep farmer with his first wife Esme is the subject of *I Bought a Mountain*. The title was intended as ironic, the mountain symbolising, for Firbank, freedom rather than possession. The memoir proved a tremendous success, and it was in its 29th edition at the time of his death. It was also the forerunner of a whole genre of books in which urban dwellers flee to the country to live a simpler, though not necessarily easier, life.

After enlisting in the Coldstream Guards on the outbreak of war, Firbank was commissioned and then, after a period of commando training in the Scottish Highlands, volunteered for the newly-formed Airborne Force. Hardened by an outdoor life, and with experience of the mountains, Firbank took readily to soldiering. As a troop commander, he proved a devotee of the maxim "train hard, fight easy". When training in Tunisia for the invasion of Italy, he took his men up into the Djurjura Alps, believing that "short of a foe in battle, there is no sterner teacher than a mountain".

His tough regime was, however, leavened with humour, in particular by the introduction of

"Carruthers", an imaginary officer possessed of all the heroic qualities whose life, opinions and probable reaction to any given situation were frequently discussed by Firbank and his comrades, even when under enemy fire.

Following the action at San Basilio, Firbank returned to England, and was then appointed GS02 (Operations) at HQ 1st Airborne Corps. In this capacity he took part in Operation Market Garden, landing by glider near Nijmegen. After the war, Firbank formed and commanded an Airborne Infantry Training Centre at Shorncliffe, Kent, and later commanded the Airborne Forces Depot on the Isle of Wight. He retired from the Army in 1948.

In 1951, he wrote a sequel to *I Bought a Mountain* entitled *I Bought a Star*, which recounted his wartime experiences. His other books included *A Country of Memorable Honour* (1953), an account of a walk from Llangollen to Cardiff, as well as mountain guides to Snowdonia. From 1954, Firbank was employed by a British engineering company, Perkins Diesel, to open up the Far East. His "parish", as he called it, comprised 20 or so states from Indonesia to China and Japan, where he was among the first British businessmen to operate after the war. He was, for a while, Secretary of the British Chamber of Commerce in Tokyo, until he wrote a typically forth-right letter to the *Times* about the incompetence of British exporters.

Firbank was an increasingly ardent Welsh nationalist, and a friend of Gwynfor Evans, the founder of Plaid Cymru. In 1984, he moved back to

Snowdonia and lived at Dolwyddelan. There he wrote many articles on conservation matters, particularly those concerning the mountains around him. He described his life as a series of reincarnations and died, as he wished, as unencumbered as a monk.

Firbank married, first, in 1935, Esme Cummins. The marriage was dissolved, and he married secondly, in 1943, Tessa Coudret, who died in 1959. He married thirdly, in 1974, Tsunemi Yagi, who survives him, together with the two daughters of his second marriage.

COLONEL
MAURICE WILLOUGHBY

Colonel Maurice Willoughby (who died on December 27 2000, aged 87) was an adventurous and unrepentant representative of the imperial breed, whose belief in the value of vigorous outdoor activity for the elderly was demonstrated when he was given his own television series. In 'Willoughby' (1981-82), the 69-year-old soldier donned a wide variety of hats, special suits and even a kilt to try his hand at gliding, climbing, canoeing, water skiing and hovercraft riding. He also drove a double-decker bus, a horse-drawn carriage and a motor mower.

In the course of these experiences the colonel, eyeglass at the ready, gave viewers the benefit of his insight into modern life. Jogging, he declared, was a "frightful bore"; during a fencing lesson he mused that it was a pity duelling was now illegal – "it makes people so much politer"; while a woman ski instructor 30 years his junior was given a lesson in the correct Army way to "present skis". Whatever the activity, the audience was assured, participation would "make your lunchtime gin and tonic taste a whole lot better".

Maurice Frederick Vere Willoughby was born at Bolarum, India, on December 23 1913, and sent to Haileybury and Sandhurst before being commissioned into the Highland Light Infantry. Although his father, grandfather and great-grandfather (who was in India during the Mutiny) had served in Highland regiments, Willoughby found peacetime soldiering frustrating. At least one third of his brother officers, he recalled, were overtly homosexual, while his batman never tired of singing the praises of his previous officer, David Niven.

There were compensations. The working day ended at 12.30 pm, leaving plenty of time to pursue a social life. In 1935, he was invited to represent the regiment at the Caledonian Ball in London. The following day, he attended King George V's last levee at St James's Palace, to which he wore pre-1914 uniform of scarlet tunic, trews and plaid secured by a large silver brooch. When his picture appeared in the newspapers, a tremendous row ensued in the regiment. Willoughby was accused of insulting the King by wearing on his head a shako with gold braid, a privilege only permitted to majors and above; he then made matters worse by observing that, if the King had noticed this *lèse majesté*, he was more observant than his uncle the Duke of Connaught, who had dined with the regiment under the impression that it was the 60th Rifles.

Willoughby was happy to return to India, which offered valuable experience patrolling the North-West Frontier, and enough risk of being killed to keep soldiers on their toes. There was also skiing in Kashmir, and jackal hunting with the Peshawar Vale Hunt. On acquiring a hunter, Willoughby asked the German consul in Calcutta for permission to call it General Goering; the following year a commission arrived, signed by Goering himself, declaring that the horse had been promoted, like its namesake, to Reichsmarschall. "Who says the Germans have no sense of humour?" commented Willoughby.

In 1941, bored by his failure to see action after the outbreak of war, Willoughby volunteered for the newly raised Glider Pilot Regiment. This offered the opportunity to learn to fly, an experience that so intoxicated him that he turned down a place at Staff College. But he was not selected for the Sicily landings, and his exasperation turned to anger when he found that half the gliders were lost at sea and most of the rest had had to land on boulders. A protest to his senior officer, who had been awarded a DSO for the operation, led to an adverse report for insubordination, but a recommendation that he be reduced from major to captain was blocked by General "Boy" Browning. Willoughby was appointed liaison officer to the French in anticipation of an invasion of Corsica, and then a ski instructor in Lebanon for an attack in the mountains of Turkey.

He finally completed his war service by being sent to join the Arab Legion.

In 1948, Willoughby represented Britain in the military pentathlon at the Winter Olympics in St Moritz. He missed three targets in a row during the pistol shooting after the man standing next to him was shot by someone else. But he took sixth place in the fencing, and was commended for his pluck in ignoring an injured shoulder to enable the British four to complete a skiing race. The following year he married Nancy Dodd, a big game hunter, and settled back into regimental duties before being posted to Field Marshal Montgomery's staff at SHAEF headquarters in Fontainebleau, and then to the Suez Canal.

Finding himself next in Khartoum, he took up an invitation to demonstrate the safety of water-skiing on the Nile, despite the crocodiles. A few nights later, a thief climbed up the drainpipe to steal his watch from his wrist as Willoughby slept on a flat roof. After some months, the watch was recovered inside a crocodile; almost 40 years on, reported Willoughby in a letter to *The Daily Telegraph*, it was still working perfectly, although the crocodile's insides had eaten away the dial.

Having come out of the Army to spend more time with his young son, Willoughby started importing ski equipment and designing dry-ski slopes. He then met David English, the future editor of the *Daily Mail*, who invited him to write about skiing and to organise trips for readers. When finally confined to his home in Sussex by two hip replacements, Willoughby let off steam by penning letters to the *Telegraph*. In these he criticised officers for taking pay rises not granted to their men, and took a dim view of regiments summoning the SAS whenever one of their men was captured, instead of mounting the rescue themselves. During the row over North Atlantic fishing he thundered, "What is this thing called the EU which is sending ultimatums on our behalf to Her Majesty's subjects in Canada?"

He took a dim view of couples leaping into bed together at the first opportunity, and found his low opinion of the namby-pamby Nineties confirmed when he recalled a beating he had received as a schoolboy for volunteering the (correct) opinion that he had mumps, and a bossy note in the *Old Haileyburian Report* declared that such recollections of corporal punishment might deter potential parents who had not been to boarding school themselves.

Yet despite appearances, Maurice Willoughby was not the archetypal old buffer. He spoke six languages, came to disapprove of hunting, shooting and fishing, and urged forgiveness of the Japanese. In 2001 he published an elegiac yet hard-headed memoir, *Echo of a Distant Drum: the Last Generation of Empire*. Willoughby was survived by his son.

MAJOR
RICHARD COKE

Major Richard Coke (who died on April 25 2001, aged 83) was awarded an MC in November 1943 and a DSO in December 1944 while serving in Italy with the Scots Guards. On November 9-10, he was second in command of F Company, 2nd Battalion, Scots Guards, when it was ordered to move to the assistance of two companies of the Grenadier Guards on Monte Camino.

This vast mountain dominated the Mignano Gap, and its capture was essential to 10 Corps' advance on Monte Cassino. The position occupied by F Company was overlooked by the enemy and under continual sniper and shell fire. After a successful night attack, the company became isolated and had to fight its own battle. The company commander was killed and Coke took charge, leading his men over very difficult terrain under constant machine-gun fire. After the three companies had suffered 70 per cent casualties on November 10, they had to regroup to hold a strongpoint.

Coke continued to command his company for three days under heavy mortar and Spandau fire and, in the words of his citation, "it was largely due to his courage and example that the position was held". F Company had gone up the hill with three officers and 105 men. Only Coke and 57 men came down unhurt, but Coke accounted for every single man to his commanding officer. For his conduct during this battle, he was awarded the MC.

By December 1944, Coke was commanding S Company of the Scots Guards, attached to the 2nd Battalion, the Coldstream Guards, which was ordered to attack Monte Penzola, a 1,300 ft peak which barred the way to Imola. Its main feature, a pinnacle guarded by perpendicular cliffs and liberally mined, was S company's objective. Under heavy shellfire, Coke brought his men around the feature's west side and, exposed to enemy action from all sides, led them – at times on hands and knees through thick mud – up the steep slopes.

A fierce hand-to-hand battle took place on the cliff tops, until, with machine-gun fire and grenades, Coke succeeded in killing or capturing all of the enemy. Fighting was intense around the enemy company headquarters where the German commander and his men put up fierce resistance until he fell, riddled with bullets. In spite of heavy and accurate shell and mortar fire, Coke's company now consolidated the position and prepared to meet the inevitable counter-attack. At 5.30 next morning, after a severe mortar and artillery concentration, the Germans attacked with elements of two companies, penetrating Coke's headquarters and inflicting heavy casualties. At this moment, he was an inspiration to his men, personally directing operations and throwing grenades in the close fighting. S Company beat off repeated attacks with heavy losses to the Germans.

In the words of the citation for his DSO: "Major Coke's magnificent leadership, his complete disregard for his personal safety under heavy shell and machine-gun fire, his determination in the face of almost insurmountable difficulties in terrain, and his heroic example had empowered his company to defeat a German battalion, which from now on was powerless to challenge our possession of the commanding feature of Monte Penzola."

Richard Lovel Coke was born at Weasenham, Norfolk, on April 3 1918. His father was the third son of the 2nd Earl of Leicester, and his maternal grandfather the 14th Lord Inchiquin. Coke was educated at Stowe, then went on to the Royal Agricultural College at Cirencester, where, in 1938, he won the Gold Medal for Forestry. As a supplementary reservist he was mobilised in 1939 and commissioned into the Scots Guards.

In 1943 he joined the 2nd Battalion in the Salerno beach-head and, apart from the period when S Company was attached to the Coldstream Guards, served with them throughout much of the heaviest fighting of the Italian campaign. An inspiring leader, Coke was also a disciplinarian who nonetheless believed in giving a man a second chance. On one occasion he was greatly pleased to see a young officer, whom he felt had let him down, reappear a few months later with an MC. Imbued from childhood with an affection for all things Italian, Coke put to good use those periods of leave in Naples, Rome and Florence (where he had relatives) when not taken up writing light-hearted letters home or paying hospital visits to his wounded Guardsmen.

Coke ended the war in Trieste, and then left the Army to run the woods at the family estate at Weasenham. His grandfather had introduced some Western American conifers – Douglas Fir, Noble Fir and Sitka Spruce – to fill gaps in the existing woods and, in 1904, his father had adopted the "uneven aged" or "continuous cover" system, whereby the wood is never clear-felled. Building on his father's achievements in forest management became Coke's life's work.

As a result of his careful management of the estate, the woods at Weasenham now combine high-quality timber production with the amenity value of ornamental trees and flowering shrubs such as rhododendrons, azaleas and magnolias. Coke had a great understanding of the countryside and was appalled at some of the imbalances of nature that have arisen in the last 20 years, in particular the damage to woodland and bird life caused by the arrival of the grey squirrel, whose effects he felt have not yet been fully appreciated. He was also an advocate of much tighter control of deer numbers. An outstanding game shot, he still holds the record of 50 brace of grouse killed with a single gun at Whitfield, Northumberland in 1957.

He became Deputy Lord Lieutenant of Norfolk in 1977 and High Sheriff in 1981. He married, in 1951, Molly Fletcher, who died in 1997. They had a daughter, who predeceased him, and two sons, who survive him.

―――――――――

MAJOR
D F STONE

Major D F Stone (who died on May 3 2001, aged 82) was awarded an MC for his service as commander of 23 Battery, the 59th (Newfoundland)

Heavy Regiment, RA. The battery was the first such Newfoundland unit to fight in Belgium, Holland and Germany, and by the end of the war Stone, who had joined the 59th on its formation in 1940, was one of the regiment's longest-serving English officers.

Douglas Frank Stone – known in peacetime as "Dougal" but as "Douggie" during the war – was born at Streatham, south London, on February 4 1919, the son of a merchant banker. He was educated at Whitgift. Planning a career in banking, after school Stone went to Germany to learn the language, and then to France to brush up his French. He joined the Army shortly after the outbreak of war.

In early 1940 Vice-Admiral Sir Humphrey Walwyn, the Governor of Newfoundland, the proudly British North Atlantic island, issued a proclamation calling for volunteers to serve in the Royal Artillery for the duration of the war. They would form two new regiments – the 57th and the 59th (Newfoundland) Heavy Regiments, RA – with most of the officers being British. By July 1941, the 59th was on coastal defence duty in Kent. B Battery, commanded by Stone, had two heavy 12in howitzers at Canterbury, as well as four French 75mm guns.

"The idea," Stone recalled, "was that when the Germans appeared in the neighbourhood of Dover, we were expected to rush out to meet them with four French 75s (the firing levers on which were very reminiscent of lavatory chains), and if we got a pasting, we were then supposed to hare back to Canterbury and fire off the two 12in howitzers." B Battery, which in 1942 was redesignated 23 Battery, remained in Kent until late April 1944, when the regiment was ordered up to Northumberland for shooting practice on the Redesdale ranges, north-west of Newcastle, and for further coastal defence duties on the North Sea near Bamburgh. On the eve of their departure for France in early July, Stone gave his men a lecture on the Wehrmacht and German uniforms, and tried unsuccessfully to teach them some French.

The battery was soon involved in the fierce fighting in the villages on the perimeter of Caen. Positioned up a church tower, which he was using as an observation post, Stone was surprised by a voice calling out from below: "Come down. This is the security police." As the accent sounded foreign, he thought it might be a trap – a suspicion which seemed confirmed when there was a burst of Sten gun fire. However, the voice turned out to belong to a French-Canadian member of a police unit – one of whose number had discharged the Sten gun by mistake.

The 59th proceeded, via the Falaise battle, to Ailly (between Louviers and Evreux), where, in late August, Stone was informed that 23 Battery was to take on an independent role under the CCRA of 12th Corps. A few days later, at a rendezvous near Amiens, his battery was ordered to the vicinity of Arras, where, with other artillery units, it became part of "Lys Force", put together to provide fire support in the Ghent area. Having maintained fire on canal bridges at Deynze to harass the enemy, 23 Battery's next stop was near Antwerp, where the

Germans still held both sides of the Scheldt estuary.

As well as firing on enemy parties ferrying across the estuary, on September 11-12 Stone's battery joined in Fire Plan "Splash", a series of bombardments against enemy artillery and mortar units. Subsequently, after providing support for "Market Garden", the airborne operation to seize crossings over the rivers and canals of southern Holland, Stone's battery crossed the Meuse-Escaut canal and entered Holland, going into action west of Eindhoven.

Thirteen miles to the north-west was the town of Tilburg, still held by the Germans. Here, Stone's primary task was to bring down fire on the Tilburg-s'Hertogenbosch road, which the Germans were using to move troops and supplies. For several days, the battery engaged targets given them by pilots of a British Artillery Reconnaissance Squadron, communicating with the aircraft by means of a VHF wireless set of which his troops had temporary use. In early October, the battery was busy in the Nijmegen area. Here, they found so many targets – mainly hostile batteries – that on a single day they had to turn their guns around three times.

By the end of the month, British troops had reached the Maas north-west of Tilburg, though the Germans still maintained their hold farther to the east. Stone's battery answered frequent calls for bombardment of enemy communications along the Maas. In late December 23 Battery, by now supporting 43rd (Wessex) Division along the Meuse, moved forward to put its guns in action west of

Liège. Here, their role was a protective one – to be in readiness to assist in preventing German columns from reaching the Meuse. In January 1945, as part of Operation Blackcock – to secure a firm base from which to advance to the Rhine – 23 Battery moved back to Sittard, close to the German frontier.

They followed 52nd Division across the frontier, and on January 21, near Hongen, their guns went into action for the first time on German soil. There followed the Reichswald battle in February, and in March the battle of the Rhine. The 59th crossed the river on March 27 and from then on, until the end of the North-West Europe campaign five weeks later, fought a succession of actions involving rapid fire and movement, all the way up to the river Elbe. By the end of the war – when the 59th was dis-banded – Stone had earned, in addition to his MC, a mention in despatches.

After the war, he made his career in the overseas department of the Bank of England, providing advice and assistance to foreign central banks, including the Bundesbank in Germany. For four years he and his family lived in Africa, where he helped to set up the Bank of Ghana after independence. When Dougal Stone took early retirement in 1975, he and his wife Madge, or "Mougal", (née Lawson), went to live on the Isle of Islay, where they had spent many happy holidays. There, Stone was for some years secretary of the Machrie Golf Club. After his wife's death in 1985, he suffered from increasingly poor health and eventually left Islay to live near a daughter in Kent, later moving with her to Pembrokeshire.

Stone was survived by two daughters – one from an earlier marriage dissolved during the war – and a son.

GENERAL
SIR WALTER WALKER

General Sir Walter Walker (who died on August 12 2001, aged 88) was an outstandingly successful commander during the Malayan Emergency in the 1950s, and as Director of Operations in Borneo between 1962 and 1965; later, he courted controversy by setting up Civil Assistance, a voluntary organisation which attracted 100,000 members.

Walker was one of the first to identify the importance of helicopters in modern military operations. "In Borneo," he reckoned, "one SAS squadron with helicopters was worth ten infantry battalions to me." Denis Healey, who became Secretary of State for Defence in 1964, considered that the Borneo campaign would be recorded as "one of the most efficient uses of military force in the history of the world". Yet the qualities that made Walker so effective in the field – clarity of vision, single-mindedness of purpose, fierce insistence on discipline, fearlessness in the face of both the enemy and his superiors – also ensured that he was a highly controversial figure.

In the early 1960s his efforts to defend the Gurkhas against plans to reduce their numbers were so forceful that he was threatened with a court martial and – under threat of losing his command in Borneo – forced to apologise to the Chief of the Imperial General Staff. In 1974 he was accused of attempting to form a private army to combat the dangers to Britain which he discerned both from without and within. The charge was absurdly exaggerated; it is undeniable, though, that he was rarely capable of trimming his views, compromising his principles, or entertaining the notion that he might be mistaken.

Walter Colyear Walker was born in India on November 11 1912, the second of four sons (there were also two daughters) of Arthur Colyear Walker, an Assam tea–planter and soldier. Family connections with the Army and India went back several generations on both sides of the family. Walker's character was well defined even in his schooldays at Blundell's, near Tiverton. "When I became head of the school's day boys," he recorded in his autobiography *Fighting On* (1997), "I found them to be a motley bunch of idle, unpatriotic, unkempt, and 'couldn't care less' type of youths. I decided to straighten them out . . ."

He went on to describe how he became "a tiger of a boxer" and decided "to sort out the school bullies, who received a straight left to the nose or an uppercut to the jaw if they insulted me, tripped me up or ruffled my hair etc". The headmaster, however, felt obliged to point out to him the difference between driving and leading.

Walker proceeded to Sandhurst with the aim of

obtaining a commission in the 1st/8th Gurkhas, which his grandfather had once commanded. He settled quickly into the discipline and austere atmosphere of the Royal Military College, though he privately doubted the wisdom of allowing so much time to be spent cleaning weapons and so little on firing them. He would have preferred to spend less time on drill, and more on weapon training, tactics, military history and map-reading. After a short attachment to the Sherwood Foresters, Walker joined the 1st/8th Gurkhas.

He had the first of his many narrow escapes from death in the Quetta earthquake of 1935, before his battalion moved up to Razmak for operations against the Fakir of Ipi. In 1939 he was recommended for a Military Cross but did not receive it as the District Commander had just approved one. One day on the frontier Walker had to retrieve some dead sepoys from an ambushed piquet, whose commander had disobeyed strict instructions. The corpses had all been horribly mutilated; for Walker this was a lesson, which he never forgot, on the importance of meticulous discipline. He was mentioned in despatches twice during this campaign.

In 1942 Walker attended the Staff College at Quetta, which had then decided to pay attention to the Far East rather than to the Middle East as before, and two years later he took over command of the 4th/8th Gurkhas, who had been involved in heavy fighting in the Arakan. The story of how he revived the morale of this battle-weary battalion and, in two months of exhaustive re-training, transformed it into the most effective fighting unit in the division has been told in *A Child At Arms* (1970) by Patrick Davis, who served as a subaltern in the battalion. Walker applied the lessons that he had learned in Waziristan, particularly in relation to ambush techniques, of which he became the supreme exponent.

His abrasive manner and painstaking attention to detail won him enemies, but in the ensuing battle with the Japanese the 4th/8th acquitted itself brilliantly. During the Burma campaign Walker was again mentioned in despatches and was also awarded the DSO. After a short period on the Staff at GHQ Delhi (where he worked closely with Wavell and Auchinleck) Walker became GSO1 in Kuala Lumpur. He was given the task of training "Ferret Force", which consisted of British, Gurkhas, Chinese, Dyaks, and ex-Force 136 soldiers. In 1948-49, as outbreaks of Communist terrorism increased in Malaya, Walker commanded the Far East Land Forces Training Centre, establishing what later became the Jungle Warfare School at Kota Tinggi. For this work he was appointed OBE.

Next he took over command of the 1st/6th Gurkhas. Walker went into the jungle with each company to determine where the mistakes were being made. He then withdrew the battalion from operations and again put them through the ruthless re-training that he had developed in Burma. After that he once more achieved startling results in jungle operations. The high standards that Walker demanded from his officers and riflemen became the yardstick in all the Gurkha regiments, greatly enhancing their reputation as the British Army's best jungle fighters. Nowhere was this better displayed than in the execution of Walker's Operation Tiger in 1958, when his 99 Gurkha Brigade eliminated the last 100 communist terrorists operating in Johore State.

Ten-day ambushes, laid on the basis of Special Branch information, became the norm, and Walker once ordered an ambush group to stay in position for 28 days. "My Special Branch man," Walker later declared, "had guaranteed the CTs [Communist terrorists] would come and after 28 days they came – and were killed in the swamp." For his work in Malaya Walker was twice mentioned in despatches, awarded a Bar to his DSO and appointed CBE.

On his return to Britain he faced a different battle in Whitehall, where the Government was reducing the size of the Army, a policy which would involve cutting Gurkha numbers by half. Walker, now a major-general, did not hesitate to call this "a betrayal". His campaign to retain Gurkha fighting strength was interrupted when he was made Director of Operations in Borneo from 1962 to 1965. Here, his versatility in fighting a defensive war with Indonesia along a 1,200-mile frontier with limited resources showed him to be a field commander of genius. Many of the tactics he employed – using four-man SAS patrols as his "eyes and ears" to give warning of border incursions, flying in howitzers by helicopter to provide support fire for forward company bases and, above all, his "Claret" operations – broke rules but were devastatingly effective. His

Claret raids into Indonesian territory, planned and executed to inflict decisive but limited damage to the enemy's forward bases, only became public knowledge a decade after the event.

Walker's great slogan was "Jointmanship". He succeeded in making all the services work together, and with the local population. Though a martinet, he became known as a "soldier's general", and the best there was. To the Gurkhas, in particular, whose talents he used to the full, he was nothing less than the hero of the age. With Whitehall it was a different story. He felt, with some justification, that his championship of the Gurkha cause was held against him – but then he made no effort to tread lightly on toes, however high in authority.

Although both the C-in-C Far East and Earl Mountbatten had recommended Walker for a knighthood, the Army Board did not approve, and he did not get it. A proposal for the CMG was also rejected, though he was appointed CB in 1964. In 1965 Walker became Deputy Chief of Staff, Army Land Forces Central Europe, in which post he supervised the removal of AFCENT to Brunssum, in Holland, after General de Gaulle had withdrawn France from Nato. Next, from 1967 to 1969, he was GOC, Northern Command, at last being appointed KBE in 1968. His final post was Commander-in-Chief, Allied Forces Northern Europe, from 1969 to 1972. Once more he found his subordinates and his allies less dedicated to their tasks than he would have wished. There were some stormy occasions.

After Walker retired from the Army in 1972, he

continued to express extreme concern (often in letters to *The Daily Telegraph*) about the dangers to Britain. At home he discerned, not least in trade unions, "the Communist Trojan horse in our midst, with its fellow travellers wriggling their maggoty way inside its belly". For wanton lawbreakers, Walker favoured corporal punishment. Abroad, Walker warned, the Soviet empire was waiting to strike.

In addition he deplored the hostility shown to Ian Smith's rebel government in Rhodesia, and attacked what he considered the feeble policy adopted towards the IRA, which he saw as a Marxist organisation inspired by Russia. "Northern Ireland should now be declared a proper operational area, or even war zone," he reckoned, "in which would-be murderers caught carrying or using arms would be subject to summary trial and execution." In an interview given in 1974 he raised the possibility that the Army might have to take over in Britain.

Soon afterwards, claiming the encouragement of (among others) Admiral of the Fleet Sir Varyl Begg, Marshal of the RAF Sir John Slessor and Michael Bentine, the former Goon, Walker set up an "anti-chaos" organisation, known at first as Unison, and later as Civil Assistance. The proclaimed aim was to create a force of "trustworthy, loyal, level-headed men", who would be ready to ensure the continuance of essential services should public order break down – as Walker considered all too likely. Though he named Enoch Powell as the right man to lead the nation, he insisted that his movement existed only to support the properly constituted authorities.

There was no question of anyone being armed.

By the end of August 1974, some 100,000 people supported his movement, and Walker spoke of the numbers rising to three million within another month. But Civil Assistance was fatally easy to mock. Journalists wrote of Lambrook–les–Deux–Eglises in reference to Walker's home in Somerset. In the *Telegraph* Maurice Weaver fashioned a master-piece of mockery from the leader's own remarks. Britain survived; Civil Assistance petered out.

Walker persisted in his jeremiads, proclaiming in 1977 that the West's only hope of salvation lay in the neutron bomb. He undertook extensive travels to lecture on the perilous world situation – above all to South Africa, which he visited six times, and to Pakistan, where the President, General Zia, was particularly friendly. Walker published two books, *The Bear at the Back Door* (1978) and *The Next Domino* (1980). But in 1985 Walker's active career was virtually ended when two botched hip replacement operations by Army and RAF surgeons left him in terrible pain. He faced this disaster with courage. The only consolation was that he received £130,000 in damages from the Ministry of Defence. Even *in extremis* his views remained as forthright as ever. The claim of homosexuals to equal treatment caused him especial distress. There could be no place for such people – "who use the main sewer of the human body as a playground" – in the Armed Forces. His own recreations were listed in *Who's Who* as "normal".

Walker married, in 1939, Beryl Johnston. She died in 1990. They had two sons and a daughter.

FIELD MARSHAL
LORD CARVER

Field Marshal Lord Carver (who died on December 9 2001, aged 86) was regarded as the cleverest soldier since the Second World War and also one of the most uncompromising senior officers of his generation. Although he made a substantial contribution to the efficiency of the British Army in both war and peace, his honesty was presented in a manner which made few concessions to the feelings and susceptibilities of others, whatever their rank.

One of Carver's more blistering attacks was on the policy of nuclear deterrence, which he described as being either bluff or suicide. He believed that the only credible method of preventing Soviet aggression was to build up adequate conventional forces on land, sea and air. The Trident missile programme seemed to him a waste of money and manpower, which could have been better utilised on conventional arms.

As for the stockpiles of 50,000 nuclear weapons, they could never be required unless the holders had decided on a policy of genocide and suicide. When the Communist regime in Eastern Europe collapsed he was critical of the plan to expand NATO, and later argued that the compensation and counselling culture was damaging the Armed Forces.

Richard Michael Power Carver was born on April 24 1915 at Bletchingley, Surrey. His father worked for Carver Brothers, the family firm of Egyptian-cotton brokers. On his mother's side, Carver was the great-great-great nephew of the 1st Duke of Wellington. He was educated at Winchester, and hoped to go to Cambridge with a view to becoming a journalist. But the family resources were at a low ebb – his father had been forced to retire by the recession – and it was clear that this would be impossible unless young Michael obtained a scholarship; this was deemed beyond his intellectual reach.

Instead, he was sent to Sandhurst, and thereafter always seemed to be striving to prove that academically he was equal to the best of university graduates. This preoccupation, combined with a considerable degree of intolerance, seemed to increase as he grew older and involved him in some bitter exchanges, not least in the correspondence columns of *The Daily Telegraph*.

In 1935 Carver was commissioned into the unfashionable Royal Tank Corps, partly because one of his brothers had friends in it and partly because he thought he could manage there on his salary. He had initially considered serving for four years, then leaving the Army for a career in the law, for which he had studied in his spare time at Sandhurst. But his military promise quickly became clear after the outbreak of war.

Starting with the 1st Royal Tank Regiment in Egypt, he won a reputation as a brave, quick-minded officer without faults, and was given a series of staff appointments with the new 30 Corps and 7th Armoured Corps, the Desert Rats. During the 1941-42 winter campaign in Cyrenaica, he was twice mentioned in despatches and awarded an MC. The citation referred to his "quick, clear thinking and calm handling of situations, which were often difficult ... Much of his staff work has been carried out under fire, or in close proximity to the enemy. This officer's coolness under fire, energy and resource were an example to those working under him."

Two years later, Carver won an immediate DSO at El Alamein, where he distinguished himself as GSO1, 7th Armoured Division. "Under difficult and arduous conditions," the citation recorded, "he has displayed outstanding skill and ability in handling the staff work of the division. Always cool and collected under fire, he has set a fine example to the rest of the staff."

Later in 1943, while in command of 22nd Armoured Brigade in Italy, Carver was awarded an immediate Bar to his DSO for having "displayed exceptionally high powers of command, initiative and foresight . . . In particular, on October 4, the enemy were strongly posted along the line of villages and it became necessary to stage an attack on Cardito. The arrangements for this attack, involving the co-operation of the infantry, tanks and guns, were most excellently organised by Lieutenant-Colonel Carver and it was certainly due to the soundness of his plan that the attack succeeded with little loss to ourselves and caused the whole enemy line to give way."

Carver later served for three weeks on the Normandy beaches, then was put in charge of 4th Armoured Brigade, making him at 29 the youngest acting brigadier in the British Army. His brigade crossed the Rhine immediately behind the leading infantry and was instrumental in affording an extra punch to achieve complete success. After that, he was always in the forefront of the advance, and conducted a most successful operation in breaking out of the bridgehead over the river Aller, and thus opening the way for the armoured division to pass through.

On stepping down in rank after the war, Carver became Grade 1 Technical Staff Officer at the Ministry of Supply, being concerned with the development of Armoured Fighting Vehicles. In 1950 he attended the Joint Services Staff College, where his habit of asking the last question at the end of a long session on Saturday mornings did not enhance his popularity. Field Marshal Montgomery, his former commander in the desert, admired Carver's military proficiency but commented drily: "This officer thinks there is nothing but dead wood between him and the Chief of the Imperial General Staff." Years later, even Carver himself admitted that he must have been "an impatient young man".

Next Carver was appointed Assistant Quarter Master General Allied Land Forces, Central Europe, at Fontainebleau, where he was less impressed by German and French hopes for a European defence community and more concerned with the evolution of nuclear tactics. At SHAPE, he ran Montgomery's annual command post exercise, and then became Deputy Chief of Staff to General Sir George Erskine in East Africa during the Mau Mau insurrection, in which he was again mentioned in despatches. He was promoted Chief of Staff to General Sir Gerald Lathbury and, in

1955, achieved his wartime rank again.

Two years later Carver was at the Imperial Defence College. He became Director of Plans, War Office, in 1958-59, then Commander of 6th Infantry Brigade Group. In 1962 he was appointed Major-General, GOC3 Division (the Army's Strategic Reserve), which took him to Cyprus as commander of the Anglo-Turkish-Greek Truce Force in 1964. On being asked as he set out whether he thought 5,000 troops were sufficient for the job, he replied: "I doubt it." But the appointment enabled him to display some diplomatic skills.

When this body was replaced by the United Nations Force in Cyprus, he became its deputy commander as well as commander of the British contingent. In September 1964 he returned to the Ministry of Defence to become Director of Army Staff Duties. With a Labour government in power, Carver's star continued in the ascent. He was devoid of sentimentality, and therefore willing to slash the Territorial Army, though his single-minded approach caused considerable resentment. "Carver by name and carver by nature," commented bitter Territorials; the organisation later had to be rebuilt at considerable expense.

In 1966 Carver was appointed lieutenant-general and took command of Far East Land Forces; this was followed in 1967 by his promotion to general as Commander-in-Chief, Far East, which was a tri-service appointment. Carver was GOC-in-C Southern Command (1969-71), Chief of the General Staff (1971-73), and Chief of the Defence

Staff (1973-76). He proved an effective Whitehall warrior, demanding less paper and fewer hand-written reports, but not as radical as his supporters had hoped. Ironically, his decision to speak in English, not Latin, at Winchester's *Ad Portas* ceremony earned him a far more severe reprimand by *The Wykehamist* than anyone in the Army would have dared to deliver.

Carver was ADC to the Queen (1969-72), Colonel Commandant of REME (1966-76), of the Royal Tank Regiment (1968-72), and of the Royal Armoured Corps (1974-77). He was also designated British Resident Commissioner for Rhodesia from 1977 to 1978 as the colony's rebellion wound down.

Even before he resigned from the Army Carver had established a reputation as a writer, earning plaudits for being "thorough but compellingly readable, scholarly but not digressively detailed". *Second to None*, his history of the Royal Scots Greys from 1919 to 1945 which was published in 1954, was followed by a steady output of books, the best of them drawing on his personal experience and first-hand knowledge. *El Alamein* (1962) earned particular praise, even from Montgomery who came in for criticism, though he added: "I often wonder what the various writers would have done themselves in the conditions of the time . . . I do not consider I would have acted differently in any way." Other works included *Tobruk* (1964); *Harding of Petherton*, a study of Carver's early patron (1978); *The Apostles of Mobility* (1979); *War Since 1945* (1980); *A Policy for Peace* (1982); *The Seven Ages of the British Army*

(1984); *Dilemmas of the Desert War* (1986); *Twentieth Century Warriors* (1987); and *Britain's Army in the Twentieth Century* (1998). There were also his memoirs *Out of Step* (1989) and an edition of *Letters of a Victorian Army Officer: Edward Wellesley, 1840-54* (1995).

In addition, Carver also reviewed for several publications, and was frequently consulted by producers of television programmes. But he declined the temptations of armchair punditry, and consistently refused to volunteer for action on television during such conflicts as the Gulf War and Bosnia.

Tall and austere in appearance, Carver was not noted for his bonhomie – some felt that he kept the cutting edge of his tongue too far forward, even in wartime – or for his sense of humour. But when, after his drastic reforms of the Territorial Army in 1974, members of the TA Council designed a tie bearing a crossed carver and hatchet in gold over the letters TA, he asked that one should be presented to him.

Carver was appointed CBE in 1945, CB in 1957, KCB in 1966, GCB in 1970 and created a life peer in 1977. He married, in 1947, Edith Lowry-Corry, who survived him with their two sons and two daughters.

John Keegan writes: Mike Carver, as he was universally known, revelled in a row and had many throughout his long Service career. He was not, however, a bully. It was the pleasure of the argument, not that of brow-beating those junior to him in intellect or rank, that he enjoyed. He knew his reputation, moreover, so that those with whom he crossed swords felt no inhibition in revealing the fact. "Getting across Mike Carver" became something of a distinction. Eventually his disputatiousness reached self-caricature; the Royal Air Force, for whose abolition he repeatedly called in the House of Lords, finally chose to ignore his speeches. As he aged he also mellowed, however, a process most evident in his writing, which acquired a grace and perceptiveness in his later essays not present in his critical histories of the desert war.

He made no compromises in friendship. Though he enjoyed my company, he gave me a terrific ticking-off for failing to attend a conference in Texas, which took place while I was fully occupied with the Gulf War. For several years I had failed to keep an appointment mismanaged by a third party, and he told any mutual acquaintance that "Keegan is completely unreliable." I bear no grudges, and I hope few are borne elsewhere. Mike Carver, in his ferocious way, was fun.

CAPTAIN
SIR RODEN CUTLER, VC

Captain Sir Roden Cutler (who died on February 21 2002, aged 85) won the Victoria Cross while fighting against the Vichy French during the Syrian campaign of 1941; later he joined the Australian diplomatic service, and then became Governor of New South Wales.

When the Australian infantry attacked French positions at Merdjayoun on June 19 1941, Lieutenant Cutler was part of an artillery forward observation team, attached to the 2nd/25th Battalion, which pushed ahead under enemy machine-gun fire to establish an outpost in an isolated hut. Cutler went out to mend a telephone line which had been cut. When he returned to the hut, he and his men came under attack from infantry and two enemy tanks; his Bren gunner was killed and a fellow officer mortally wounded.

With one of his gunners, Cutler returned fire with anti-tank rifles, which had little effect. They then took up a rifle and a Bren .303 machine-gun and succeeded, temporarily, in driving back the attack. When the enemy tanks returned, their main guns firing, Cutler hit the turret of one with an anti-tank rifle. This, too, was ineffective, so he diverted his fire to its tracks, and forced both tanks and infantry to withdraw. As the surviving Australians themselves fell back, Cutler personally supervised the evacuation of the wounded. But realising that the enemy was confused, he pressed on into the town accompanied by a small party of volunteers.

With one man, Cutler established an observation post among rocks at the town's north-west corner, overlooking the only road by which enemy transport could approach. He directed his battery's fire on to the enemy's positions, although aware that they were massing to the left for a counter-attack. After being cut off, he hid until dark then made his way back through enemy lines. Cutler's success in registering the exact position of the road turned the battle in the Australians' favour.

On the night of June 23 he took charge of a 25lb field gun which, the next day, he positioned in front of the Australian infantry, enabling it to fire point-blank on the French. Two weeks later, Cutler was attached to the 2nd/16th Battalion as a forward observation officer when the enemy was sighted at Damour, where the Australian infantry had been pinned down by heavy machine-gun fire; he captured several Vichy French from three machine-gun posts. Then, when his infantry's wireless would not work in the hilly country, he volunteered to carry the telephone line to forward positions. But on the way he was severely wounded in the leg and lay, isolated and exposed, for 26 hours. By the time he was rescued the leg had become septic and had to be amputated.

Cutler's VC was awarded for conspicuous and sustained gallantry over these 18 days. He was the only Australian artilleryman to win the VC, and his courage and determination became a byword among forward troops.

The descendant of a carpenter who had emigrated from London as a free settler in 1833, Arthur Roden Cutler was born on May 24 1916 at Manly, New South Wales. He was educated at Sydney High School and Sydney University, where he read Economics. He went to work at the Public Trust Office in 1934. After war was declared, Cutler was posted to the 2nd/5th Field Regiment of the 78

Division Artillery, which trained in Palestine and Egypt before going to Syria.

After being invalided home in 1941, Cutler received his Victoria Cross from the Governor-General the Earl of Gowrie, also a VC. He first became State Secretary of the Returned Sailors', Soldiers' and Airmen's Imperial League of Australia, though some members complained that the post should have gone to a First World War veteran. Next, he was chosen to be a member of the aliens' classification and advisory committee, and then an assistant deputy director of the Australian Security Service.

After the war Cutler was appointed Australian High Commissioner in New Zealand. He was then posted to Ceylon, where he found the High Commissioner's residence crawling with bugs attracted by food that had been dumped there after a food exhibition. As High Commissioner, he defended his country's "white Australia" policy, and restored morale by insisting that his staff were properly organised and wore white suits; but he also incurred the unions' wrath at home by granting visas to Ceylonese.

Cutler's experience as a man of action proved useful when he was appointed minister to Egypt just as the Suez Crisis began. One of his first decisions was to remove the large number of weapons from the basement of his residence, on the grounds that it could not, in any case, be easily defended. He quickly discovered that the Western powers were not only divided, but totally ill-prepared to cope with Nasser. The British Prime Minister, Anthony Eden, and the

American Secretary of State, John Foster Dulles, were hostile to each other, and both were in poor health; the Canadians were rudderless after their minister in Cairo had committed suicide; and the Australian Prime Minister, Robert Menzies, was displaying unjustifiable optimism about what the allies could do.

With an invasion about to take place, Cutler sent home all but four of his staff. The British were slower, and Cutler watched from the roof of the British embassy with the ambassador, Sir Humphrey Trevelyan, as the airport, by which they had hoped to escape, was being bombed. Since the British embassy was now cut off and short of food, Cutler and his commercial secretary drove at high speed to a bazaar where they bought rice and a whole sheep. On returning to the embassy, where an Egyptian soldier stood guard before a hostile crowd, Cutler distracted the soldier while his colleague passed over the purchases.

After the Anglo-French invasion was called off, Cutler joined other diplomats on a stinking train which wove its way slowly through the battlefields of Mersa Matruh, El Alamein and Sidi Barrani to reach Libya. Cutler became Secretary-General to the South-East Asia Treaty Organisation (SEATO) Conference of Ministers and chief of protocol at the Department of External Affairs in Canberra; he was then appointed High Commissioner to Pakistan, and Consul General in New York from 1961 to 1965. After a brief spell as ambassador to the Netherlands, he returned home in 1966 to become Governor of

New South Wales for 15 years. He greeted the press with Hilaire Belloc's lines, "But as it is, my language fails,/Go out and govern New South Wales!"

Cutler popularised the institution of the governorship without compromising its essential character by declaring that he would not have a uniform, since it would cost £600 and the public did not expect it. He had to change his mind some years later when Sir Michael Adeane, the Queen's Private Secretary, told him it would be required when the Queen arrived for the Cook bicentenary celebrations. Cutler believed that "proper protocol is what I call natural courtesy".

There were nods of approval when the practice of ladies withdrawing at the end of formal Government House dinners was reintroduced, but some expressions of surprise when he broadened invitation lists to include both nuns and Communist trade union leaders. One of his earliest engagements was a visit to Sydney Trades Hall, which was thought to be the first by a Governor since the 3rd Lord Carrington in 1888. He approved of worker participation in company decisions, and believed in strict guidelines for foreign investment and stricter supervision of the nuclear industry.

Having grown up in the Depression, Cutler put creating jobs for young people before controlling the inflation rate, and upset the Liberal Prime Minister Malcolm Fraser by criticising federal economic policy in a speech opening the State Parliament. The speech had been written by the state's Labour premier so Cutler correctly maintained that he was bound to deliver it. He was once confronted by some anti-Vietnam War protesters, one of whom fell down in front of him, then complained that he had been kicked. "A man with one leg cannot kick anyone," explained Cutler, "even his dog."

Roden Cutler served as overseas vice-chairman of the VC and GC Association from 1986 to 1991, and deputy president from 1991. He was chairman of the State Bank of New South Wales from 1981 to 1986, honorary colonel of the Royal New South Wales Regiment, and honorary air commodore of the Royal Australian Air Force. He was appointed CBE in 1957; KCMG in 1965; KCVO in 1970; and AK in 1981.

He married first, in 1946, Helen Morris, who died in 1990; they had four sons. He married secondly, in 1993, Joan Goodwin, who survives him.

FIELD MARSHAL
SIR NIGEL BAGNALL

Field Marshal Sir Nigel Bagnall (who died on April 8 2002, aged 75) won an MC and Bar in the Malayan jungle, and spent the latter part of his career defending the Army against the cuts demanded by politicians as they increased its responsibilities after the collapse of the Soviet Union.

The most gifted thinker among the post-war generation of soldiers, Bagnall played an important role in developing the concept of operational warfare, encouraging the modernisation of training, and warning that the three services' quarrels over a depleting defence budget was only hurting their cause. His immense popularity with both officers and men was earned by an early concern that the steadily increasing demands on the modern Army were damaging both the morale and the marriages of personnel.

With the nickname "Ginge" – reflecting a peppery nature as well as the red hair of his youth – Bagnall was prevented from making the ultimate step to the top from Chief of General Staff to Chief of Defence Staff, partly because it was felt that the Ministry of Defence would have a quieter life without him. He had little time for tactical nuclear weapons. His reluctance to go along with the policy of fudge as expressed in the document *Options for Change*, led him to be mauled by Mrs Thatcher in the presence of the Defence Secretary and other members of the Chiefs of Staff Committee; thereafter he was regarded as "unreliable" – though many thought he was right.

The son of an officer in the Green Howards, Nigel Thomas Bagnall was born in India on February 10 1927 and educated at Wellington. Joining the Army at 18, he was granted a regular army emergency commission in the Green Howards in 1946, then transferred to the Parachute Regiment with whose 8th Battalion he served in Palestine; he later went to the 1st Battalion the Duke of Wellington's Regiment. Bagnall returned to the Green Howards in time to serve with the 1st Battalion in the Malayan Emergency.

For much of the time, he was in an isolated position at Kampong Menchis. When he took over the position, the whole area was effectively under terrorist control; in less than two months combing the area with his small force, he captured 11 terrorist agents and located and destroyed 16 terrorist camps. By Christmas 1949, the area had been sufficiently pacified for the police to relieve military forces. On May 27 1950, Bagnall led a night patrol into a terrorist-infested area. With cool patience he located the terrorist camp, and then led a small encircling party through dense jungle.

After an hour, they reached an assault position 30 yards from a terrorist-occupied hut. Bagnall then threw a grenade into the hut, flushing out three terrorists, whom he and his patrol shot dead. Praising what he described as his "gallantry, coolness and ruthless energy", Bagnall's commanding officer said, in the citation for his Military Cross, that he was a "source of inspiration to his platoon and company, and an example which can seldom have been surpassed".

By January 1952 Bagnall was operating in the Tampin area as an Intelligence officer, and being employed on any difficult operations requiring exceptional skill. With a combination of carefully planned fighting patrols and improvised track-side ambushes, he and his men killed a total of 18 terrorists, including a Communist branch committee member, whom Bagnall shot personally. They also wounded one enemy and captured another. In a conflict in which the killing of a single terrorist was considered a major success, Bagnall's operations devastated the local Communist network. The citation to the Bar of his MC commented: "This officer's brilliant tactical leadership, his skilful tracking and complete disregard for his personal safety are a byword throughout the battalion and also, according to surrendered terrorists in the Tampin area, among the enemy themselves."

On returning home, Bagnall had a personal setback when he was found guilty of dangerous driving and disqualified for three years after an accident in which a cyclist was killed. But after a period as an instructor at the OCTU at Eaton Hall, Cheshire, he was posted to his regiment's 2nd Battalion, serving with them in the Suez Canal Zone and Cyprus. There he was again involved in counter-insurgency operations, this time against the Greek Cypriot terrorist organisation Eoka. Bagnall transferred to the 4th/7th Royal Dragoon Guards and attended the Staff College, Camberley.

From 1960 to 1961 he served at the Directorate of Military Operations at the War Office before going on to attend the Joint Services Staff College. There followed a period of regimental duty until he became military assistant to the Vice-Chief of the Defence Staff. In March 1966 he became GSO1 (Intelligence) at the Directorate of Borneo Operations, and GSO1 at Headquarters, Far Eastern Command, as military assistant to the Commander-in-Chief, Sir Michael Carver. A month later he was back with his regiment as Commanding Officer, first in Omagh, and then at Sennelager, West Germany, where he supervised the regiment's conversion from armoured cars to main battle tanks. After serving as an instructor in the Joint Services Staff College, Bagnall was appointed Commander, Royal Armoured Corps, in 1st (British) Corps, BAOR.

In 1972 his reputation as an expert on armoured warfare led him to be given a Defence Fellowship at Balliol College, Oxford, and then made secretary of the Chiefs of Staff Committee at the Ministry of Defence. After being GOC, 4th Division, he returned to the MoD in 1978 as Assistant Chief of Defence Staff (Policy), then was given command of 1st (British) Corps before being appointed Commander-in-Chief, BAOR. The following year he became Commander of NATO's Northern Army Group, in which post he inaugurated and oversaw major changes in NATO's operational doctrine. A fluent German speaker, he had unprecedented success in persuading the German military leadership to agree that, in the event of a Soviet attack, the alliance's troops could withdraw to a fallback position which would be an effective killing ground.

Bagnall was finally Chief of General Staff for three years until his retirement in 1988 with the rank of Field Marshal. He was Colonel Commandant of the Royal Armoured Corps from 1985 to 1988; of the Army Physical Training Corps from 1981 to 1988; and an honorary fellow of Balliol College, Oxford, the honour which he said gave him greatest pleasure. In retirement, Nigel Bagnall became an enthusiastic duck breeder. He also published *The Punic Wars* (1990), in which he brought a soldier's insight to bear on the struggle between Rome and Carthage, and drew lessons for our time on the importance of military preparedness, and clear and consistent strategic planning. Enoch Powell, who reviewed the book in *The Daily Telegraph*, regretted that the author had deployed the matter-of-fact "aloofness of a Staff College lecturer addressing a class of Camberley students". But it was well received elsewhere, particularly in Germany, and he worked on a book about the Peloponnesian Wars during his last years.

Although intolerant of incompetent staff officers, Bagnall was loyal to those who lasted the course; he was so tone deaf that he depended on them to ensure that he saluted an anthem at the right moment. He disliked wearing what he called his "f------ jewellery", and preferred to walk with a shuffle instead of a crisp military strut. Bagnall was appointed CVO in 1978, KCB in 1981, and GCB in 1985. He married, in 1959, Anna Caroline Church, who survives him with their two daughters.

Sir John Keegan writes: Nigel Bagnall was a most unusual soldier. He had a real personal following in the Army, and news of his death brought sorrow to hundreds of his comrades-in-arms. Quick-tempered but warm-hearted, he aroused much more affection than fear, and was also greatly admired for his intellect and academic bent. Not only did he introduce the Army to "the operational level", a concept borrowed from the panzer generals which he successfully domesticated by brilliant exposition, he also made the study of war respectable and transformed the outlook of a whole generation of officers. Civilians greatly liked him also, and he was very popular at Balliol, as shown by his election to an honorary fellowship.

He was blessed by an exceptionally happy family life, in partnership with his beloved Anna and two boisterous daughters. The girls' explosions of impatience with official pomposity may have been a safety valve for his own. His complete down-to-earth nature made him greatly loved, and he will be missed by a very wide circle of friends, men and women, in and out of the Army.

LIEUTENANT-COLONEL
HENRY VAN STRAUBENZEE

Lieutenant-Colonel Henry van Straubenzee (who died on April 12 2002, aged 88) earned a DSO while commanding 12th Royal Tank Regiment in support of the Canadians' assault on the heavily fortified Gothic Line which was spread across northern Italy during the autumn of 1944.

Although it was suggested that the operation could be swift, the weather was atrocious and the mountainous terrain difficult. The attackers had to contend not only with swollen rivers, mined roads and demolished bridges, but also with stubborn resistance from two of the most resolute German units, the 1st and 4th Parachute Divisions. For weeks van Straubenzee spent much of his time outside his tank, liaising on foot with the infantry. He first showed initiative and coolness in organising Canadian 1st Division's crossing of the river Arzilla; he then organised the capture of the key height of Monte Luro under very heavy fire.

In the confusion of battle, he once found himself mistaken for his Canadian cousin Casimir van Straubenzee, in command of the Three Rivers Armoured Division. Another time he rushed back to his tank under shellfire and got into the wrong vehicle, and he was blown off the top of his turret by a shell which tore off his epaulette and grazed his shoulder. Even when he was wounded in the head and hand he refused to retire to a dressing station. The citation to his DSO declared that he had inspired "by his fine example and by his indomitable resolution to help the infantry at all times."

However, much to his annoyance, van Straubenzee was moved to Palestine as GSO1, HQ 1st Division, six weeks before the war ended. On VE Day, he and another officer became so exasperated over dinner with their only other companion, a padre, that they tied him up in a rug then went off to drink more in Haifa. When they returned in high spirits John Butler, the future Anglican Bishop of Tuam, had fallen over and the two feared the worst until they realised that he was asleep; they carried him to bed. At the following Sunday's service, Butler looked pointedly at them as he preached on the text: "Yea, though I walk through the valley of the shadow of death I will fear no evil."

Henry Hamilton van Straubenzee was born on

March 7 1914 in Johannesburg, where his father, the managing director of an engineering firm, died soon after his birth. Henry and his brother Philip were taken by their South African mother to live with their van Straubenzee grandfather, a retired general, in Yorkshire. Young Henry went to Winchester, where he became a keen fisherman, and won a scholarship to Sandhurst.

In 1934 he was commissioned into the Oxford-shire and Buckinghamshire Light Infantry, which gave him the opportunity to play 50 cricket matches a year for a wide variety of teams, including Sandhurst, the Army and Essex, right up to the outbreak of war; in one game he and his brother Philip shared an opening partnership of 100 for the Light Infantry against the Greenjackets. When the Oxford and Bucks went to France with the British Expeditionary Force, van Straubenzee was briefly detached from his regiment to command a platoon of the Northumberland Fusiliers; he was mentioned in despatches. Before finally wading out to sea at Dunkirk to be picked up by a paddle steamer, he buried his I Zingari jersey in a slit trench to ensure that it would never end up on a German.

Back in England, van Straubenzee was selected for the Staff College, Camberley, after which he was posted to 126th Brigade when it was being mechanised. Like many successful officers, he gave much credit to his soldier servant, Dennis Smith – "Smith 200", as he called him – who was an invaluable guide to the feelings of the other ranks. On one occasion van Straubenzee returned to his quarters to find a chauffeured Rolls-Royce waiting outside for "Mr Smith"; Dennis apologetically explained that he had been asked to play centre forward for a civilian team on Saturday afternoons.

Van Straubenzee was posted next to the Northamptonshire Yeomanry and 10th Division in Syria, before going to Italy. At the end of the war, he was appointed GSO1 at HQ 1st Division in Palestine, but soon moved on to take command of the 2nd Battalion, Oxford and Bucks, at Bethlehem. He was uneasy about taking over an infantry unit, and hardly reassured by a lance-corporal's recollection that the regiment had mutinied in Canada under one of his ancestors in the 19th century; but he enjoyed the job until he was suddenly recalled to HQ 6th Airborne Division, which was engaged in the anti-terrorist role in Palestine. On his return home he was awarded an OBE.

Subsequent appointments included two years as an instructor at the Staff College, Camberley, and another spell as GSO1 with 11th Armoured Division in Germany. After that, he was military assistant to two successive Chiefs of the Imperial General Staff, Field Marshal Lord Harding and Field Marshal Sir Gerald Templer. Van Straubenzee was then given command of the 4th/7th Royal Dragoon Guards in Germany. But although he was a popular, respected and efficient commanding officer, the back trouble resulting from his wounds caused him to be medically down-graded, thus limiting his career prospects.

In 1957 van Straubenzee retired early to join W H

Smith, where he first took charge of shop fittings and eventually became managing director. For nearly 20 years he also served on the executive committee of the Army Benevolent Fund. He remained an enthusiastic fly fisherman and helped to form a syndicate made up of military friends on the river Test. In the mid-1990s, he was asked to take part in a series of Staff College discussions on the operations conducted in the Falklands and the Gulf, entitled "The Realities of War."

Henry van Straubenzee married, in 1943, Angela Fenwick, who died in 2000; they had a daughter and three sons, one of whom is circulation manager of *The Spectator*.

MAJOR-GENERAL SVERRE BRATLAND

Major-General Sverre Bratland (who died on April 29 2002, aged 84) established such a high reputation by his conduct during the Narvik campaign in 1940 that he was subsequently commissioned into the King's Shropshire Light Infantry, with whom he served gallantly in Normandy.

In the course of training in Yorkshire with the 4th Battalion KSLI, Bratland quickly gained the confidence of his men, who preferred to call him by the nickname "Jimmy". However, his still limited mastery of English caused confusion when he gave orders over the radio. This was particularly the case in

Normandy, where he landed as part of 11th Armoured Division, eight days after D-Day. On more than one occasion the radio transmissions of D Company, 4 KSLI, were thought to have been intercepted by the enemy.

As the battalion became heavily engaged in the fighting around Caen, Lieutenant Bratland established a reputation for cool courage and sound leadership as a platoon commander. He was wounded during the battalion's baptism of fire at Baron-sur-Odon, and evacuated to England. A month later he returned to consolidate his reputation as a dashing platoon commander. When Antwerp was taken, Bratland, who spoke excellent German, was detailed to accept the surrender of the kommandant. The German, however, refused to surrender to a mere subaltern, and so the company commander had to do the honours.

Bratland was also involved in the capture of large numbers of German prisoners, who were subsequently locked up in the lions' cages at Antwerp Zoo; the Germans sent a note of protest to London, implying that the lions had not been removed beforehand. On September 22 1944, in the course of some of 4 KSLI's fiercest fighting during the crossing of key canals in Holland, Bratland led a platoon attack near Asten, for which he was awarded the Military Cross.

His company commander, Major Ned Thornburn, recalled that Bratland was "never happier than when he was crawling on his stomach, and since the advance had perforce to be in single-file along the ditch, it was in very truth Jimmy who, single-handed, drove the enemy slowly back down the road. Every few minutes he would have a grenade-lobbing competition with the Germans further up the ditch, after which they gave him best and withdrew another 25 yards; and in this manner some 250 yards was cleared, sufficient to provide D Company with elbowroom for manoeuvre."

Bratland fought with the battalion right up to the end of 11th Armoured Division's advance into northern Germany, and was wounded once more shortly before the capture of Hitler's successor, Grand Admiral Doenitz, at Flensburg.

Sverre Bratland was born at Utskarpen, northern Norway, on June 2 1917, one of the 11 children of a farmer and fisherman. He left school at 14 to work on the family farm while continuing his education by correspondence course. At 18 Bratland saw an advertisement for an Army-sponsored course, and more than three years later emerged as its top student. He then joined the Norwegian 6th Division Under-Officers' Training School at Harstad. By 1939 he had reached the rank of sergeant.

In April 1940, Bratland was mobilised as a member of a ski-borne rifle company which was deployed to Gratangen, just north of Narvik, and his company engaged the enemy in skirmishes to slow up the German advance. He was then transferred to Bodo, south-west of Narvik, where he was wounded during a German air raid; a piece of shrapnel remained lodged in his shoulder for the rest of his life. While in hospital, he was less than pleased to be sharing a room with a downed Luftwaffe pilot, but took the opportunity to improve his German.

In the summer of 1941 Bratland fled to Sweden, where he co-ordinated the activities of various Norwegian refugee camps. The following spring he left to train with the Norwegian Brigade in Scotland. Later he was posted to the Norwegian Military Academy, housed in Kensington Palace, and passed out as a commissioned officer. In December 1943, Bratland was one of a dozen young Norwegian officers who passed a War Office selection board before being commissioned in 4 KSLI.

After his war service, for which he was appointed Chevalier de la Legion d'Honneur and awarded the St Olav Medal with Oak Leaf, Bratland had a successful military career in Norway. This included a two-year course as a captain at the Swedish Military High School in Stockholm, command of a battalion in the Southern Norway Brigade, appointment as Chief of Staff to C-in-C Northern Norway, and command, in the rank of major-general, of the Norwegian 6th Division. He also held the NATO appointment of Deputy Commander AFNORTH. His final appointment was Commander, Land Forces Southern Norway, before he retired in 1982. Bratland continued to give frequent lectures to the Norwegian Military Academy in Oslo.

He was a consistently strong advocate of the British style of command and training for war, which encouraged flexibility of thought and individual initiative. This periodically placed him at odds with other senior commanders who favoured the more formal and inflexible tactical doctrine of the post-war Swedish and German armies. Only two weeks before his death he made his last visit to Normandy with his personal staff officer and former members of both 2nd and 4th Battalions KSLI, who found him as clear-thinking, robust and engaging as ever.

"Jimmy" Bratland was a widower for some years, and was pre-deceased by one son and one daughter; he is survived by two daughters.

———

MAJOR
ARTHUR FEARNLEY

Major Arthur Fearnley (who died on May 5 2002, aged 91) was awarded an immediate MC in 1942 while serving with 2nd Royal Tank Regiment in Burma. On March 5 1942, it was learned that the brigadier commanding 63rd Infantry Brigade and members of his staff, all newly arrived from India, were surrounded by the Japanese at Pegu, a small town on the railway line between Rangoon and northern Burma.

Fearnley was ordered to take his troop of three light Stuart tanks to escort them to their brigade several miles to the south. Pegu had been heavily bombed, and little beside the houses on the main street remained standing. As Fearnley's troop arrived the following day, Japanese infantry were streaming into the town, and he had some difficulty persuading the officers to begin their journey instead of staying to engage the enemy. He took one of them as a passenger in his tank; the rest travelled in two Indian armoured scout cars.

Half a mile south of the town, the troop found their way partially blocked by a shot-up British truck. The leading tank got through the gap, but as Fearnley's tank reached the truck, it came under heavy machine-gun fire from the thick jungle on either side. It then lurched off the road, and ran down a steep embankment before coming to rest in a ditch. Spotting two Japanese soldiers crawling towards them through the undergrowth, Fearnley shot at them with his revolver, and ordered his corporal to fire his Browning. "What at, sir?" asked the corporal, who hadn't seen them. "Never mind what at!" roared Fearnley, "Just fire the bloody thing!" The corporal fired a few bursts and then fell back, wounded in his chest.

Fearnley now discovered that his driver had been killed, and believed that, at any moment, the Japanese might lob a grenade through the top of the turret. When it proved impossible to get the driver out of his seat, he had to sit on the dead man's lap to re-start the engine, and get the tank moving again. As it climbed back on to the road, they came under intense fire once more. Since bullets had frosted the glass panel in front of him, Fearnley had to follow instructions shouted to him by his wireless operator in order to steer. They managed to manoeuvre around the road block, but a few minutes later they were brought to a halt by another, formed by two large trucks which had been placed end to end across the road.

Fearnley revved his engine and, by repeatedly ramming one of the trucks, made a gap which they were able to squeeze through and, eventually, rejoin their squadron. Despite being awarded an immediate MC, Fearnley felt an overwhelming sense of failure since the brigadier and three battalion commanders who were placed in his charge had lost their lives.

Arthur James Fearnley was born on June 19 1910 at Salford, Lancashire. He went to Ackworth, a Quaker boarding school in Yorkshire, before going into the family building business, in which he served his apprenticeship as a joiner. In 1940, he volunteered for the Army and, after four months intensive training, passed out of the cavalry wing of Sandhurst. Posted to the Fife and Forfar Yeomanry, Fearnley became an instructor on the American Stuart light tank. The expertise gained, he said afterwards, saved his life two years later.

In 1941, he joined the 2nd Royal Tank Regiment in Cairo and, after a short time in the Canal Zone, moved with his regiment to Rangoon as part of the 7th Armoured Brigade. Shortly after the action in which he won his MC, Fearnley and his comrades demobilised their tanks and, armed with their Smith and Wesson revolvers, acted as rearguard to the retreating Army on the long trek northwards. Fearnley's experience convinced him that the biggest advantage the Japanese possessed was not their air superiority but their abundance of horses. The British armour, confined to the few roads, was of limited use; the enemy could deploy and supply their units throughout the jungle terrain.

After three months in India, he went next with his regiment to Basra, as part of Paiforce, to patrol the southern borders of Turkey. In April 1943, his regiment embarked for Bari and, on arrival in Italy, took over the tanks and transport of 6 RTR. Fearnley was appointed Intelligence officer and assistant adjutant, but the non-combatant role did not suit him, and he transferred to B Squadron as second captain. In 1944 he was promoted to major, and took command of A Squadron. His regiment fought its way north, ridge by ridge, and finished the war in Padua.

A few well-placed officers, Fearnley recalled, had managed to cushion the austerities of a soldier's life with consolations denied to their comrades. One was the brigade dental officer, who had acquired an attractive girlfriend in the south of the country and, being reluctant to lose her companionship as the Allies advanced, secured the use of an ambulance in which he moved her from one brigade area to another.

Arthur Fearnley retired from the Army in 1945 and re-joined the family firm. A man of considerable charm and good humour, he enjoyed taking part in amateur theatrical and opera performances. For some years he sat on the Salford magistrate's bench. He married, in 1951, Patricia Holcroft, who survived him, together with two sons and a daughter.

SERGEANT-MAJOR
LEONARD GRIFFITHS

Sergeant-Major Leonard Griffiths (who died on June 28 2002, aged 83) won the Military Medal during the British Expeditionary Force's retreat from Dunkirk and the Distinguished Conduct Medal while serving with General Slim's 14th Army in Burma.

In 1940 Griffiths was, as a 22-year-old dispatch rider, one of the few men left in an anti-tank regiment which had suffered particularly heavy casualties at the Battle of Cassel. The conditions under which he had to ride his motorcycle were extremely arduous, and he had already seen enemy aircraft machine-gunning schoolchildren whom he had helped to save by procuring an ambulance. When it became essential to supply provisions for his hard-pressed unit, he was given what his battery commander described as the "impossible task" of reaching a ration truck and bringing it back to their position.

This involved riding on an appalling road surface under fire. He was constantly thrown from his machine, which became badly damaged. Nevertheless, Griffiths finally managed to locate the ration truck, which he brought back, again under heavy fire, to his unit – where it was promptly blown up. By now the Germans were very close, and Griffiths realised that he had to escape. He set off on foot for Dunkirk. "Leg weary, hungry, cold and dying for want of sleep, I came across a horse," he recalled. "This I mounted, and for 15 miles across France this steed gave me the necessary rest so that I could finish the journey on foot". The citation to his MM refers to his "conspicuous bravery and devotion under heavy fire."

By the time Griffiths was awarded his DCM in Burma in 1944, he was a battery sergeant-major serving with 22nd Anti-aircraft/Anti-tank Regiment, Royal Artillery. In January that year Slim had visited the Arakan front. He knew that the Japanese intended to attack and that 7th Indian Infantry Division would be a prime target; he also knew that the weak spot was its administrative base at East Mayu, and that this was where the enemy would strike. On February 11, at 1 pm, the Japanese launched an assault against a defensive position on a hill occupied by 284 anti-tank battery.

Griffiths, who was in charge of the position, rallied his men against repeated attacks. He decided to signal his intention to withdraw, but was told to hold on and that help was on its way. Eventually, a small number of men arrived, led by an officer who was immediately killed by a machine-gun burst to the head. Griffiths's response was single-handedly to attack the machine-gun and put it out of action.

Even so, by two o'clock the position was surrounded and Griffiths himself had been badly wounded, having taken a bullet through his right heel and another in the right shoulder. He also had a multiple wound close to his left hip. Only five men were left defending the position. But when the Japanese launched what they anticipated would be their final charge, Griffiths jumped on to the parapet shouting "Come on boys, give them a cheer!" "The resulting volley," said his citation, "broke the Jap charge."

A brewer's son, Leonard George Griffiths was born on October 26 1918 at Stourbridge, Worcestershire. He began working as a sales assistant in a shop at 14, and by the outbreak of war had risen to become manager of a furniture store at Kidderminster. After demobilisation Griffiths joined the Civil Service as an apprentice joiner with the Ministry of Works (cabinet making being his lifelong hobby). He became superintending technical officer, and in 1969 was responsible for the furnishing at the investiture of the Prince of Wales at Caernarvon Castle. During his time in the post, he was also responsible for the refurbishment of the House of Commons and of 10 Downing Street.

Griffiths was a committed Methodist who, while living at Brierley Hill, his wife's home town near Dudley, was the Sunday School superintendent at Bank Street Methodist Church before they moved to Sidcup. He married Georgina Gennard in 1941, a week after receiving his Military Medal from the King. The ceremony took place at the thirteenth hour of April 13; the bridesmaids sported 13 buttons on the backs of their dresses. The couple, needless to say, were not superstitious. Leonard Griffiths was survived by her and their three children.

LIEUTENANT-COLONEL "RONNIE" DEGG

Lieutenant-Colonel "Ronnie" Degg (who died on July 27 2001, aged 92) was one of the outstanding battalion commanders of the Second World War; in 1944 he won a DSO while commanding the 1st Battalion, the South Staffordshire Regiment, on Chindit operations in Burma.

Degg, who after school worked in the coal mines, had enlisted in the ranks during the General Strike. He went on to be commissioned in the field and appointed second-in-command of his battalion when it formed part of Brigadier Mike Calvert's 77th Brigade – one of five brigades in Special Force, which was committed to action behind Japanese lines in 1944.

There was a plan – the brainchild of General Orde Wingate – to establish a strong position astride Japanese lines of communication, cutting the Mandalay-Myitkyina railway. A force would be flown in and re-supplied by air, acting in support of General "Vinegar Joe" Stilwell's American-led Chinese troops in their advance on Myitkyina; at the same time they would divert Japanese troops from their advance on India. The South Staffordshires were split into two columns – 38, commanded by Lieutenant-Colonel Richards, and 80, by Degg.

The force landed by aircraft and gliders in bright moonlight at a clearing known to the troops as "Broadway". From there Degg's 80 was to move off and establish a block on the Mandalay railway at

Henu. The objective – "Stafford Hill" – proved to be occupied by a large force of Japanese, and as Degg established the column's position they at once came under fire. All night they were attacked by parties of Japanese who managed to infiltrate their meagre defences. They held off the enemy until the morning when they were joined by 38 and a column of Gurkhas, who were in time to repel a far stronger attack.

When Calvert arrived he ordered an attack on Japanese positions, which involved fierce hand-to-hand fighting and the use of man-pack flamethrowers. After a re-supply drop on March 18, Calvert moved his headquarters to "White City" (a reference to the many parachutes which draped the tall trees), where the Staffords defended the northern and eastern sectors. Three nights later, the Japanese launched a full-scale attack on this position, showering it with grenades and mortar fire. In the early hours of the morning, Colonel Richards was killed leading a counter-attack, leaving Degg to take command of the whole battalion. The Japanese assault was beaten off with heavy losses.

Special Force, though under constant attack, now controlled 30 miles of railway, cutting the lifeline of the Japanese in the north. But casualties had been heavy and Calvert decided to move to "Blackpool", a new defensive perimeter, further north between Mawlu and Mogaung. But before they could get there, Blackpool fell to the enemy, and Calvert learnt that the Chinese and Americans were approaching Myitkyina, and received orders that his brigade was to attack Mogaung. By now 77th Brigade had only 550 effective soldiers, many of them wounded and nearly all suffering from malaria, jungle sores or swollen feet. Even so, Mogaung was taken in a midnight assault with the Staffords and Gurkhas wading through rivers and marshes and clearing hills and ridges in close-quarter fighting.

Throughout this period Degg proved himself a courageous and skilful commander, whose drive and energy proved an inspiration to a battalion reduced to a third of its strength by casualties and sickness. Moreover, the loss of so many officers meant that Degg took part in all attacks, and was constantly in the front line of battle. "Under his leadership," Degg's DSO citation proclaimed, "his battalion never failed in attack or lost ground in defence. The battalion has continually outmatched the Japanese in courage, in defence, endurance and bravery, and this has been largely due to Lieutenant-Colonel Degg's skill and stubbornness."

Roland Degg was born on February 10 1909 at Hednesford, Staffordshire, and educated at Chadsmoor Boys' School. At 13 he went to work at the Huntington Colliery as a "nipper", looking after the pit ponies. During the General Strike in 1926, he left the pit to enlist in the South Staffordshire Regiment, initially to get three square meals a day. His early service was with the 2nd Battalion in Malta, Palestine, Egypt and India. He was a lance-corporal in 1931, later a full corporal in A Company, and captained the battalion football team in 1934.

Next year his football skills were responsible for his

posting to the 1st Battalion at Aldershot as they made a bid for the Army Cup. He remained with the 1st Battalion and by 1937 was a sergeant, one of only three selected as escort to the regimental colours of King George VI. He continued to serve with the battalion in Palestine until the outbreak of war, and in May 1940, by now company sergeant-major of D Company, he moved with them to the Western Desert.

In December 1940, as part of "Selby Force", Degg and his battalion took part in the assault on the strongly-defended Italian positions at Sidi Barrani, for which the regiment gained a battle honour – and at the end of which the CO jumped into Degg's slit trench and presented him with two pips. Promotion had been slow in the pre-war Army; it had taken Degg 10 years to reach the rank of sergeant. Now, in less than four years he would be promoted to acting lieutenant-colonel. In 1941 the battalion moved to India, with duties in internal security and in protecting supplies and transport from Indian dissidents.

After the capture of Mogaung at the end of the operation in Burma, the South Staffordshires were flown back to India. Peace found Degg training Dutch troops at Chichester, Sussex. He then attended Staff College and took up a staff appointment in Western Command. In 1951 he returned to the 1st Battalion of his regiment as CO, taking it to Hong Kong, Northern Ireland and Germany, before handing over the command in April 1954.

Retiring from the Army that year, he became

personnel manager of Horseley Bridge and Thomas Piggott Engineers, at Tipton in the Midlands, remaining with the company until final retirement in 1975. Ronnie Degg was a footballer, swimmer, water-polo player and all–round athlete. Even at 45 he was considered to be his battalion's best hammer-thrower. Brigadier Mike Calvert described him as "a very fine solid unshakeable type, which the South Staffordshire Regiment appears to breed".

He married first, in 1937, Ellen Spires, who died in 1960. He married secondly, in 1963, Sheila Spires, his first wife's niece. She survives him, together with two sons and four daughters from his first marriage.

MAJOR
BOB MAGUIRE

Major Bob Maguire (who died on October 13 2001, aged 87) first won a Military Medal in North Africa in 1942 as a sergeant in the 12th Royal Lancers (Prince of Wales's), and then received a battlefield commission followed by a Military Cross.

"Guns" Maguire, as he was known in his regiment, was the type of soldier whose solution to the hazard of minefields was to batten down the hatches of his armoured car and simply to charge across them. Yet the circumstances in which he won his Military Medal showed that, far from being a hothead, he was a highly competent troop leader capable of sustained effort over a long period.

With the change in Middle East Command in August 1942 and the arrival in North Africa of Generals Alexander and Montgomery, it was essential for the British to know what Rommel was doing. The Germans were still a force to reckon with but, as well as engaging the enemy, it was important to report on their whereabouts and strength. The 12th Lancers were therefore given an offensive reconnaissance role, and it was one at which Maguire excelled.

His reports on enemy movements and formations over a seven-month period in the latter half of 1942 earned him his Military Medal; his accounts were said to be monuments to accuracy despite being gained in conditions of great difficulty, with Maguire being deprived of sleep, as well as under constant fire. At all times, says his citation, Sergeant Maguire never failed to give all that was required, and more. In addition, although he engaged the enemy on numerous occasions, inflicting many casualties, Maguire never allowed himself to get embroiled in a dog fight.

On one occasion he showed the utmost coolness when told to try to recover another troop's armoured car which had been knocked out at close range by anti-tank gunfire. He achieved this by putting the vehicle on tow while being under heavy shell fire. Throughout this entire period, says Maguire's citation for the MM, he maintained an outstanding record and devotion to duty. When attached to another brigade, Maguire made a similar impression earning special commendation. Not surprisingly, therefore, when General Alexander, on a visit to 12th Lancers, met Sergeant Maguire he was sufficiently impressed to send a special signal recommending that Maguire be accepted for commission.

After being commissioned Guns Maguire continued to make his mark. In Tunisia a fellow officer, Lieutenant (later Major-General) Arthur Brockhurst, was ambushed by Germans armed with anti-tank guns and captured. Brockhurst seized a tommy-gun, shot three of his captors, and escaped, being picked up by Maguire in his armoured car.

By June 1944 the 12th Lancers were in Italy, heavily involved in the pursuit of a retreating German Army that was still capable of hitting back. On June 21 Maguire was in command of a troop of armoured cars occupying an observation position at a village called Morro and watching for enemy movement. At 5 am Maguire was suddenly attacked by a patrol of some 50 Germans who advanced from a flank covered by very heavy fire from several machine-guns, pinning Maguire to the ground. Disregarding the intense fire, Maguire managed to reach an armoured car and immediately engaged the enemy, now less than 200 yards away and advancing rapidly.

The fact that his sighting periscope was damaged did not prevent him from bringing accurate fire upon the German forces. They continued to advance until they were forced to take cover not more than 100 yards away from Maguire's position. Maguire continued to fire on the enemy, forcing them to withdraw. Later, 24 dead were counted. The speed with which Lieutenant Maguire acted, with no regard for his personal safety, and the skill and accuracy he displayed in handling his weapons had proved decisive; Maguire was awarded the Military Cross.

Four days later Maguire was captured, and the 12th Lancers lost one of its most effective and aggressive troop leaders. He was ambushed and wounded when his armoured car was hit while on patrol, and spent the rest of the war in captivity.

Robert Cecil Maguire was born in Hampshire on December 11 1913, the only child of a stable worker. He attended Ross-on-Wye Grammar School, enlisting in the 12th Royal Lancers (Prince of Wales's) aged 17. After the war Maguire continued to serve with the 12th Lancers, remaining with them following the amalgamation in 1960 with the newly-formed 9th/12th Lancers (Prince of Wales's). He retired in 1966.

Maguire retained his connection with the regiment, becoming a case worker on the Board of Trustees of the 9th/12th Lancers' Charitable Association; his responsibility was to investigate applications for grants by soldiers who were in need. It was a role that brought him much satisfaction. He met his future wife Babs before the Second World War at a wedding where he was best man and she a bridesmaid. But, with war imminent, Maguire was not inclined to embark upon marriage; instead, he decided to wait until 1945. His wife and a daughter survived him.

BRIGADIER
"PUDDING" PYE

Brigadier "Pudding" Pye (who died on August 21 2002, aged 97) was awarded an immediate DSO in April 1943 while commanding the 2nd Battalion, the Sherwood Foresters, in the attack on a strategically vital hill in Tunisia known as Point 174.

The position had been taken by British troops on two previous occasions, but was lost again in German counter-attacks. Under heavy artillery, mortar and machine-gun fire, Pye first went forward to find barbed wire and a minefield at the bottom of the hill. After ordering a barrage by the divisional artillery and a mortar platoon, which covered his men with smoke, Pye had the wire cut, and Lieutenant St J M Brachi was killed walking up the hill.

With a disregard for the heavy casualties, Pye then showed great determination and coolness in leading a charge over the crest of the hill to occupy the forward slopes. The action secured the objective, and prevented the enemy from forming up to make another attack. But the Foresters continued to be harried by fire from six Tiger tanks 300 yards down on the other side until the Germans withdrew at nightfall.

Pye's citation said that his outstanding personal bravery and leadership was an inspiration to all and undoubtedly led to the success of this extremely difficult operation. The Germans, who were surprised and scattered by his final charge, would probably have been even more surprised if they could have known that after the war this fearsome figure would later breed budgerigars.

Randall Thomas Kellow Pye was the only son of Colonel W E Pye, who served in the 1897 Kirah expedition, the Chinese war of 1900 and the First World War. He was born on October 2 1904 at Aurangabad, India. Known to his mother and father as Randall but to everyone else as "Pudding", he was sent home at seven and, because of the First World War, did not see his parents for another eight years. Initially he stayed with his grandparents, and then, after their return to India, with the family of a fellow pupil at the New Beacon School, Crowborough.

He went on to Wellington and Sandhurst before being commissioned into the Sherwood Foresters in 1924. Pye was posted to the 1st Battalion, which moved to Ballykinlar, Northern Ireland, and while they were there, he was instrumental in forming the Londonderry Garrison Drag Hunt, of which he was a whip. In 1931 he was posted to the 2nd Battalion in India and subsequently served at Multan and in the Sudan. Seven years later, he graduated from the Staff College at Camberley, and was posted to HQ Aldershot Command before being appointed Brigade Major of 164 Infantry Brigade.

From August 1940 to June 1941 he was on the staff at GHQ, Home Forces, and then for six months served as second-in-command of the 4th Battalion Oxford and Bucks Light Infantry. In March 1942 he was GSO1 at HQ First Army and in July was given command of 2nd Battalion, the Sherwood Foresters. He remained with the 2nd Foresters, which were assigned to take part in the attack on Pantellaria, a rocky island 60 miles south of Sicily. Although possessed of formidable coast artillery and a garrison of 15,000 Italians, it surrendered after a heavy aerial and sea bombardment without any fighting. The Foresters had one casualty, a corporal bitten by a mule. In July 1943 Pye became GSO1 (Operations) at HQ 15 Army Group then, after the Sicily campaign, was made GSO1 in Italy with 5 Division, during which time he was appointed OBE and mentioned in despatches, before joining the staff at Middle East Land Forces.

With the return of peace he attended the Senior Officers' War Course held at the Royal Naval College, and after a year in Germany was appointed to command 6th Infantry Brigade in Malaya where he was again mentioned in despatches. Pye was that rare combination, an excellent CO of fighting troops and first class staff officer. The citation for his OBE in Italy noted that "he had ensured the smooth running of the divisional machine at all times and gained the well-merited competence of all subordinate commanders. He has dealt with equal facility and accuracy with the differing problems presented by the defence of the Anzio beachhead, the subsequent advance, and the initiation and organisation of training. He was self-effacing, but forceful and accurate when needed."

After retiring to Sussex in 1952, Pye set up in business breeding budgerigars with his brother-in-law. He hunted with the Old Surrey and Burstow; was a churchwarden for 19 years and chairman of the local church school. Pye married, in 1937, Peggy Muriel Sagar-Musgrave-Brooksbank, who predeceased him; they had a son and two daughters.

―――――――――

COLONEL
JIMMY JOHNSON

Colonel Jimmy Johnson (who died on August 30 2002, aged 92) was wounded and taken prisoner in France in 1940; he was then awarded an MC for his escape to Spain, and received the DSO in 1945 for his leadership and gallantry in command of the 2nd/4th Battalion King's Own Yorkshire Light Infantry in Italy.

Johnson went to France with the 1st Battalion, Royal Welch Fusiliers, as a company commander, shortly after the outbreak of the Second World War. His battalion was one of those holding the outer ring of the Dunkirk defences and, after being wounded by a sniper, he was captured at Robecq, south-east of St Omer. Johnson was interrogated at German divisional headquarters before being taken to a French emergency hospital in a motorcycle combination. But while being transferred to a hospital at Camiers, near Boulogne, he and a comrade, Captain Trythall, cut a hole in the peri-meter wire during the lunch hour and got away in broad daylight under the noses of the German sentries.

After three days of walking, sleeping in barns and

under haystacks, they reached Liomer, near Amiens, where they obtained two cheap bicycles. The Germans were everywhere and all the main bridges were guarded; but, with the help of a farmer, they crossed the river Cher, the boundary between occupied and unoccupied France. But when they tried to acquire travel documents in Chateauroux, the pair were arrested and sent to a concentration camp at St Cyprien. Johnson and Trythall managed to obtain some money from the Swiss consul at Geneva, then bribed their way out of the camp to cross the Pyrenees by a smugglers' path.

But after travelling more than 700 miles on foot and by bicycle, they were arrested by the Spanish for smuggling currency and entering the country illegally, and thrown into the local gaol. After 10 days, they made contact with the British consul at Barcelona who arranged for their removal to the military prison at Figueras, where they were held for a further five days before being put on a train to Gibraltar. They arrived on September 22, three months after their escape from hospital. Several battleships, including *Warspite*, were in the harbour and, three days later, the house in which Johnson and Trythall were staying received a direct hit during a heavy bombing raid. Trythall was killed, and Johnson was wounded in the hand. For their courage and resourcefulness, both men were awarded the MC; Trythall posthumously.

James Robert Johnson was born in London on January 6 1910 to Australian parents; his father commanded a battalion of the Royal Welch Fusiliers in the First World War and was awarded the DSO. Jimmy was educated at Charterhouse where he excelled at cricket, squash and tennis, he also became Public Schools and Sandhurst racquets champion. In 1932, Johnson accompanied the 2nd Battalion, Royal Welch Fusiliers, to Gibraltar. It was there that he met his future wife, Diana, the eldest daughter of Admiral of the Fleet Sir Roger Keyes, at a polo match.

After two years in Hong Kong, he was appointed ADC to the Governor of Tasmania, Sir Ernest Clark. In October 1940, Johnson returned to England and joined 8 RWF before transferring to 9 RWF as second-in-command the following year. In 1943, he was appointed GSO2 at 1st Army HQ and took part in the landings in North Africa in November. After short periods with the 16th Battalion Durham Light Infantry and the 2nd/5th Battalion, Sherwood Foresters, he took command of 2nd/4th Battalion, King's Own Yorkshire Light Infantry, in Italy in February 1944.

The battalion had been in action for six months, all the senior officers were either in hospital or had been evacuated, and the men were exhausted and close to breaking point. Johnson visited his companies every day despite continuous shelling and mortaring of the battalion positions, often slogging across a No Man's Land in which patrol clashes were frequent, to reach a detached company. His courage, cheerfulness and energy put new heart into the battalion at a very critical time. In early September 1944, during the breakthrough of the Gothic Line in northern Italy, Johnson reorganised his companies from a forward position while under heavy shelling from a self-propelled gun and launched an attack which enabled a bridgehead to be established over the river Ventena at Ponte Rosso.

During the winter months, the German 90th PG Division counter-attacked the battalion positions over the river Lamone, west of Faenza. Johnson immediately visited his forward company, which had borne the brunt of the assault and reorganised its defences. His leadership over many months was recognised by the award of a DSO.

The 2nd/4th KOYLI were in Austria at the end of the war, and Johnson was appointed GSO1 (Operations) at HQ at Klagenfurt and then in Vienna. In 1948, he moved to the School of Infantry, Warminster, as chief instructor, before attending the Joint Services Staff College. Three years later, Johnson rejoined the 1st Battalion, Royal Welch Fusiliers, as commanding officer at Kingston, Jamaica. During his tour, detachments from 1 RWF were sent to Grenada and Antigua on internal security duties and, when the situation became serious, Johnson assumed direct command. His unit was also employed for a month on hurricane relief work and, in 1953, was involved in ceremonial and security arrangements for the Queen's visit and the Three Powers Conference.

Johnson was posted to BAOR in 1954 as GSO1 at HQ 2nd Infantry Division before moving to Washington as GSO1 (Operations and Intelligence) with the British Joint Services Mission. After serving as military attaché in Athens, he retired from the

Army in 1961. Through a chance meeting on a pre-retirement course, Johnson discovered that Darryl Zanuck, the Hollywood film producer, was looking for a British military expert to advise on his adaptation of *The Longest Day*, an account of the first 24 hours of the Normandy invasion by *The Daily Telegraph* correspondent Cornelius Ryan. The fact that Johnson had not taken part in the Normandy landings was considered an advantage, and he was given the job. He also advised Samuel Bronston on *55 Days at Peking*, a film about the Boxer Rebellion, during which both his father and father-in-law had been in Peking.

After retiring, Johnson bought the Keyes family's former home in Buckinghamshire. He and Diana converted the stables and built up a successful pottery business over the next few years. He continued to play at the Royal Tennis court in Oxford until he was well into his sixties, and enjoyed travelling until close to 90.

Jimmy Johnson was appointed OBE in 1954. His wife, whom he married in 1936, died in 1983; he is survived by two sons and a daughter.

MAJOR
DOUGLAS WITHERINGTON

Major Douglas Witherington (who died on September 21 2002, aged 82) played an important role in devising a humane way of parachuting mules to the Chindits behind Japanese lines in Burma.

The Americans had conducted experiments earlier in the Second World War by attaching parachutes to the animals, then pushing them out of an aircraft. Unfortunately, the first six beasts were fatally injured when the jerk of the opening parachute ruptured their mesentery artery, which feeds blood to the intestines. The remaining mules wisely resisted all efforts to make them follow. Major Witherington and Lieutenant-Colonel Ken Barlow, Royal Army Veterinary Corps, felt they could do better.

They adapted a small inflatable assault dinghy, $6^{1}/_2$ ft by 4 ft, into which a mule, heavily sedated with chloral hydrate, could be placed, with special padding to protect its private parts. Inside the plane a launching track was made to ensure the smooth departure of the mule in its "raft" with six para-chutes, which then floated down from about 600 ft.

In the course of six experimental drops, they had one fatality, when a mule became caught up in a cluster of parachutes at the tail of the aircraft, broke free and made a precipitate descent, with the result that it sustained a spinal fracture and had to be destroyed in the dropping zone. The other five experiments, however, were successful. When the animals had their straps released they got up, showing some signs of sweating and stiffness, but no real distress; and they were ready to carry heavy wireless equipment, ammunition and flame throwers.

Although some animal lovers today might argue that the beasts were not volunteers, Witherington adopted the view that both men and mules are expendable in war.

Douglas Harold Witherington was born on February 16 1920 and educated at Moulton Grammar School. He went to the Royal Veterinary College and was a temporary inspector for foot and mouth in Devon and Oxfordshire before joining the Royal Army Veterinary Corps in 1942. After marrying his fellow veterinary student, Christina Grieve, he was posted to northern India.

On the Chindits' first expedition behind Japanese lines, their mules had alerted the enemy to their positions by braying; so, when Witherington volunteered for the second, as part of 14th Brigade, he was given the task of muting the force's beasts by removing their vocal cords under general anaesthetic. In the field the Japanese recognised that mules were more important targets than men, since they carried the radio equipment on which operations depended for instructions. They proved more resilient than ponies and were indifferent to shells, though nervous of small arms fire.

The drivers became so fond of their animals that they sometimes named them after Grand National winners. However exhausting the day's march, Witherington noted, both drivers and accompanying troops would immediately start cutting grass for the animals after unloading. He himself was shaken when his own mule, carrying veterinary equipment, was killed after a Japanese patrol suddenly fired on them.

During his six months behind the lines, Witherington kept up his spirits by writing to his wife in letters scribbled with a sharpened bamboo, using gentian violet. He eventually contracted typhus, and was left with a sergeant in a jungle clearing, expected to die. But an American flying overhead in a single-seater plane spotted them, and arranged for them to be taken to hospital. It was while recuperating on a houseboat in Srinigar that Witherington wrote a full account of his experiences, which recognised the vital importance of being able to replace the injured animals. As a result he and Barlow began their experiments in anticipation of a third Chindit attack behind the lines; but it proved unnecessary after the Americans dropped the atomic bombs on Hiroshima and Nagasaki.

After the war, Witherington became a veterinary officer at Kuala Lumpur, and then chief veterinary officer for Singapore, where he and his wife worked together to develop an animal infirmary. They returned to Britain in 1951, briefly to run a small practice at Whitley Bay, before the National Hunt Committee appointed Witherington its veterinary officer; his duties were soon extended to include flat racing. When the Jockey Club became concerned in the early 1960s about the increase in the incidence of doping racehorses, Witherington began to collaborate with the Animal Health Trust (AHT), a forensic laboratory at Soham House, Newmarket.

He published a booklet on the markings of horses, which was an invaluable aid at an international meeting of racing authorities held in Paris in 1972. Later there were a number of incidents involving top-quality thoroughbreds, which performed unexpectedly badly during races. With the aid of research workers at Bristol veterinary school, Witherington developed a heart monitor that recorded an electro-cardiogram, which could then be transmitted from the racecourse to a receiver in Bristol, thus enabling rapid diagnosis. He also worked closely with Michael Scott at the AHT's blood typing laboratory to ensure that horses' markings could be cross-checked, thus guaranteeing the accuracy of the Weatherby's general stud book.

Retiring from the Jockey Club at 65, Witherington worked for Tattersalls, ensuring that horses entered for sale could be identified accurately, until 1999. Having led a team of vets in Cheshire during the 1967 outbreak of foot and mouth, he was greatly disturbed by the mass slaughter of healthy animals in the 2001 epidemic.

Witherington was awarded the Dalrymple Champneys Medal by the British Veterinary Association in 1981 and appointed OBE in 1985. He was survived by his wife, whom he married in 1943, and a daughter.

SERGEANT
WILLIAM PARKES

Sergeant William Parkes (who died at Napa, California, on October 7 2002, aged 106) was one of the last survivors of the Welsh Bantam Brigade, formed for troops between 5 ft and 5 ft 3 in tall, which was involved in some of the heaviest fighting on the Western Front during the First World War.

Although two inches over the prescribed height when he joined the 12th Battalion of the 24th Regiment, South Wales Borderers, Parkes and two other men regularly went out on night reconnaissance patrols together in No Man's Land because it was believed that their lack of stature made them harder to see; a tall officer who once accompanied them on patrol concluded that this was right, and wanted to turn back.

Parkes's most disturbing experience was a lone patrol on which he brushed the snow from the face of a dead German in a crater, and found that it strongly resembled that of one of his own brothers. The toughest action in which he was involved was the taking of the formidable defences of Fifteen Ravine at Gonnelieu, south east of Cambrai; by the end of that action he was commanding his company after all the officers were killed. When Parkes was wounded in the leg by shrapnel in April 1917, he urged his dresser to bind him up tightly so he could return to his men; it was only when he stood up that he realised that he could not walk.

One of an iron moulder's 11 children, William Parkes was born on January 18 1896 at Newport, Monmouthshire, and went to Bolt Street School before becoming a barber's assistant and then a sailor. On the outbreak of war, he was turned down by the Royal Navy because he was too small. But, in March 1915, he joined up with the Borderers, training as a machine-gunner at Aldershot.

After his leg injury, Parkes became an instructor at
Sniggerly Camp, outside Liverpool, and started
training for a commission; but he concluded that he
was not well enough educated and returned to the
Front. After the war he found work in the docks,
then emigrated to America, where he was employed
in the Pennsylvania coal mines until he decided to go
to California. Parkes first became a plasterer. He was
nicknamed "The Speedy Welshman" by the *San
Francisco Chronicle* when he began playing soccer in
his spare time with the San Francisco Barbarians,
who won the state championship in 1922-3. After he
was involved in a scuffle, the paper changed this to
"The Battling Welshman".

Parkes settled in Napa Valley, where he became an
orderly at the state hospital, and rose to become
superintendent in charge of outpatients' day jobs. It
was there that he met his wife Dolly Nelsen, who
was then married to Roy Gardner, a mail train
robber imprisoned in Alcatraz. When Gardner
committed suicide after being released, he left a
note asking Parkes to look after Dolly. After their
marriage in 1938, Parkes built a house opposite the
hospital. He tried to join up with the American
forces on the day of Pearl Harbor, but suffered a
minor heart attack.

Parkes sang in the choir of his local Episcopalian
church, and, after retiring at 58, concentrated on
cultivating his one-acre garden of vegetables and
fruit trees; he also cautiously dabbled in the Stock
Market until the early 1990s, when he decided that
the risks were becoming too great. After his wife's

death in 1979, he lived alone in their house.

Parkes, who retained his Welsh accent but regarded himself as English, became an American citizen. He never returned to Britain, but he sponsored the emigration of a niece who married an American and later looked after her uncle. Parkes joined the Royal Canadian Legion, because there was no British Legion branch nearby, and in 2000 was appointed a member of the French Legion d'Honneur.

INDEX OF PERSONALITIES

(Italics denotes main entry)